African Arguments

Written by experts with an unrivalled knowledge of the continent, *African Arguments* is a series of concise, engaging books that address the key issues currently facing Africa. Topical and thought-provoking, accessible but in-depth, they provide essential reading for anyone interested in getting to the heart of both why contemporary Africa is the way it is and how it is changing.

African Arguments Online

African Arguments Online is a pan-African platform for news, investigation and opinion, managed by the Royal African Society, www.africanarguments.org

Published by Zed Books and the IAI with the support of the following organisations:

The principal aim of the **International African Institute** is to promote scholarly understanding of Africa, notably its changing societies, cultures and languages. Founded in 1926 and based in London, it supports a range of seminars and publications including the journal *Africa*.
www.internationalafricaninstitute.org

The **Royal African Society** is a membership organisation that provides opportunities for people to connect, celebrate and engage critically with a wide range of topics and ideas about Africa today. Through events, publications and digital channels it shares insight, instigates debate and facilitates mutual understanding between the UK and Africa. The society amplifies African voices and interests in academia, business, politics, the arts and education, reaching a network of more than one million people globally.
www.royalafricansociety.org

The **World Peace Foundation**, founded in 1910, is located at the Fletcher School, Tufts University. The Foundation's mission is to promote innovative research and teaching, believing that these are critical to the challenges of making peace around the world, and should go hand in hand with advocacy and practical engagement with the toughest issues. Its central theme is 'reinventing peace' for the twenty-first century.
www.worldpeacefoundation.org

About the author

Nanjala Nyabola is a Kenyan writer, humanitarian advocate and political analyst currently based in Nairobi, Kenya. Her writing and research focus on refugee issues and humanitarian interventions, as well as technology and media in Africa. She is the co-editor of *Where Women Are: Gender and the 2017 Kenyan Election* and a frequent contributor to numerous publications and platforms including Al Jazeera, Foreign Policy, Foreign Affairs, IRIN, New African, The Africa Report and the BBC's 'Focus on Africa', as well as numerous books. Nyabola holds a BA in African Studies and Political Science from the University of Birmingham (UK), an MSc in Forced Migration and an MSc in African Studies, both from the University of Oxford, where she studied as a Rhodes Scholar, as well as a J.D. from Harvard Law School.

DIGITAL DEMOCRACY, ANALOGUE POLITICS

HOW THE INTERNET ERA IS TRANSFORMING POLITICS IN KENYA

NANJALA NYABOLA

In association with
International African Institute
Royal African Society
World Peace Foundation

ZED

Digital Democracy, Analogue Politics: How the Internet Era is Transforming Politics in Kenya was first published in 2018 by Zed Books Ltd, The Foundry, 17 Oval Way, London SE11 5RR, UK.

www.zedbooks.net

Typeset in Haarlemmer by seagulls.net
Index by Ed Emery
Cover design by Jonathan Pelham

Cover image credit:
Eddy Kamuanga Ilunga, Reconnaissance II, 2016
Acrylic and oil on canvas
Courtesy of October Gallery
James Zang collection

A catalogue record for this book is available from the British Library

ISBN 978-1-78699-430-1 hb
ISBN 978-1-78699-431-8 pb
ISBN 978-1-78699-432-5 pdf
ISBN 978-1-78699-433-2 epub
ISBN 978-1-78699-434-9 mobi

Printed and bound by CPI Group (UK) Ltd, Croydon, CR0 4YY

*For my family, who don't always understand
but support me anyway.*

CONTENTS

Part III: History not learned from

ACKNOWLEDGEMENTS

This book has been over ten years in the making, beginning with my experiences of the 2007 election violence in Kenya and my own frustrating interactions with the Western canon on Africa that discouraged me from pursuing this subject while at university. Ten years since that crisis, I'm ecstatic to finally be able to put these thoughts into the world, and glad to see that my instincts were right – technology is indeed playing a disproportionate role in shaping Kenyan politics.

It takes a village to complete a project of this depth and breadth, and I am especially grateful to my little e-village that has believed in me and in this project. I would especially like to thank Dr Keguro Macharia, who is more of a mentor to me than he realises and constantly pushes me to be a more generous, questioning and engaged thinker. To the radical feminists of Kenyan Twitter – Ory Okolloh Mwangi, Aisha Ali, Kellie Murungi, Nanjira Sambuli, Dr Wambui Mwangi, Dr Wandia Njoya, Dr Njoki Ngumi, Dr Grace Musila and countless others whose daily conversations are filled with wit and wisdom that every day reifies my belief in our broken little country. You are ungovernable, and Kenya needs more of you. And to Dr Yolande Bouka, Dr Malebogo Ngoepe, Jina Moore and Katrin Siedel, who listened.

Research anywhere is a difficult process, but especially so in a developing country and outside the bounds of a bricks and mortar institution (we need open access now!). The painful process of trying to make this project happen under these circumstances has reified my belief that to truly decolonise the university and the academy we must work on access to knowledge. I would like to thank everyone who sent journal articles, carried books in their luggage or sent e-books to my e-reader. I would also like to thank the Foreign Policy Interrupted Fellowship that started me on this journey, the Logan Non-Fiction fellowship at the Carey Institute for Global Good and the European Journalism Centre for the fellowship that allowed me the time and space to finish the advanced draft of this text.

This is not an academic book in the traditional sense: for example, the language is deliberately simple. I wrote it outside the academy for a general audience even while using academic methodology and techniques: my contribution to the growing push to decolonise and diversify the academy. A massive thank you to Stephanie Kitchen, managing editor of African Arguments, and Ken Barlow at Zed Books, who have been patient and supportive of an idea that has been nurtured over multiple iterations. I'd also like to thank my reviewers for their insightful and challenging feedback. James Wan, you know what you did – thank you forever. For all its flaws (and there are many) social media has brought many wonderful people into my life – too many to list here – and I am grateful for every connection, conversation and opportunity.

LIST OF FIGURES
AND TABLES

LIST OF ABBREVIATIONS

API	Application Programming Interface
BAKE	Bloggers Association of Kenya
BVR	Biometric Voter Registration
CA	Cambridge Analytica
CBD	Central Business District
CBK	Central Bank of Kenya
CCK	Communications Commission of Kenya (defunct)
CEDAW	Convention for the Elimination of All Forms of Discrimination Against Women
CIPEV	Commission of Inquiry into Post Election Violence (Waki Commission)
CORD	Coalition for Reforms and Democracy
CTC	Constituency Tallying Centre
DM	Direct Message
ECK	Electoral Commission of Kenya (state agency that oversaw elections until 2010)
EVIDs	Electronic Voter Identity Devices
GDPR	General Data Protection Regulation
ICC	International Criminal Court
ICT	Information and Communications Technology
IDPs	internally displaced persons
IEBC	Independent Elections and Boundaries Commission
IFMIS	Integrated Financial Management Information System
IREC	Independent Review Commission (Kriegler Commission)

KANU   Kenya African National Union (political party)
KBC   Kenya Broadcasting Corporation
KIEMS Kenya Integrated Elections Management System
KNCHR Kenya National Commission on Human Rights
KPTC   Kenya Posts and Telecommunications Corporation
KPU   Kenya People's Union
KRA   Kenya Revenue Authority
KTN   Kenya Television Network
NARC   National Rainbow Coalition (political party)
NASA   National Super Alliance (main opposition coalition in
       the 2017 election)
NCIC   National Cohesion and Integration Commission
NHIF   National Health Insurance Fund
NMG   Nation Media Group
NSSF   National Social Security Fund
NTC   National Tallying Centre
NTSA   The National Transportation Services Authority
NYS   National Youth Service
ODM   Orange Democratic Movement (political party)
PSCU   Presidential Strategic Communications Unit
PEV   Post-Election Violence
PNU   Party of National Unity
POS   point-of-sale
RTS   Results Transmission System
SMS   short messaging service
SNS   social networking systems
USAID United States Agency for International Development
VPNs   Virtual Private Networks

PREFACE

By the end of my graduate degree in African Studies in 2011, I had a gnawing frustration.

Despite the large volume of books and articles I devoured about Kenya specifically and Africa in general, no matter how hard I looked, I couldn't see myself in any of the literature that I was reading about the continent and communities I called home. It sometimes felt as if Africa had stopped moving after the end of the Cold War, and the only version worth reading about was poor, violent, sickly, hungry and ultimately existed only through the benevolence of international organisations and governments.

That may very well have been a product of where I was studying, yet in my own life and in my extensive travels on the continent I knew that this was an incomplete story. In Ghana, at the University of Kumasi, I worked with a team setting up a project to allow more engineering students to travel to other African countries and exchange ideas. In Sudan, I walked the streets with a brilliant feminist activist who deliberately and happily invited the ire of the morality police by occupying her city in bright red lipstick, skinny jeans and a perfect high bun. And in Kenya I witnessed an idea born from a blogpost quickly evolve into the pioneering crisis-mapping app, Ushahidi.

It's not that Africa has no problems. But I knew that a different side to Africa existed, even if none of the books on the reading list saw it. People are doing more than just surviving. I left university with the sense that I needed to put some of my energy into helping that Africa get heard.

This book is born out of that desire to bring something specific about contemporary Africa into the conversation. Much of the work that has already been done about the intersection between technology and politics in Africa has been in composite: edited collections about Africa that don't permit the depth the subject increasingly requires. Moreover, existing studies that dominate the discourse and are grounded in technology or developmentalism tend to be overly optimistic about the terrain simply because they ignore politics, or the political agency of the state. Yet beyond the reductive conversation on mobile money in Kenya, young Africans especially are embracing technology and digital platforms as spaces to have their opinions articulated and amplified, as well as to speak directly to Power in their respective societies. Technology is impacting normative ideas about the relationship between generations – allowing young people especially to speak out of turn, find and amplify each other. And in public spheres that still routinely silence the voices of women, digital spaces are making it possible for women to scream into the void.

These and other changes sit comfortably in the realm of 'democracy' but that's a big word that needs to be unpacked – to manage the expectation that simply providing technology will address the structural issues that have kept this energy out of the public sphere. Power is complicated. The more people move into these spaces to raise their voices, the more power pushes back. It's necessary to understand the contours of this pushback too.

So this book isn't about technology per se. It's about the collision between politics and technology, and the ways in which technology has shifted power dynamics within a specific society. It's about how people are using technology to participate in and change political spaces in their country. It's about how individuals are finding methods to interrogate the social and political system they live in. It's about how new identities and ideas of self are developing in reaction and resistance to what went before. It's also about the extent to which we can say that what is being developed online is a real reflection of the state of affairs offline.

I set two methodological challenges for myself when I started this project. For the most part, it's descriptive rather than prescriptive – recounting the state of affairs rather than proposing a 'way forward'. This is deliberate. The book discusses a single country as a place to be understood on its own terms, avoiding the dangers of a single, over-simplified 'African' story. This decision is a challenge to myself as well as the reader. Think about it. If this were a book about how a new technology is being used in Europe or North America, it would not be controversial to focus on a single country, but most readers still find it perfectly natural to collapse Africa's 53 countries and thousands of nations into a single volume.

Another methodological challenge I set for myself was to work against this idea of Africa as a problem to be solved. So much of the intellectual inquiry into African politics begins from a presumption that the only interesting stories that come from Africa are those that have to do with failing structures and I wanted to start with a discussion on what is working before moving into what is not. Markets and industries, governments and universities are interesting enough, but so too are spaces where people are simply existing. What changes when we start with the people rather than the structures? There is agency. There is creativity. There is negotiation.

Contemporary political analysis of African countries is stunted by a crisis of imagination, I believe. Much political analysis of the continent sees countries as existing in one of three states: the developmental state, the conflict state and the post-conflict state. For instance, a simple search for books about Kenya will produce a pretty long list of books that are mostly confined to a handful of themes. Outside fiction books we have themes like state violence – colonial or post-colonial. Authoritarianism. Development crises. Security. Encounters with animals. Africa as a backdrop to someone else's story. A handful of themes that necessarily squeeze out the colour or depth to life that we know – love, joy, hope, frustration, ambition, community. For those who live, work and love here, we know that life is far more complex than that.

The impact of this constricted field of vision is significant. It is apparent in policy work; in received wisdom of how systems work; and in what opportunities are imagined for social and political action. This failure to imagine agency leads to the development of amazing policies or innovations that have nothing to do with the reality of people's lives. Particularly in relation to technology, constantly portraying Africans as passive recipients of seemingly benign things like medical interventions or technological innovation renders them passive. It silences us. Life, it seems, simply happens to Africans and isn't shaped by them or guided by their hopes, dreams, desires and wishes.

In this book I tell a story of how individuals in an African country were using new spaces to shape their realities in novel ways. I show how a community that I am a part of and also know as a researcher is taking control over the narrative of their lives and recasting it on their own terms. I wanted to explore these realities in some depth and flip some of the logic on its head.

The book is also shaped by my own career as a political analyst. One of the strangest things an African scholar can do is move to Europe to study Africa. The cognitive dissonance of moving from solely seeing oneself as an individual or at the broadest as a member of an ethnic group, to being held up as the token representative of the second largest continent on earth is difficult to overstate. I was asked to speak for places I had never seen or imagined. If what I said resonated with what the inquirer wanted to hear, it would be taken as truth even if it had no basis beyond a hunch. But if it didn't resonate with the inquirer's worldview, I was told that I didn't live in or know the 'real Africa', even when I had empirical proof.

Still, it was in this disorientation that I found some academic freedom. I decided that I did not want to 'perform Africa' for my professors or for my peers. I did not want to merely go through the motions of reifying what I was being taught to think. I wanted to define this thing Africa for myself in a way that made sense in terms of what I knew and what I didn't yet know. This wasn't a quest for 'truth' but a decision to orient my thinking in a certain way; a way that I hoped was open, ready to be surprised, and ready to be proven right or wrong, whatever the case may be.

These two points of departure have shaped my work, including this book. I think a lot about Sékou Touré's words:

> In order to achieve real action, you must yourself be a living part of Africa and of her thought; you must be an element of that popular energy which is entirely called forth for the freeing, the progress and the happiness of Africa. There is no place outside that fight for the artist or for the intellectual who is not himself (or herself) concerned with, and completely at one with the people in the great battle for Africa.[1]

'Great battle for Africa' is a weighty term but it captures the intellectual push and pull currently in play over who has the right to speak for Africa and what they have a right to say. To me, the great battle here is to find and describe systems, processes, events or spaces in Africa in a way that speaks as close to the truth as possible about quotidian life on the continent without reducing Africans to caricatures. It's about telling a story that isn't condescending, wilfully partial and that does not perpetuate the pedagogy of colonisation. The great battle for Africa is for honest and earnest intellectual inquiry. It's about decolonising knowledge about the continent.

African Studies as a discipline, in so far as it exists,[2] continues to resist decolonisation and this resistance bleeds into the way journalism and political analysis of the continent is conducted. The complications of funding and institutional support mean that the terrain of study is often defined in Europe and North America. Gatekeepers with rigid standards for deciding what counts as worthy or unworthy of thought in Africa abound. Some of the comments I've received for my own work include 'no one cares about Sudan' or 'this story about Kenya's political history isn't sexy enough'. People have a version of Africa that they want to read about and it's hard to get people to think about things differently.

What we read about Africa is a version of reality that is inevitably shaped by the interests of gatekeepers who are not necessarily intimately connected to Touré's 'popular energy'. And this is a major obstacle to 'real action' – to discourse about Africa that is truly oriented towards freedom (economic, social, political) on the continent.

How do we unpack the phrase 'popular energy'? Popular energy is the zeitgeist – the energy that defines a society at a particular moment. Popular energy is the things that dominate conversations, shape action, or direct attention and efforts. Popular energy is the forces that set the tone for social or political action by members of a community at any moment. Popular energy consists of the social and political issues that motivate action in the private and the public realm. Popular energy is the pulse of a society at any given moment.

Digital spaces have increasingly become part of Africa's popular energy and that is why it is important to understand how these spaces function, and not just in Africa. In the last few years social media has not only led to plenty of significant political action on the continent but also triggered a reaction from the state which has tried to re-establish control over it. Popular energy can change a situation rapidly – taking us from a couple of disgruntled tweets to a full-fledged revolution in a matter of days, as in Egypt during the Arab Spring. It is important to understand the individuals and collectives that comprise these spaces, and the ways they direct collective action towards certain goals.

Why are so many governments threatened by the widespread embrace of such spaces? Why would prominent personalities turn to this space to conduct important political conversations? How does social media lead to concerted offline action in a country where the majority of the population does not have internet access at home? How much can engaging on social media really do for people? What happens when bad guys take advantage of the digital spaces to undermine the offline world?

These are some of the questions that this book explores. Each country in Africa is unique in history and experience so the book has focused attention on just one as an entry point for a bigger conversation about political organisation in digital spaces around the world. Kenya is an example, but the book argues that fundamentally this is a conversation about how citizens everywhere are expanding their definitions of democracy, and building a corporative public sphere that reflects their interests and passions.

It's about how technologies alter the distribution of power in complex societies. Kenya stands in contrast with Ethiopia, for example, where the massive state machinery has historically suppressed political organisation by citizens on- and offline, or with neighbouring Somalia, with no centralised state control and where digital spaces are giving citizens a chance to redefine a political and national Somali identity without the traditional structures that precede such developments. Meanwhile, consideration of the 2016 US general election and the 2016 Brexit vote in the UK underscores that the debate around digital democracy is far from settled. Detours like these show that specific developments in Kenya are part of a bigger story about digital democracy even if specificity is needed to ask the right questions. Is more social media good or bad? Should some people be denied access to platforms that make it easier to disseminate toxic doctrines? How do we protect impressionable adults – and should we?

Kenya gives us an excellent sample for this conversation because so many Kenyans are active online. Millions of Kenyans have active accounts on social media platforms. Zooming in on how democracy is playing out in digital spaces is a weathervane of how similar issues will play out offline. Many traditional conversations on technology adoption in the developing world have singled out Kenya as a place where there are possibilities for building a profitable digital and digitised democracy.[3] This country has everything to gain by consolidating a robust public sphere but is also investing a great deal of time and money into policing online behaviour: what does this say about our ideas of digital democracy?

This book is not meant to be a complete conversation. It is bookended by two pivotal political moments and dwells primarily on the impact of the Internet age on politics in Kenya, but the key theme is not election conflict – it is agency. It is designed as a starting point for a better dialogue on the new political spaces that Africans are creating and why, as well as what it is they want them for. It is a preliminary discussion of what politics in the digital age does and could look like in Kenya and beyond – more a rough guide to this new terrain than a comprehensive atlas. It's not about preaching solutions or pointing fingers. It's about shifting perspective on an African country to recognise agency and acknowledge the right to simply be – in all our complexity – and moving towards more informed reflection on how Kenyan society works. It's about moving away from gut instincts and speculation, towards a more informed analysis of the ways in which contemporary Africa defines and deploys its agency.

Overall, this is a book about how people in an unexpected country in an unexpected continent are making use of technologies that were not designed with them in mind in order to shape their political destinies. It's about the new ways in which information travels and how this interacts with existing structures in a society. It's about the lessons that Kenya can give the world, and a break from the stream of publications highlighting what the world can teach Kenya. This is a book about an African country in the twenty-first century that acknowledges history but is not constrained by it. Overall, the book looks beyond 'Africa rising' or 'Africa failing' narratives to 'Africa being' stories – stories reflecting the ambivalence, complexity, challenges and opportunities of an African society in an increasingly connected world.

INTRODUCTION

It began with a rumour.

Late on the night of Sunday 3 April 2016, messages tore through Kenya's numerous WhatsApp groups that one of the country's best known mid-sized banks – Chase Bank – was in trouble. By Tuesday, 5 April, the news had leapt onto Twitter. User Mumbi Seraki (@ Mumbi Kenya) tweeted 'After Imperial, CBK focused ON forensic audits and found a similar ALLEGED FRAUD at Chase Bank where close to 15b is missing from the books'.[1] Each of the 14 tweets responding to Seraki demanded evidence and called on her to prove her allegations, with some going as far as inviting Chase Bank to prosecute Seraki for allegedly defaming the bank.

Even though Seraki is a relatively well-known personality, the initial instinct was to disbelieve her because Chase Bank was no small outlier bank. Unaffiliated with the US bank of the same name, the Kenyan bank was incorporated in 1995 as a mid-sized bank primarily serving low-income earners, small and medium-sized enterprises and other underserved communities.[2] It had one of the largest sharia compliant banking units in the region and served many businesses in Kenya that traded primarily with the Middle East.[3] At its peak, Chase Bank was one of the most successful indigenous banks in the largest banking sector in East Africa.

Fear of a bank collapse was close to many people's minds as Kenya's bank sector was in flux in 2016. A few months earlier, Imperial Bank, another indigenous mid-sized bank had gone under owing to fraud and mismanagement, taking with it billions of shillings of customers' money. A long-running exposé by Kenyan writer and blogger Owaah revealed the extent of the rot at Imperial, a conspiracy by the bank's managing director against the bank and its depositors that went all the way up to the governor of the Central Bank of Kenya (CBK).[4] In one of the most shared blog posts of the year, the blogger laid out the guts of the Imperial Bank saga, pointing out the complete erosion of systems of accountability, rampant systemic corruption and the abandonment of depositors once the rot was exposed. The blog post was so popular that the mainstream media, which had been ignoring the story up this point, finally followed up with their own exposé.

Some Facebook posts alleged that major depositors heard about the Chase Bank rumours prior to the Twitter revelations and immediately withdrew their money. For the majority of customers, however, the first sign that something truly was wrong didn't come until Seraki's tweet on 5 April. The Chase Bank social media accounts were running as normal. Users frantically tagged the bank in Seraki's tweets, urging them to respond. The people managing the bank's social media urged customers to ignore such rumours: 'that information is completely false and we urge the public to ignore it'.[5] The bank drafted and issued a press statement asserting that Chase Bank was 'strong, sound and transparent'.[6]

Forty-eight hours later, on 7 April 2016 Chase Bank was under receivership – taken over by the Central Bank – with all accounts frozen, and the CEO and Managing Director suspended pending investigations.

Customers who went to branches in the morning found the doors locked, heavy steel chains wrapped around the sparkling chrome door handles, knotted together by angry, iron padlocks. Every branch had a notice posted above the locks announcing that the bank was closed until further notice. Some customers hopped online to try and access their accounts, with no luck. The bank's online banking site was down. Staff members suffered the double burden of having to explain a situation they didn't fully understand

and were also directly affected by through the closure themselves due to the requirement that they have accounts with the bank so their salaries could be paid into them. Crowds gathered at bank branch entrances, waiting and hoping that someone would come out and say something, but no one did. For the next week, Chase Bank would remain closed.

Irate customers, probably feeling unheard as official communication was so slow in coming, took to social media to express their frustration. For those who weren't customers, it gave insight into the scale of the loss. It was the first week of the month – bills, rents and salaries were due. Some people had lost everything. There were tweets about having to beg landlords for more time. Others wondered what to do about school fees and school supplies that were due soon. For one person, it was all too much: 'Fuck you Chase Bank' he or she wrote in permanent marker across the glass doors of the bank's branch in the Nairobi Central Business District. The picture was loaded onto Twitter and Facebook and quickly went viral. Another user tweeted: 'fuck chasebank fuck chasebank directors fuck whoever knew what was going on and decided to keep quiet fuck you fuck you fuck you. fuck you!'[7] Chase Bank was dying and taking entire lives down with it, but unlike Imperial Bank much of the country now had a front-row seat to the carnage.

Who tried to kill Chase Bank?

According to the Central Bank, social media was definitely an accessory to the attempted murder. In the 7 April press release announcing the receivership, the CBK argued 'Chase Bank Limited experienced liquidity difficulties, *following inaccurate social media reports* [emphasis added] and the stepping aside of two of its directors'.[8] The CBK argued that the social media rumours triggered a bank run that ultimately tipped the scales and led to the bank's collapse. It's a charge that many of Kenya's best-known social media users and experts vehemently deny. Social media doesn't cause bank collapses, they say, corruption and fraud do. In a response piece, Nanjira Sambuli, the former head of research at Nairobi's iHub, which was at the time the largest tech incubator and co-working space in the country, argued that social media merely accelerated what turned out to be accurate reports that the bank was in trouble.[9] It wasn't malicious; the stories were true. And this is exactly what social media is designed to do – help tell stories further and faster without the barriers facing traditional media. Chase Bank tried to kill itself.

The truth, as always, is probably somewhere in the middle. Like all banks, Chase didn't physically have all the money in its accounting books. A bank's financial position is a mix of money borrowed, owed and expected, as well as physical deposits. Some of it is paper and metal, but most of it is IOUs or promises of money in the form of interest and loans. When the rumours of an imminent collapse went viral, those who held physical deposits in the bank panicked and rushed to withdraw their money. But most of that money was out in the universe, given to people in the form of loans or invested as part of the bank's portfolio. As customers withdrew the limited physical deposits that were held in the bank, the bank was left holding a bunch of IOUs – worthless currency that makes it impossible for a financial institution to operate. The immediate cause of the run on Chase Bank was definitely panic.

However, the bank run was a symptom of a much deeper malaise within Chase Bank: the first tipping domino that brought down the whole structure. Chase Bank was holding far more IOUs in proportion to real money than is allowed in Kenyan law and indeed by financial prudence. A big part of this was large loans to staff members, which are often given at much lower interest rates and more generous terms than those given to the general public. Banks in Kenya are only allowed to lend up to 25% of their loan book to staff members. Independent audits by private firms are supposed to review the bank's financial position every year and let investors know if these rules are broken. Chase Bank had been lying to its independent auditors about insider loans, which were underreported by over 300%.[10] Up to 8 billion shillings in insider loans was hidden in the audit – far more than is allowed.[11]

Chase Bank was already in a bad way, long before the story broke on social media, having overextended itself in a highly risky way, particularly by extending most of its loan book to insiders (staff members and directors). This meant that not only was the money being given away but it was being given away at concessionary rates.

The common denominator in these seemingly irreconcilable positions on what exactly triggered the collapse of Chase Bank is that they all see a connection between the advent of social media and the speed at which the bank collapsed. Chase Bank broke Kenyan banking laws but was already weak.[12] Had Chase Bank had a better financial structure there is every reason to believe that, despite the bank run, the bank's collapse would not have happened so quickly and so thoroughly. The speed at which information was provided by institutions and individuals online did add more fuel to fears of the bank's demise. There was an accelerator effect that made the inevitable happen faster.

This story of Chase Bank is part of the broader ten-year narrative in which digital spaces generally, and social media especially, emerge as one of the most potent political spaces in Kenya. The virtual spaces created through Twitter, WhatsApp, Facebook and other platforms are today a collective powerful force that institutions have been forced to reckon with. A 2016 study of Twitter in Africa showed that in general Twitter accounts in Africa tend to be more political than those from other countries – 8.6% of the total number of tweets to 2% in the US and the UK.[13] For Kenyans, social media is not simply a space to post pictures of new clothes or delicious food, or to have conversations about sports. It is a space where some of the most exuberant and insightful political conversations are happening. Digital spaces have been used to conceive of world-changing technology, to plan and execute protests, to shape academic discourse, as well as to shift political conversations in ways that include and exclude power. Social media especially has become a weathervane of the political winds in Kenya, giving more space to voices that are ordinarily left out of political conversations offline.

Sensing the increasing importance of digital spaces, the government has tried to get in on the act. In 2014, the Kenya government launched the e-citizen platform. The portal is supposed to be a one-stop shop for government information and services. Several key agencies have transferred much of their work onto the portal. As of 2017, Kenyans need an e-citizen account to apply for a passport, driver's licence or identity card, to register a new business or for health insurance. Other agencies have also developed similar platforms that are not integrated with the e-citizen platform. The Kenya Revenue Authority (KRA), which collects taxes in Kenya has an e-platform where individuals request tax IDs and file their tax returns. The National Transportation Services Authority (NTSA) also runs its own platform for motor vehicle registration, for example when a person buys or sells a car and needs documentation to support the transaction.

However, it's not all rosy. Social media platforms can be toxic spaces that replicate offline harm. Violent acts are encouraged and distributed on these platforms, such as politicians threatening physical violence against their opponents. Video recordings of physical and sexual assaults, particularly against women, have gone viral – disseminated by thousands of people – on Kenyan social media. Ethnic chauvinism is frequently played and replayed, especially around elections. Abuse levelled at individuals and institutions is prevalent. Rules around privacy and against defamation of character have been ignored. Paid shills for specific political voices have bought followers and built pulpits from which those followers are bullied and whipped into a frenzy for their political paymasters, crowding out more meaningful discussion.

Meanwhile, there are major concerns about elaborate operations to collect and store citizen data without an effective data management and security policy. As of 2017, the Kenyan government had failed to pass a data protection law even while it continued to amass citizen data. The Independent Elections and Boundaries Commission (IEBC) keeps mobile phone and biometric data for all eligible voters in the country. This information is supposed to be confidential, but voters still periodically receive unsolicited text messages from political parties, raising questions about the lack of data privacy. Some individuals have also accused mobile phone companies of allowing the government access to location information of various individuals through their mobile phones. Kenyan mobile phone users frequently complain about having to unsubscribe from services to which they never subscribed. There are also increasing concerns about the state using its vast data collection operation, particularly through mobile giant Safaricom, for unchecked citizen surveillance.[14]

Kenya is not unique globally. Around the world, the internet is the latest frontline in the never-ending tango between citizens and their states. Social media is making it impossible to pretend not to notice anger or claims of disaffection, and vast data siphoning operations are being built under the guise of security. Digital technology is allowing relative freedom of speech in societies where such freedoms are resisted. Furthermore, it is allowing people to be angry – vocally, visibly and virulently – in a way which traditional media is unable to capture or articulate. Some of the most powerful moments of the last ten years – from the Black Lives Matter movement, to the cataloguing of deaths of migrants and refugees on the high seas of the Mediterranean and the South China Sea – start on these platforms. And because of this – because governments contain fragile egos that do not respond well to such criticisms – there are many palpable fears that this is a space that must be curtailed and controlled.

Between 2016 and 2017, social media had profound but ill-understood impacts on key political moments around the world. Significant evidence emerged that Facebook and its news Application

Programming Interface (API) affected the outcome of the US election as well as the Brexit vote through the manipulation and consolidation of echo chambers and accelerated diffusion of 'fake news' – an ill-defined term that in popular parlance comprises everything from propaganda, spin and other forms of misinformation to real news that the listener doesn't want to hear. Yet social media has also been used to raise the profile of political protests in the Gambia, the Democratic Republic of Congo (DRC), Ethiopia, Sudan, Chad, Gabon, Congo-Brazzaville and other less reported-on countries where local media is subject to state capture. These countries and more have used the sites to track activists who have been arrested and tortured for their work. A picture of three-year-old Aylan Kurdi, dead on the shores of the Aegean sea after fleeing the war in Syria, went viral on social media and triggered a change in refugee policy in Europe.[15] Social media has allowed people to publicly grieve for the ongoing military sieges in Syria, Yemen and other countries, with images of starving children arguably shaming the international community into intervening.

Around the world, unsure of what this new force represents and what it could do, governments have fought back. In 2016 alone the internet was shut down 54 times in 27 countries.[16] In Africa especially, it is open season on digital platforms, and specifically social media. Uganda, Chad and Congo-Brazzaville, fearing that young people and activists would use the platforms to organise anti-regime protests countrywide, shut down all systems for up to two weeks around contentious election periods. In Ethiopia hundreds of activists across the country were arrested during nationwide protests against the regime, as were Ethiopian-based relatives of Ethiopian nationals abroad who posted materials that they considered supportive of the protests.[17] Activists in Zimbabwe and Hong Kong have been arrested for their Facebook posts. Something about the way information is generated and shared on social media has governments around the world quaking in their boots.

*

Figure 1 Map of African countries where the internet was shut down in 2016

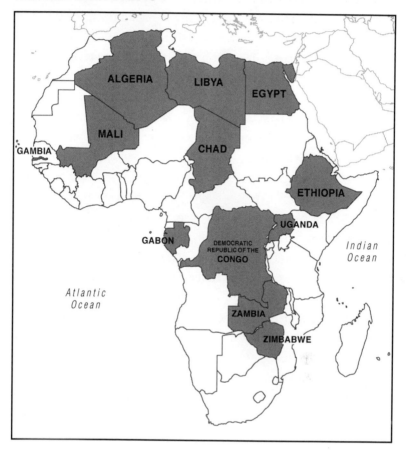

Many governments find themselves stuck in a paradox. On one hand, there is tremendous pressure to control social media and the internet. On the other, there is significant pressure to keep up with other countries by moving key government services online and to leave space open for 'innovation'. 'Digital government' is one of the most powerful development buzzwords, where citizens are expected to use government-designed website portals to access information and services. In India, the centralised Aadhaar system – similar to Kenya's e-citizen platform but collecting far more biometric data – has been both criticised and celebrated.[18] Supporters say it will allow the state to streamline the provision of government services. Critics say that it creates more obstacles between the low-literacy citizen and the state, thereby creating a two-tier state. They are also concerned about the scale of data collection involved in setting up the system. The state therefore has a significant interest in promoting digital literacy in the general population but is wary of a more informed public, while there are segments of the population who based on historical experience do not believe that a project of this scale has their interests at heart.

It was in this context – this oscillation between open-hearted embrace and outright fear – that the Kenyan government promised that the 2017 election in Kenya would be the first truly digital election in the country. As part of that promise, the IEBC developed an elaborate infrastructure to collect voter data from the various polling centres and transmit them to the National Tallying Centre (NTC) in Nairobi. This system – the Kenya Integrated Elections Management System (KIEMS) – was supposed to be a game changer in the context of a history of violent and unpredictable elections. In addition, the IEBC deployed a website known as the Results Transmission System (RTS), which was supposed to allow members of the public to access real-time information about the election.

Every one of these systems failed spectacularly during the actual election, primarily due to human interference. Of the 40,883 KIEMS kits that were distributed to polling stations around the country, at least 11,000 were not used because of the alleged unreliability of the network signal at these stations – charges that members of the public disputed, publicly and vocally, on social media.[19] Several more malfunctioned on site on voting day.[20] During court proceedings that led to the invalidation of the presidential election result, the IEBC itself disowned the results that were transmitted on the RTS platform, which differed significantly from those that were finally announced on 11 August. Lawyers for the commission said that they were not the actual electoral results but 'statistics'.[21]

*

Does the Kenyan state want digital government or not? On the one hand, the illusion of digital government is good for a narrative of modernity that they are desperately courting. On the other, electronic platforms come with a significant loss of control. Given the reliance on digital spaces in Kenya, a countrywide shutdown of the internet like those in Ethiopia or Gabon, or a shutdown of social media as in Uganda would be impossible. However Kenya is not so democratic that the fear wasn't palpable. In the build-up to the 2017 election, this was one of the many questions that was repeated to the Cabinet Secretary for Information and Communications Technology Joe Mucheru: would Kenya switch off the internet during the election given that so many similarly situated countries did? To his and Kenya's credit they did not,[22] but fears of throttling – when an Internet Service Provider deliberately slows down internet speeds – led to heightened monitoring[23] throughout the extended election period. Fears of a shutdown were also fuelled by past practice. The Kenyan government, for instance, switched off access to internet and mobile networks in parliament in early December 2016 during a contentious parliamentary debate on funding for the highly anticipated 2017 elections.[24]

If social media can bring down a bank, can it bring down a government? Can a tweet launch a revolution? Can a digital election finally deliver an uneventful election in Kenya? These were perhaps the questions the Kenyan government was asking itself watching the Chase Bank saga unfold. Considerably rattled, as if they reasoned by analogy that they were also on shaky ground, many government-friendly bloggers and social media users pushed out a patriotic counter-narrative to reassure the undecided. The hashtag #IStandWithChaseBank was created to encourage people to keep their deposits with the bank and have faith in its directors. It reeked of desperation, and the facts of the scenario hint at the absurdity of the push. Bank directors were private citizens deceiving depositors and regulators. Why should you keep your money with a bank led by people who were not patriotic enough not to steal from their clients? Wouldn't patriotism demand accountability on behalf of depositors who were facing the threat of losing their homes, businesses and life savings?

Chase Bank did finally survive the storm. At the time of writing the CBK receivership was still in place as it prepared to sell the bank as a going concern. Small-scale deposits were guaranteed by the CBK while larger investors were asked to be patient as the situation resolved itself. The entire saga was a lesson in why fear of social media is warranted and yet often misguided. Unlike Imperial Bank months before, which limped towards receivership with marginal media coverage, Chase Bank nearly died on the national stage. It took only two days between rumours of investigations of bank directors of Chase Bank and its imminent collapse. Social media was definitely a part of this story. Would Chase Bank have collapsed without social media? Probably. But would it have happened so fast and so spectacularly? Possibly not. The only unambiguous lesson from the Chase Bank fallout is that we need to spend a little more time understanding how digital platforms in Kenya interact with offline politics.

This book, then, is an attempt to locate Kenya on the spectrum of state reactions to emerging digital spaces: from the brusque and authoritarian, to the liberal and accommodating. It is written as a detailed account of Kenya's first digital decade, the ten-year period between Kenya's election violence in 2007 and the shambolic 2017 vote, to map the advances and regressions that have occurred in the political space. In the first section, the book establishes the contours of Kenya's public sphere and the challenges that triggered the digitisation push during this decade. In the second section, the book maps the positive and negative impact of this forced yet accidental collision between the digital and the analogue. Finally the book ends on the uncertainty triggered by the chaotic 2017 election, particularly highlighting scandalous revelations of fraud and foreign manipulation in the face of heightened political consciousness and conversation online.

Very few countries in Africa have been so deeply entangled in the global panic over the role of technology in politics as has Kenya. On one hand, it is only one of four countries in the greater Eastern African region (including the Indian Ocean islands) that has had regular changes of government through elections. The economy is growing steadily if not dramatically. Kenya's digital boom is part of an effort to diversify an economy that until now has never had hydrocarbons to rely on.

However, every general election in Kenya since 1997 has had incidents of electoral violence. Between August and October 2017, the police killed at least 36 people in violence connected to the election,[25] and this has a great deal to do with the uncertainty created by the failure of digital tools and proof of irregularities and illegalities documented on social media. Spaces for freedom of expression are shrinking dramatically even as economic gains continue. The media is struggling to find its independence; bloggers and journalists are being killed, arrested or otherwise intimidated. Significantly, global firms like Cambridge Analytica that have been involved in digital engagements overseas are present in the country, to the detriment of Kenyan people. No amount of digital innovation can paper over analogue failures, deliberate or otherwise, and so the collision of digital democracy and analogue politics in Kenya between 2007 and 2017 is the epitome of three steps forward, two steps back.

Part I

ANALOGUE
POLITICS

Chapter 1

2007: THE VIOLENT ORIGINS OF KENYA'S DIGITAL DECADE

'Kenya is not one of those countries where people win elections by 99% of the votes', Kenya's Deputy President William Ruto declared to a room of foreign correspondents based in Nairobi.[1] It was 17 October 2017, ten days before a presidential election rerun, and Ruto was speaking at a briefing for the Foreign Correspondents Association of East Africa on progress towards the election following the invalidation of the election of 8 August. In an unprecedented turn of events, the Supreme Court of Kenya had ruled in a 4–2 decision that there were too many irregularities and illegalities to allow the first vote to stand. Kenyans needed a second presidential election, which was set for 26 October, so that the winner could have a clear mandate. Ruto had gathered the foreign correspondents at his office so he could assure them and their audiences that Kenya's painful march towards full democracy was still on. Because the briefing was only for foreign correspondents the comment didn't get much traction. It would be more significant after 26 October.

The story of Kenya's 2017 election is the story of politics and technology promising great things and completely failing to deliver. By some estimates, this was the most expensive election in African history at $28 per capita before the rerun, which cost another $12 million.[2] A big part of this cost was the development of an IT infrastructure for voter identification and result transmission.

The KIEMS featured the Electronic Voter Identification Devices (EVIDs),[3] in which 40,883 tablets were used for biometric identification of voters. It also periodically transmitted aggregate statistics on turnout and participation to the National Tallying Centre in Nairobi. Combined with the RTS,[4] the idea was that enhancing the technology would enhance the transparency of the election – a win–win for everyone.

During the tallying process, it became clear that the RTS system did update periodically as required by the IEBC's regulations, and that the statistics it was displaying had nothing to do with the vote. I personally monitored statistics on the rejected votes – that is, votes that were cast but rejected by party agents for small lapses like checking outside the box or checking two boxes – and by the time counting ended, it was up to 400,454 nationwide.[5] Later, during the Supreme Court proceedings triggered by the petition challenging the result, the IEBC disavowed the results, calling them 'statistics'.[6] The final number of rejected votes submitted and verified by the IEBC was 81,000, a significant decrease.

The period between the announcement of the result and the second presidential election on 26 October 2017 was filled with uncertainty, violence and fears of violence, as well as institutional failures by the IEBC. In the roughly two months between the invalidation of the 8 August vote and the October rerun, IEBC Commissioner Dr Roselyn Akombe resigned and left the country after receiving numerous death threats.[7] She said that she was wary of overseeing both elections because of her concerns over the integrity of the process.[8] Akombe claimed that the Commission was resistant to criticism and reform following the scathing Supreme Court decision, ignoring many of the amendments they were required to make, including on the use of digital systems in the election. But she was also scared for her life and didn't think that the risk was worth it. The day after she resigned, the chair of the Commission Wafula Chebukati seemed to agree, telling a press conference that he could not guarantee a credible election.[9] Some days after that, the CEO of the Commission went on three weeks' leave, meaning that three senior officials at the Commission would not be present during the actual vote.[10]

Ruto probably regretted his hubris on 30 October, when less than two weeks after he made his statement, his running mate Uhuru Kenyatta was declared the winner of the election with 98% of the votes cast.[11] In Eastern Africa, only the authoritarian Paul Kagame in Rwanda had a more improbable winning margin (garnering 98.6% of the vote[12]). In part, the outcome was because the opposition coalition National Super Alliance (NASA) had called for a boycott and main opposition challenger Raila Odinga withdrew from the race. According to figures released by the IEBC, turnout for the October rerun was 37.99%, down from 79.5% in August, meaning that more than half of the people who voted in August did not vote again in October.[13] And even those figures were highly contested as individuals took to Twitter and Facebook to share pictures of electoral forms they claimed had been manipulated in various parts of the country, inflating the tally considerably.

It was even worse during the October rerun. The Commission did not use results from the KIEMS kits at all, and there was no RTS.[14] The only digital element of the election was that the commission uploaded digital copies of the tallying forms onto the website, which allowed members of the public to scrutinise them.

Kenya's big digital election was an enormous flop.

It is impossible to understand Kenya's fixation with computer-aided politics without understanding its political history. The country's first digital decade, bookended by two highly contentious elections in 2007 and 2017, triggered tremendous social and political changes in the broader society. Some of these changes include the birth and success of mobile money, the creation of Africa's most vibrant tech scene, or the decision to computerise the election process. All of this is shaped directly – much more so than in similarly situated countries – by Kenya's electoral politics.

At independence in 1963, Kenya was a multiparty state, but after a spectacular falling out between then-President Jomo Kenyatta and his Vice-President Jaramogi Oginga Odinga, a ban on Odinga's Kenya People's Union (KPU) meant Kenya became a de facto one-party state.[15] After Kenyatta's death in 1978, his Vice-President Daniel Toroitich Arap Moi took over and formalised the one-party system four years later.[16] In 1982, there was an attempted coup by the air force, supported by some university students.[17] Consequently, Moi clamped down not just on the coup plotters but on the public sphere and any centres of power that he saw as challenging his authority.[18]

Between 1986 and 1992, thousands of Kenyans who dared to organise against the one-party state were arrested, detained, tortured or forced into exile.[19] Many of these were journalists and academics like the late satirist Wahome Mutahi, former chief justice Willy Mutunga, Ngugi wa Thiong'o and opposition leader Raila Odinga – Jaramogi Oginga Odinga's son. The resulting climate of fear allowed the regime to survive for 16 years, but by the end of the 1980s the demands for multiparty democracy were too strident and focused to be ignored.[20] Moi finally relented and at a party conference at the Kasarani Sports Stadium in December 1991, he announced that Section 2A of the constitution that made Kenya a one-party state was repealed.[21]

The first ten years of multiparty democracy in Kenya were characterised by an incremental opening up of the public sphere in the face of intense organising and resistance by the opposition, civil society and student groups.[22] Although Moi had permitted parties to be organised, his ruling party Kenya African National Union (KANU) destroyed or compromised many of the public institutions that were necessary to a functional democracy, like the judiciary.[23] Elections in 1992 and 1997 were characterised by widespread rigging and political violence that left hundreds dead and displaced. Although media was diversified, the state still retained majority control of the fourth estate through shareholding and state broadcasters.

However, in 2002 the fragmented opposition finally united to support a single candidate, Mwai Kibaki, a long-serving minister and vice-president under Moi who had defected to the opposition soon after Section 2A was repealed. In an unprecedented victory and in what would go down in history as Kenya's most peaceful general election to date, Kibaki won against Uhuru Kenyatta – Jomo's youngest son and Moi's chosen successor.[24] Kenyans were ecstatic. Kibaki's swearing in was one of the best-attended public events in recent memory. The resulting euphoria challenged the ominous threats that Moi had been making since 1991 that multi-party democracy was inherently destructive in an ethnically pluralist society like Kenya.

The euphoria was short lived. By 2004 the coalition that had brought Kibaki into power was fraying, notably around the implementation of a new constitution which had been one of the opposition's unifying issues.[25] Kibaki had promised a new constitution within 100 days of taking power, but a national conference to debate the contours of such a constitution didn't take place until April 2003.[26] The debates were acrimonious and a draft document was not consolidated until March 2004, known as the Bomas Draft. After representatives from NGOs and from government walked out of talks, the remaining delegates designed a draft that ignored Kibaki's reservations and created a strong prime ministerial position.[27] Legislators loyal to Kibaki then passed a law giving themselves the power to amend the draft before subjecting it to a referendum as required by a court decision.[28]

At a retreat to finalise their proposed drafts to the constitution, legislators watered down the proposed Bomas Draft considerably, much to the chagrin of critics who saw it as political horse-trading rather than constitution making.[29] Despite these and other criticisms, in 2005 the draft went to a referendum as required by law. Following an acrimonious campaign period characterised by protest, ethnic mobilisation and misrepresentation of the content of the document, the draft was rejected by voters.[30]

The referendum result would destroy the ruling coalition. As they were campaigning outside their parties, the electoral commission assigned each side a fruit as a symbol. Those in favour of the watered down draft campaigned as team banana. Those against were team orange. It was one of the most hotly contested electoral races in the country's history. In the end, those against the draft won by 58% to 42% against, with a nearly 54% turnout.[31]

The result electrified Odinga and his supporters, who promptly left government to establish their own political outfit called the Orange Democratic Movement (ODM). It united those who were frustrated with what they saw as increasing ethnicisation of government under Kibaki and those who regretted staying with KANU after Moi's retirement only to be locked out of government. For Odinga, it hinted at the possibility that the presidency that had eluded him in 1997 and 2002 could finally be his in 2007.

2006 was a tumultuous year for Kenya that in many ways foreshadowed the disaster that would be the 2007 general election. Panicked by the loss of the referendum, Kibaki and his supporters began to undo many of the freedoms that had catapulted them into office. Notably, they went to war with the press. For example, in March 2006, armed and masked individuals raided the Standard Media Group offices in Nairobi.[32] The then Minister for Internal Security, John Michuki, said the police raided the Standard Group because they were going to publish and broadcast a series of stories that would be damaging to the state. This upped the ante on the impending election, and put the press on a warpath with the state.

By the time the December 2007 election came round, Kenya was highly polarised. The government was nervous and on the defensive. The opposition was electrified and cocky. The press was predisposed to go against the government after a year of constant tension and humiliation. The stage was set for something major to happen.

*

The 2007 election created the conditions for Kenya's most seismic social and digital change. On 29 December 2007, Kenya began its descent into what would later be called its worst crisis in history, shattering its reputation as an island of stability in a tough neighbourhood.[33] By 27 December, when voting took place, none of the major political outfits from the 2002 election were still viable political vehicles. KANU, which had ruled the country since independence, was now a small opposition party and its party leader Kenyatta had defected and joined Kibaki on the campaign trail.[34] President Kibaki himself abandoned his National Rainbow Coalition (NARC) for the Party of National Unity (PNU).[35] Odinga had been removed from his ministerial role and was running as leader of ODM, taking with him several other ministers fired by Kibaki for supporting the orange campaign during the referendum.[36] He was joined by William Ruto from KANU, who had served as a senior government official under Moi. Kalonzo Musyoka, who had served as a minister under both Moi and Kibaki, formed his own party, the Orange Democratic Party – Kenya, which reflected his decision to support the 'no' vote but remain independent.[37] The tectonic plates had shifted, and some lava was about to make it to the surface.

On 27 December itself millions of Kenyans braved the scorching December heat to cast their ballots – the exact number remains unknown because the Electoral Commission of Kenya (ECK) never made the results public. Although the campaign had been hard fought, voting day itself was peaceful. In the shadow of the successful 2002 election and the 2005 referendum, there was a great deal of expectation in the air. The sense was that Kenya was on track for another hotly contested but ultimately peaceful and representative election.

In the evening of the 27th the first set of results began to trickle in. Odinga slowly but surely began to take the lead against Kibaki. Some irregularities emerged.[38] For example, constituencies in both government and opposition strongholds were returning results of 110% or 109% voter turnout, suggesting that the ballot stuffing that had been rampant under Moi had reared its head again.[39] But because it was happening on both sides, the expectation was that the impact of one would cancel the other out.

In the early stages of the tallying process, Odinga had a seemingly unassailable lead of over 1 million votes.[40] But by the morning of the 29th, this lead had evaporated. Five electoral commissioners publicly claimed that there was major fraud underway.[41] The opposition descended on the national tallying centre at the Kenyatta International Conference Centre in downtown Nairobi and alleged widespread alteration of constitutional tallies. They insisted that they had proof, which stalled the chair of the ECK for a while, though not too long.

Significantly, this was all playing out on live television and radio across the country. At one moment, a returning officer with the electoral commission emerged from the backroom where votes were being tallied and declared on camera that there was widespread result alteration occurring.[42] Much of his testimony was captured on camera before security officials rushed him away and a scuffle involving some of Kenya's most visible political figures ensued. As part of the effort to regain control, all media was ejected from the national tallying centre. Odinga gave a speech on the steps of the tallying centre asserting that electoral results were being falsified with the collusion of the ECK. He wanted the count and the announcement of the results to stop.

The chair of the ECK, Samuel Kivuitu, would later allege that he was not privy to everything that was happening outside the tallying centre.[43] He insisted that he was only reading the results as offered to him. On 30 December it was announced that incumbent Mwai Kibaki had won the election. Curiously, Kibaki was sworn in late at night in the State House grounds and in the absence of the general public.[44] Once again, this was all captured on television and radio.

Odinga quickly called for protests against what he saw as deceit aided by the electoral commission. He was met with a strong state response. Michuki promptly banned any kind of protest in the country, which only aggravated Odinga's supporters further.[45]

Michuki also tried to rein in the press, banning any form of live broadcast and threatening heavy penalties for ignoring his order.[46]

This was the first time Nairobi and Mombasa had been brought into the election violence that had troubled Kenya since 1992. Clashes between Odinga and Kibaki supporters, ostensibly along ethnic lines, flared up in informal settlements in Nairobi. In Lang'ata, where I lived, we watched the sky over Kibera, often dubbed the largest informal settlement in the world, glow orange as individuals set fire to their neighbours' homes.[47] The downtown area of Nairobi as well as several informal settlements were barricaded by the police. Food ran low in supermarkets as the main markets that supply fresh produce in the city – Wakulima Market and City Market – were inaccessible. As uncertainty grew, so too did the scale and spread of the violence.

Attacks and rumours of attacks quickly fed into counterattacks against putatively hostile ethnic groups. Outside Nairobi, the main Nairobi–Kisumu highway was impassable between the two agricultural towns of Naivasha and Eldoret. Gangs of youths of various ethnicities raided buses and *matatus* (14-seater minibuses used for public transit) looking for 'enemies', and eventually buses refused to ply the route. Rumours and evidence of forced circumcisions of Luos in towns in the Rift Valley drove counterattacks of non-Luo businesses in Kisumu, which in turn fuelled more attacks against them in towns where they were the minority. Kikuyu businesses and homes were destroyed in Eldoret and Nakuru, triggering reprisals in Naivasha and Kiambu.

The worst episode of civilian-inflicted harm in independent Kenya was on 1 January 2008. In Eldoret, Kikuyu families who had moved to the area under the first Kenyatta's resettlement scheme had founded a small church they called Kiambaa Church after a similarly named region in Central Kenya. When the violence began, many displaced worshippers sought refuge in the Kenya Assemblies of God Pentecostal church. Hundreds of men, women and children were sleeping on mattresses strewn across the floor[48] when the sound of distant chanting echoed through the building.

Earlier in the day, a gang of about 200 armed youth had been stomping through the town demanding to see everyone's identity cards so that they could punish those who belonged to ethnic groups that had supported Kibaki – primarily Kikuyu.[49] After tearing through the town, they finally descended on the church. The internally displaced persons (IDPs) at the church were sitting ducks. According to a witness, when they saw the large gang approaching, many of the IDPs ran into the church, effectively into a trap.[50] Some of the men tried to repel the gang but were quickly overpowered. The gang poured petrol on any mattresses they could reach, stuffed them into the windows and set the church on fire. By the time the flames had died down, 30 people were dead.[51]

Militia groups coalesced around three major ethnic groups in the country – Kikuyu, Luo and Kalenjin – and ran amok in various towns and cities, particularly in Nairobi and Mombasa's informal settlements, as well as Kisumu, Eldoret and other towns in the Rift Valley. Messages alleging attacks and counterattacks proliferated in text messages and on local language radio stations. Attempting to restore order, the police joined in the fray, summarily executing hundreds of young men in places they believed were hotspots.[52] According to Human Rights Watch, amongst other victims, the police summarily executed 44 people in Kisumu – Odinga's stronghold – and another 34 in Mathare informal settlement in Nairobi.[53]

Despite many local-level peace-making attempts, only the international intervention of mediators like former UN Secretary General Kofi Annan and the threat of litigation at the then-robust International Criminal Court (ICC) stopped the violence. In February 2008, Kibaki and Odinga signed a series of accords to bring a political settlement and urge them to calm their supporters.[54] By this time, according to official estimates, which are markedly lower than those of non-governmental organisations, over 1,000 people had lost their lives and 150,000 homes had been destroyed in the most widespread violence in Kenya since independence.[55]

*

The 2007/08 post-election violence would dramatically alter Kenya's politics and public life. For the media, the ban on live broadcasts meant that they were unable to keep up with the speed of broadcast by international stations during this period.[56] Moreover, as tensions escalated, media houses internalised blame for spreading what was later deemed inflammatory information. Rather than continue to criticise political actors, they chose to broadcast pacifying, pre-approved messages. Although they continued to share information, it seemed meagre compared to the dramatic coverage being offered by international media.

One group of Kenyans grew particularly frustrated with the situation. During the economic and political deterioration between 1992 and 1997, millions of Kenyans had left the country, resulting in one of the largest African diasporas. By 2005/06 there were 2.3 million Kenyans living abroad, of whom an estimated 46.6% were 'highly educated'.[57] As a result, 16% of the country's highly educated people were in countries as disparate as the US, UK, India, China, Turkey, Russia and South Africa, watching as the country burned.[58] Information from Western media houses screamed that Armageddon was underway while local media grew inaccessible. I personally recall a sense of being stuck between the thumping rage of the international media and the state-sterilised narrative of local media on the internet. Reliable and verifiable information was scarce, and the main source of information for those tracking the developments was the internet.

As part of a broader, uncoordinated effort to retain links with Kenya, many in the diaspora and at home had by 2007 become active bloggers. Some of the blogs that had hitherto had apolitical briefs became more political as access to reliable information remained scarce.[59] Internet forums like Mashada or the Concerned Kenyan Writers group became heated sites for conversations and argument, some of it extremely productive and some of it replicating the contours of the offline violence.[60] On the whole, online forums opened up a new space for political discourse in Kenya that was being stifled in the traditional media and offline society.

The social and political rapture caused by the post-election violence (PEV) had ripple effects beyond the physical and material damage that it did to the country. The image of Kenya as a haven of peace was shattered. In a country where so much of what is taught as history is actually highly sanitised, pro-government propaganda, the post-election violence caught lumbering government agencies unawares and left spaces for new narratives of statehood and identity. There was a sense that what the government was saying was inaccurate, and for the first time new spaces emerged where this narrative could be challenged. Traditional media lost a significant amount of credibility because of its reluctance to confront issues head-on, leaving a population thirsty for some version of the truth. It was in this context that online media very quickly became a substitute for print media in particular.

As part of the political settlement that ended the violence, a number of special commissions were established to look deeper into the causes of violence. One of these was the Independent Review Commission (IREC), also known as the Kriegler Commission.[61] This commission focused on the flaws in the election system that had fuelled the mistrust and frustration that triggered violence in the first place. The commission unpacked every stage of the election from registration, to tallying, to verification, to announcement of results.

The Kriegler Commission concluded that the ECK 'did not live up to the standards of a transparent, free and fair election'.[62] The commission recommended in part that, in order to increase trust in the process, Kenyans needed to consider increased digitisation of elections. It recommended an integrated and secure tallying and data transmission system – ideally computerised – so that there could be simultaneous transmission of data to the national tallying centre. The commission also recommended the integration of this system with a progressive election result announcement system. It wanted the media to have full access to this system even if the

ECK retained overall control of it. It also requested more time for the verification of provisional results to correct frivolous errors and hear complaints of non-frivolous objections.

In short, the eventual computerisation of Kenya's 2017 election was not simply the function of the state's natural expansion. It was directly demanded by the settlement that followed the most intense political upheaval in the country's election. The Kriegler Commission recognised that the flagrant, systemic abuse of the ECK systems in 2007 had deeply ruptured trust in the political system, which could lead to further political upheaval down the line. The Commission thought that technology could bridge that trust gap.

In retrospect, the Commission underestimated the depth to which trust in electoral institutions had been damaged, and the tenacity with which Kenyan politicians would continually try to manipulate systems to win elections. Even though the ECK was disbanded and replaced by the IEBC, many of the practices that led to the former's demise recurred in 2013 and more violently in 2017. This was part of the reason why the Supreme Court threw out the 8 August election result. It was not conducted to the standards recommended by the Kriegler Commission and later operationalised in laws like the new 2010 constitution and the Elections Act (2012). Moreover, when the IEBC more or less ignored the KIEMS and the RTS system, it basically ignored the heart of the political settlement.

The 2007 election in Kenya fuelled a thirst for new politics, new discourses and new places to have them, the contours of which would soon mimic global shifts in how political information is created and delivered.

Chapter 2

AVATARS IN THE SQUARE: THEORISING KENYA'S PUBLIC SPHERE

What is possible online is dependent on what exists offline. Any freedom, interest or capacity with which people are able to use digital spaces to advance their political interests is entirely dependent on a number of offline factors, from practical ones like availability of infrastructure to more ideational factors like the state of the public political participation in the society in question. In many countries around the world it also depends on the extent to which, democratic consolidation, has occurred – how close the society gets to the one person, one voice ideal. Our digital public lives are predicated on our lives offline.

The typical wisdom on the digitisation of politics is that more technology will inevitably lead to more democracy.[1] Technology and science have been portrayed as neutral, abstract, transparent and predictable things that can bring order to the chaos of human life. This has fuelled a presumption in policy that systems built on technology are superior to those that rely on humans or human intervention, as more predictability means more order, and more order is always better. An election conducted electronically is theoretically superior to one run primarily by humans: a banking system that relies on technology is said to be superior to one that still relies on tellers and bean counters.

A pedestrian definition of a democracy is a society in which all eligible members are able to meaningfully participate in public discourses regarding issues and situations that pertain to the society as a whole. A democracy in this case isn't simply a place where people are able to cast ballots – there are many countries where people vote repeatedly and their vote is practically meaningless because it does nothing to change political outcomes. Participation must be meaningful in order to influence the political trajectory of the society in question. It's about the extent to which individuals are able to shape their societies.

The phrase 'digital democracy' was coined precisely to both make the case and provide evidence that technology enhances democracy. In some policy language, the fact that so much protest and political resistance is happening online and on social media platforms is provided as evidence that more access to technology is increasing citizen participation in their societies. And in many ways it is. However, the phrase is also used in a normative sense to advocate for increasing access to these digital platforms, positioning them as affordable alternatives to their analogue predecessors. It all depends on how you define democracy and what you see as the obstacles to full democratic participation in the society in question.

Implicit in both these definitions of digital democracy is the belief that technology is neutral – it is not good or bad in and of itself. But this technological consensus is fraying based on inequalities and biases built into the system, and also on overarching questions of access. The supposed neutrality of technology can no longer be taken for granted.

A brief discussion on algorithms demonstrates how digital technology can have biases built into it from the outset. Algorithms are essentially a set of rules or operations that determine the process of solving a problem. A computer system, when presented with a set of data, subjects the data to a series of specified operations that deliver a set of outcomes. For example, you put in a set of résumés at one end, the computer crunches them, and at the other end comes out a ranking of the résumés based on whatever rules you programmed the computer to use. An algorithm is this set of rules. It determines how various operations interact with each other. What factors should your programme consider? Do you add first and then subtract or vice versa? What happens when the first number is bigger than the second number? Algorithms don't have to be numbers either. They could be names, or cities of birth, or colour. As long as it can be translated into computer code, it can be handled by an algorithm.

In her 2017 book,[2] data scientist Cathy O'Neil writes persuasively about the dangers inherent in much algorithm-based automation. She talks about the data economy or the significant shift towards using mathematical formulae to perform functions that would previously been done by humans. At first, this was limited to mechanical or rote functions, like sorting through large volumes of loan applications and putting the most promising on the top of the pile, ready for review by the person who would actually approve them. With the increasing reliance on computers, these formulae or the rules through which data is processed and sorted have become more complex and less understandable.

Until a few years ago, algorithms were very much hidden from public conversation. It was the kind of nerdy thing that all computer specialists knew but the public didn't feel had anything to do with them. The advent of social media changed that. For the first time, lay people could see instantly what a difference changing the rules could have on their lives. For example, when it first started Facebook simply showed the user everything that was being shared by their Facebook friends in real time. After a few years, users began to complain that they were spending far too much time on the site and threatened to ignore or close down their accounts in order to boost their productivity.

In response, in 2009 Facebook altered the algorithm that runs a user's home page – the news feed – so that information was sorted not by time, but by various subtle operations.[3] First, it got rid of the chronological order. Second, you only saw information from people you regularly interacted with on the platform, established by the number of times you posted on each other's walls or messaged each other etc. Third, it allowed people to pay for access to your newsfeed so that you would also see content from people or businesses you weren't necessarily following. These and other changes essentially meant that Facebook was in a better position to push certain content to the top of the user's attention span. It gave the site more control over the information you consumed.

O'Neil points out that today algorithms are used in banking, human resources and employment, in large school and university operations – pretty much every facet of our lives that can be subjugated to a computer programme. Critically, as more governments and corporations shift to electronic systems, they will be able to use these functions to subtly influence our experiences on these platforms. O'Neil argues that algorithms always reflect the biases and limitations of those who build them and are just as capable of racial, gender or age biases as human beings because they are designed to mimic human behaviour. In fact, purely technology-based systems might be worse in the long run because they lack empathy and cannot see context.

With regard to social media, an in-built limitation to its usefulness for democracy is the question of profitability. In October 2017, senior executives at Facebook, Google and Twitter were summoned to the US Congress to testify about the extent to which their platforms had contributed to Russian interference in the 2016 US presidential election.[4] During the hearing it emerged that the Internet Research Agency, auspiciously named but essentially a bot farm – groups of individuals or organisations that capitalise on the nuances of these platforms to churn out massive amounts of often identical content optimised for social media or to boost the popularity of existing content[5] – had spent about $126 million on advertising on these platforms towards this purpose.

Bot farms can only exist and prosper because these sites are designed to make money, and the algorithms that run Facebook, Google and Twitter are designed to privilege paid-for content. So those with deeper pockets obviously get more access to users. This is anathema to the flattening democratic principle of one person, one vote. It more closely resembles feudalism, where the moneyed landlords have a greater influence on the content and timbre of politics than the lowly serfs. The connection between advertising and algorithms on these platforms undermines their claims of enhancing democracy.

Following the 2016 presidential election in the US and the ascendance of computer-generated political victories like Brexit in Europe there is increasing apprehension that digitisation has been bad for Western democracies. Because these platforms don't adequately discriminate between whose money they take and whose they reject, they have given space to groups that would ordinarily be marginalised, such as racist groups in the US that have bought significant airtime on these platforms.[6]

Still, it would be absurd to generalise these findings around the world because the core presumptions simply don't apply across the board. For one thing, the US and European nations have relatively more people online as a proportion of the general population than many other societies around the world. This gives digital platforms disproportionate space to influence offline politics. Secondly, much of what has been done to these societies was deliberate and targeted, almost as a form of modern combat between the West and Russia. This was digital warfare. There is much less interest in conducting similar warfare in countries like Togo. Even so, it would be naive to dismiss the risk altogether. Certainly the case of Kenya analysed in greater depth in subsequent chapters suggests that the risks are still salient.

This ties to the question of access – can it truly be a digital democracy if it excludes much of a country or society? Kenya is a leader in the developing world but is still lagging behind in regard to digital access. Those who are making politics online are a subset of a subset of yet another subset – those who have access to electricity, then those who have access to the internet, and finally those who have accounts on social media.

The internet first became available in Kenya in 1993 but full access through dial-up connections was not available until 1995.[7] In the first few years, growth was slow – stymied by the high cost of both access and equipment. By 2000, there were only 200,000 internet connections in Kenya for a population of 31.25 million. This began to change with the liberalisation of the telecommunications sector and the introduction of the National Optic Fibre Backbone – a nationwide network of fibre-optic cables that also connects Kenya to international networks. Significantly, the emergence of mobile internet has further lowered the costs of connectivity.

Still, 2012 statistics reaffirm that there are major access disparities not just of Information and Communications Technology (ICT) but of electricity in general.[8] In 2011/12 only 60.1% of Kenyan households had access to electricity, a higher number than neighbouring Ethiopia at 18.1% but lower than Ghana at 73%. Similarly, only 12.7% of homes in Kenya had access to the internet and to a computer, higher than both Ghana (2.7%) and Ethiopia (0.5%). Interestingly, Kenya had one of the highest rates of increase in internet access on the continent between 2007/08 and 2011/12 – 10.5%, compared to Ethiopia's 0.4%, Rwanda's 0.7% (but lower than South Africa's 14.9% and close to Namibia's 8.5%).

By 2017, there were 30.8 million internet subscriptions in Kenya but because it is possible for a single institution or individual to hold a subscription, it is difficult to extrapolate per capita.[9] What is clear is that most Kenyans access the internet through their mobile phones. Kenya has one of the highest mobile phone penetration rates in the developing world at a staggering 88% in 2017.[10] Given population dynamics, we can assume that many of these mobile phone users are teenagers. In 2017 43% of Kenya's population was below the age of 15, and approximately 60% of Kenya's population is below the age of 30.[11] In 2012, 74% of Kenyans over the age of 15 owned mobile phones, of which 32.3% were capable of accessing the internet and 24.5% of using social media.[12]

By 2017, these estimates had grown considerably. According to the Bloggers Association of Kenya (BAKE) there are an estimated

Table 1 Kenya key ICT indicators

Indicators	Apr–Jun 2017 Q4	Jul–Sep 2017 Q1	% change Q4 to Q1
Mobile subscriptions (millions)	40.259	41.028	1.9
Fixed subscriptions	71,307	71,118	-0.3
Mobile penetration	88.7	90.4	1.9
Fixed telephone penetration	0.16	0.16	0.0
SMS on-net (billions)	14.670	18.754	27.8
Mobile money transfer services			
Number of mobile money subscriptions (millions)	28.074	28.192	0.4
Number of registered mobile money agents	180,657	184,537	2.1
Number of transactions-sending and withdrawal (millions)	480.585	537.242	11.8
Value of transactions- sending and withdrawal (Ksh in trillions)	1.218	1.659	36.2
Data/Internet services			
Data/Internet subscriptions (millions)	29.624	30.891	4.3
Total available international bandwidth (Gbps)	2,906.87	2909.512	0.1
Total used international bandwidth (Gbps)	882.573	887.187	0.5
Internet penetration	100.2	112.7	12.5
Broadband penetration	34.2	38.8	13.5
Broadcasting services			
Number of free-to-air TV channels	66	62	-6.1
Number of radio FM stations	178	178	0.0

Source: Communications Authority of Kenya, First Quarter Sector Statistics Report for the Financial Year 2017/2018 (July–September 2017).

12 million Kenyans using WhatsApp, 7.1 million on Facebook, 4 million on Instagram and another 1 million on Twitter.[13] Of course some of these are individuals with multiple accounts, e.g. people running both business and private accounts, and given the country's youth-skewing population curve, most of these people are likely to

Figure 2 Changes in mobile subscriptions and mobile penetration in Kenya

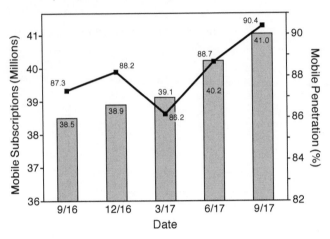

be under the voting age of 18. This means that it is impossible to argue definitively that social media has a direct effect on Kenya's electoral politics. Moreover, digging deeper into the geographical patterns of use of both major social media apps, we see that the majority of Kenyans online are from Nairobi, with the second city of Mombasa a distant second. Still, every year, more and more social media savvy users will mature who most likely do not consume traditional media the way their parents do and this constituency will become increasingly important.

Banda argues that much of the discussion on technology in Africa fails to take into account the unique terrain in which the technology is deployed.[14] In Kenya, the interaction between digital technology and media has thrown up several unexpected outcomes, where new media is increasingly encroaching on territory abdicated by traditional media and is forcing both power and the fourth estate to adapt. In the beginning, traditional media generally ignored social media. However, realising that they were losing readers to these platforms many sites tried to replicate them on their own webpages, creating closed networks of consumers. Eventually detente was reached when traditional media realised that it could use the structures of social media to disseminate its own content. Lately, this delicate balance has come under threat as social media platforms begin producing their own content and broadcasting or distributing it directly to consumers.[15]

This connection between media and democracy is about information generally and communication specifically as the basis for political behaviour.[16] Think of political behaviour as a series of reactions to information. We hear news about a certain candidate's success in their previous position as an economic advisor and we decide to vote for them as president in the hope that those skills will translate into their position as head of state. We hear of a certain threat from community A and we in community B mobilise so we can diminish that threat. The channels through which information is carried therefore become important tools of control. If you control the channel you can selectively amplify or diminish content at will. So those who control narratives around key events are in many ways responsible for the conduct of those who consume that information. Gatekeepers – journalists, editors, publishers, owners – have a disproportionate role in shaping political outcomes.

At the same time, the process of governance is essentially a series of conversations between groups that hold power and those who live under them. People can either signal their acceptance of what power does by remaining silent or they can express their frustration through voting, protest or exit. Those who want political power produce stories or information and project it in public, and those who would be governed respond to it. People that govern might adjust their stance or reject the response of the governed – hence a conversation. Information travels back and forth between the two groups and they react to it (or not), and the sum total of all of that is governance.

The space in which these conversations happen is what is known as 'the public sphere'. Jürgen Habermas defined the public sphere as 'the realm of our social life in which something approaching a public opinion can be reached'.[17] The public sphere is the space in which all conversations with power across and between various groups collide and some kind of national narrative is produced. Our national narrative will be whatever results from the mix of voices and is of course determined by who is best able to get heard. Habermas argued that public opinion is created by conversation and that the media – the platforms that carry these conversations – is integral to this public sphere.

The public sphere is an idea produced by ideas.[18] For example, people only participate in the national conversation if they believe that their voice matters. We don't all need to trek to parliament to participate in the national conversation. We simply need systems that allow us to hear from our leaders and – critically – communicate back to them what we are thinking or feeling. A public sphere also needs space where individual ideas can come together. This could be a physical space like a park in the case of Speakers' Corner in Hyde Park or Jantar Mantar in India. But it could also be an intangible space like the convergence of millions of people reading the same newspaper, or an electronic space like the internet.

Public opinion is therefore the outcome of the ongoing debate on what a society should look like – the push and pull between what states do and what citizens are willing to put up with. Habermas called this push–pull the 'rational-critical debate' and argued that the educated middle class who could both read and have the time to engage in this debate therefore became the most influential segment of the public sphere.[19] This was probably a reflection of the intellectual preoccupations of the time which tended to believe that anyone who wasn't speaking the language of power wasn't participating in the rational-critical debate. Today, we have a more nuanced perspective on these issues. As Arundhati Roy says, 'there's really no such thing as the voiceless. Only the unheard'.[20]

The late Nigerian scholar Raufu Mustapha expanded this criticism by arguing that there are in fact many public spheres that reflect the social and cultural boundaries – e.g. class, ethnicity, age, gender – that cut across our lives.[21] This resonates with the feminist idea of the personal as political, in that the public sphere cannot be restricted to the formal political realm that is dominated by patriarchal power structures. Mustapha argued that these multiple spheres are reconciled by their intent – that the philosophical goal of all of these spaces is deliberation and the goal of building more representative societies. And this is why the media is particularly important as a site that enables deliberation. Lauren Langman, a media theorist, thinks that class is an issue too. She links the idea of media to identity building, arguing that the media's role is 'communicating news, ideas, theories and analyses ... "public spheres" created places ... for fostering modern bourgeois identities'.[22] The stories we choose to tell and the ways we choose to tell them are central to how we see our place in our state.

It's interesting that when thinking about the rational-critical debate, Habermas thought that 'media' was anyone who produced and shared ideas generally. Yunusa Y'au, a Nigerian scholar, thinks that the debate and discussion that make up the public sphere need dialogue, and dialogue by definition requires interactivity.[23] He sees a tension between highly interactive spaces like digital platforms that have low reach and low-interactivity spaces like traditional media that have much greater reach, and argues that a robust public sphere needs both. The tension is that the highly interactive platforms are vulnerable to state capture because of their centralisation, which can compromise the quality of the public sphere in general. In Kenya, 'media' is privately owned media corporations, while physical spaces that might have offered alternative platforms – parks, speakers' corners – are on the decline. The state broadcaster that is supposed to balance out the conversation by offering a not-for-profit platform that can compete with private capital is deliberately starved of resources. Digital platforms arise as a replacement for the latter but are increasingly morphing to take up room reserved for the former.

The sociologist Peter Ekeh argues that in the Western political tradition, politics comprises a public and a private realm, while a lasting impact of colonisation was that politics in colonised societies was divided into three realms – the public, the civic and the primordial (or the traditional).[24] The public and primordial spheres roughly correspond with Habermas' public/private divide, but the civic sphere is the hybrid space where an African bourgeois class 'accepts the principles implicit in colonialism but rejects the foreign class imposing them ... competent enough to rule but with no traditional legitimacy'.[25]

In Kenya, these distinctions perhaps explain why despite its relative profitability the media has struggled to emerge as a viable site for expressing public opinion. The political conversation that happens in Kenya's media rarely reflects the full spectrum of public opinion; it often feels hackneyed or hollow. This is made clear when you look at the role of language, where English is treated as the natural language for political discourse even though in Kenya political discourse in English sounds stilted and forced. Often, politicians and media personalities will switch to *sheng'* (patois) or their traditional languages to 'truly connect' with audiences. Even Swahili is considered by many to be too difficult and too formal. Yet under the Moi administration especially, *sheng'* was illegal, and that says something about the extent to which patriarchal power will go to keep voters' immediate concerns off the political agenda.

The underlying idea that if you couldn't read or afford a television or radio then you were not consuming 'media' is faulty because many people consume political information through other formats. This also explains why new media has become such a potent force in political discourse in Kenya – because it allows for the collision between Ekeh's public, civic and 'primordial'. It allows Kenyans to present the fullness of their political identities by transcending the boundaries between the private and the public spheres. It is private because everyone is creating and curating their own feed but Ekeh's public because this curation is done for a public. In many societies 'media' also includes plays, music performances, rumours and informal channels of communication – much of the HIV/AIDS awareness education that happens in the global south is predicated on this – and so new media emerges in a context that is already open to consuming political news in diverse formats.

By definition, therefore, those who dominate public debate are extremely influential. Individual opinions can differ substantially from public opinions, but public opinion will reflect the views of those whose voices prevail. Ideally public opinion is not determined by outliers, even though some outliers are able to exert disproportionate influence, particularly by buying it. This explains why the idea of 'Kenya as a haven of peace' persisted. It is a bourgeois concept that is integral to the nation-building project that did not necessarily reflect the reality of life for many Kenyans. The authoritarian state co-opted rather than suffocated the media so that the story told of Kenya is one the state is comfortable with, regardless that the story was partial, inaccurate and laced with government propaganda. Traces of this *'sahani za wageni'* approach to political discourse – sanitising the official narrative to make Kenya look good for outsiders – persist.

Langman believes that media is inherently an exclusive, elitist bourgeois space because the middle class dominates it. If the process of information production or dissemination is controlled by a specific class, the society will construct identities aligned to that dominant class. So if the Kenyan media keeps asserting that 'Kibera is the largest slum in Africa' and that its inhabitants are 'the poorest people in the continent', those inhabitants will continue to see themselves as such and to conduct their social transactions within the public sphere from this position. If the West continues to control narratives about Africa as a backward and terrifying place, Africans will continue to see themselves as essentially backward and terrifying. The media is inherently partial and subject to class interests, especially where it is so thoroughly controlled by a single class, and the dominant class has no interest in rendering complexity to those it dominates.

In many parts of the world, new media has done a lot of damage to this original structure. It has lowered the barriers of entry to the rational-critical debate so that if you have a Twitter account and interest you can build an audience and insert yourself into the public sphere. Yochai Benkler calls this new iteration of the public sphere the networked public sphere.[26] He argues that the networked public sphere introduces two fundamental changes. First, there is a 'shift from a hub-and-spoke architecture with unidirectional links to the end points in the mass media, to distributed architecture with multidirectional connections among all nodes in the networked information environment'.[27] Consumers are now creating and generating their own content and feeding it back to the centre, or sometimes subverting the centre altogether and communicating to each other directly. News outlets rely on social media to gauge what's trendy before covering it on their outlets. Bloggers are sought out to give their opinions on key political issues. We are no longer waiting for the media to tell us what we think about specific phenomena, but reacting to the phenomena and building stories around it that shape all future thinking or behaviour around these phenomena.

Second, the networked public sphere has led to 'the practical elimination of communication costs as a barrier to speaking across associational boundaries'.[28] We're not only communicating more efficiently but we're doing it much cheaper than has ever been done before, meaning that anyone with enough passion and commitment to the process can position themselves as a content creator and become part of the media. This undercuts revenue streams for traditional outlets and forces them to be even more responsive to online communities.

A major criticism of Habermas' work is that it saw public opinion solely from the perspective of the bourgeois white man.[29]

Boaventura de Sousa Santos, a sociologist, thinks that the idea that people have leisure time to spend in coffee houses, salons and clubs etc. in order to create the ideas that would go into public opinion reflect a very specific lived experience; does that mean that societies or groups that didn't have these opportunities didn't have a public sphere? He says not, and that the real strength in Habermas' theory is the idea of communicative action – of conversations or interactions that translate into political action.

De Sousa Santos also reminds us that we have to be ready to take apart the concepts or ideas that Habermas presents as a given in his thinking and see what Habermas himself acknowledges that he was unable to see.[30] So, for example, when Habermas argued that all members of the society should have an opportunity to participate in the rational-critical debate relevant to their public lives he wasn't paying attention to class and gender disparities.[31] And when we say that decentralised spaces, like blogs or social networks, are a 'virtual public sphere' where all people who want to can interact in virtual communities or sub-cultures, we also have to see those people who cannot or will not participate to round out the theory.[32]

Banda agrees that the switch to internet-based platforms in theory means that more of us get a say in the conversation between citizen and state – an improvement on the conception of the state that keeps governance behind institutional barriers.[33] Something important is happening, especially because the internet allows individuals space to construct alternative identities and new group identities. We can be 'Concerned Kenyan Writers' – an online coalition of writers who independently documented the 2008 post-election violence – independent of our ethnic or racial identities, or 'techies who tweet' and express strong political opinions that are less burdened by ethnic or other affiliations.[34] The internet should ideally be more egalitarian; giving more voice to individuals that don't have it.

But the internet does not flatten all the social cues that make offline exclusion or discrimination possible. Women on social media report being systemically harassed by men online for strongly expressing their opinions, much as would happen offline.[35] In Kenya, where ethnic identities are often used as a proxy or shorthand for political affiliations, social media has been unable to completely override these positions, especially where people use their real identities online.[36]

Moreover, new media has some key limitations embedded within it. First it doesn't play by the same set of rules regarding truth, integrity and verification as newspapers, television or magazines. A person publishing on these pages, running a blog or a Twitter account only needs to master the art of amplification. The discrepancy means that stories are generated on new media platforms much faster than on traditional media. Until recently, this discrepancy simply pushed traditional media to lower the bar on their behaviour. They created citizen journalism spaces like the Standard Group in Kenya's U-Report that were exempted from fact-checking practices.

This undermines the rational-critical debate because we cannot have a constructive debate if we are not operating with the same set of 'facts'. Just because someone declares something with authority or with an attractive font doesn't necessarily mean their claim is true or useful. Comedian Stephen Colbert coined the term 'truthiness' to refer to things that sound true but aren't.[37] Truthiness is an excellent way of describing much of the content that is generated outside the confines of traditional media: it has the patina of truth but is actually untrue.

Worryingly, instead of defending this competitive advantage, today much of the traditional media is engaged in a race to the bottom on this front. There is growing influence of propaganda on traditional media all around the world. Of course this is hardly unprecedented. Propaganda has always been part and parcel of the public sphere, but its persistence today defies long-held beliefs about what the corporatisation and privatisation of traditional media would lead to. Turning traditional media into corporations rather than state-owned enterprises was supposed to make them run better. Instead it has just made them more vulnerable to manipulation.

The 2016 US election and the Brexit vote in the UK made public the depth of corporate influence and manipulation on new media.[38] This is not only threatening the survival of existing social media sites but fuelling pressure on them to develop new methods of verifying or flagging unverified information. As such, Facebook and Twitter have been developing methods of filtering information from groups considered harmful to the public sphere.[39] However, these sites aren't taking down the misinformation, merely controlling how it is seen.[40] This shifts the burden of verification from the content producer to the content consumer. It is up to conscientious users to flag content that they deem offensive or problematic. With traditional media the idea was that you could at least take the journalist at their word. Now, if you're getting most of your news online you have to fact-check it yourself.

New media also reinforces information silos that media is supposed to break. Consumers on these platforms start relying on their insular networks for information – they are primarily getting their information from people they already know and trust in the interests of sparing themselves the extra labour. In the long run, it compromises the quality of any debate or discussion in the public sphere.

In effect, new media makes individuals reliant on echo chambers. Add in the fact that debate on new media spaces tends to have less decorum and respect than face-to-face discussion or written positions in traditional print media – to the point of death and rape threats – and you end up with people building higher and higher barriers to those who hold differing opinions from them. Where politics occurs along ethnic lines, reliance on new media for information reinforces ethnic divisions. Where gender excludes participation in politics, new media often exacerbates this. New media may handily dispose of the expensive elements that encumbered traditional media, but it also gets rid of the less obvious advantages of consuming information produced with a broad audience in mind.

So the extent to which new media creates a positive space for the public sphere in a specific country depends on how hard members of the public are willing to work to compensate for the missing functions. In the US, where the public was accustomed to depending on traditional media for verified information, the public was vulnerable to widespread manipulation. In Kenya, where the distinction between the public, civic and primordial is embedded in the society, people have always treated official narratives with more scepticism. New media has only deepened people's natural scepticism in relation to information produced by traditional media and the state. The avatars and self-constructed narratives have empowered individuals to use their alternative identities to articulate their opinions, mould those of others and challenge state and media narratives. In Kenya, the rise of social media has led to an expansion of the public sphere, and this is having tangible impacts on politics and public opinion across the country.

Chapter 3

COLLISION COURSE: WHERE ANALOGUE MEETS DIGITAL[1]

Whenever a major political upheaval occurs, that society confronts presumptions about itself, why it exists and the ways it hopes to move forward. Kenya after the 2007/08 post-election violence was no different. The violence rattled Kenyan society in many dramatic ways. There was public death and destruction inflicted by civilians on other civilians on a scale not seen since independence. Tangible things like bodies and properties were irreparably damaged; so also were intangible ideas and principles that had organised the society thus far. The media especially found itself in unprecedented territory, having lost considerable power to the state and the public as the new online forums devoured space that they considered naturally theirs.

Print media took the biggest hit, although radio and television soon followed. During and after the violence journalists perceptibly toned down the tenor of their critiques of the state. Public debate was already muted but the loss of the media meant that there was nowhere for people to access vibrant discussion on what they were living through. The diaspora was especially starved because they couldn't see or feel for themselves, even though they lived with the anxiety of the period. Grasping for informative content they increasingly moved online for political dialogue and criticism, and the people in Kenya soon followed, noticing the lack of similarly sharp analysis and debate in traditional media. Blogs and other social media platforms very quickly became a substitute for print media that was still beholden to political interests and unable to accommodate new voices. Over time, this migration would change the power dynamic between online voices, traditional media and political actors in Kenya, long before similar patterns were observed in other parts of the developing world.

Kenya was always going to be one of the first African countries to move political debate online. The country has a particularly high literacy rate of 82%,[2] and after radio, print media has historically been a key platform through which individuals access news in general and political information especially. Given the belief that print publishing is underpinned by practices like investigation, verification and authentication, print is viewed as relatively more trustworthy.[3] You can also keep a newspaper in a way that you can't keep a news broadcast: it has a relative permanence. The combination of breadth and depth that one gets with a single newspaper is almost impossible to mimic on radio or on television. And to reiterate, with the rapid uptake of mobile internet Kenya also has the highest rate of internet penetration in Africa,[4] again contingent on the large, diffused population that can read and navigate written material online.

Indeed, on paper Kenya has one of the most robust and economically vibrant print media sectors in the developing world, and these publications operate with a strong profit incentive. One 2015 survey found that the *Daily Nation*, which commands 40% of the nationwide readership, was read an average 4.379 million times per day. Its main rival, *the Standard* commands 20% of the national audience and was read 2.223 million times per day in the same period.[5] Compare that with the highly fragmented South African market where the highest circulating newspaper, the Zulu language *Isolezewe*, is only read 943,000 times a day.[6] These are not purely public interest organisations – sustained growth and profit are major priorities.

Despite or perhaps because of these impressive figures, print media in Kenya has always had a complex and often problematic relationship with the state. As in any other country in the world, print outlets in Kenya have struggled to retain audiences, especially with the emergence of online news. By 2007, all the major newspapers in Kenya had already seen their audiences dwindle significantly. At the same time, newspapers rely on government advertising and access to survive. For example, a full-page spread in a daily newspaper can cost the advertiser up to 1 million shillings (approximately $10,000 as of 2017). Government institutions are the only ones that can afford to do this repeatedly, for instance sending out congratulations to the president during public holidays.

These factors fuel a practice known in media circles as 'fiscing'. The Committee to Protect Journalist defines fiscing as financially induced self-censorship that is used to rein in journalists.[7] After 2015, when the government created an agency through which it would send out all of its advertising, fiscing became even more common in Kenya. This centralised body allowed the government to stop placing adverts in publications or on platforms that provided unwelcome coverage.

In a 2011 article, Kenyan researcher George Ogola traced the key stages of the development of Kenya's media, arguing that a complex network of power and interests has stifled the development of a truly robust and free press in the country and left a significant public information vacuum.[8] The two newspapers that dominate the market in Kenya were both founded before 1963 – prior to independence. The *Nation* began in 1958 as a private venture of the Aga Khan, the spiritual leader of Ismaili Muslims who have a strong presence in the country. Meanwhile, the *Standard* started in 1902 as a mouthpiece of African elites on the coast until it was sold to investor Tiny Rowland and subsequently became a mouthpiece for the racist, white settler community. At independence, the *Nation* grew in size and audience while the *Standard* floundered and began to 'curry favour with the government' in order to regain a foothold in the market.[9] This was the first major compromise in the way information was processed and presented to the public.

The earliest years of the republic under the first President Kenyatta (1963–78) were characterised by rampant state capture, assassinations and excommunications of key political figures opposing then President Kenyatta's excesses.[10] As mentioned, this led to significant political fractures within the ruling party KANU. The tension intensified and culminated in the 1969 Kisumu Massacre, when police opened fire on crowds jeering President Kenyatta as he visited the largest referral hospital in Kisumu, built with Russian funding coordinated by Oginga Odinga; 26 school-children were killed by the police.[11]

To curb public criticism, the government pushed an intense, propaganda-heavy, nation-building project in which the media was a key partner. This was the era of 'developmental journalism' where media houses 'privileged narratives of national unity' over hard-hitting news. In effect, they censored themselves by avoiding politically contentious issues. Instead of working to develop their own content, media houses relied on information from state-owned news agencies like the Presidential Press Unit, and rather than invest editorial capacity in researching these releases, they often reprinted them word for word. They also propagated state-sponsored language and ideas – e.g. referring to the president as the 'father of the nation'. However, there was also active censorship in the form of repressive laws, the shutting down of independent outlets and intimidation of journalists, all of which worked together to suffo-cate the freedom of the nascent press but not its profitability.[12]

After Kenyatta's death, the Moi years (1978–2002) were char-acterised by a doubling down on repression, particularly of print media, which remained the most robust information outlet. The government also consolidated its monopoly on radio and televi-sion. Moi was keen to reinforce Kenyatta's nation-building agenda, and clamped down on any outlets he could not control, particularly those publishing in indigenous languages. Ogola notes that in the two-year period between 1988 and 1990, almost 20 publications were banned in Kenya.[13] Both the *Nation* and the *Standard* survived this period for identical reasons – Moi controlled them. Through a holding company, he bought a large number of shares in the *Standard*, which then turned into a mouthpiece for state propaganda, and while he was unable to wrest control of the *Nation* from the Aga Khan, he exerted considerable influence over it by leveraging the spiritual leader's other business interests in the country.[14] Under Moi, the Aga Khan and Roland 'Tiny' Rowland, the largest shareholders at the *Nation* and the *Standard* respectively, became the two largest investors in Kenya.[15]

The media became more independent during the democratisation years (1990–2002), in part because the country's economy was collapsing under the strain of corruption and state capture. As dissent grew more vocal, non-traditional forms of political criticism thrived. Comedy, and particularly satire, was a major outlet for political resistance, even in the big newspapers. Satirists like Whispers and cartoonists like Gado and Maddo, who had been targets for punishment before 1992, found that they were able to criticise the state more directly than their prose counterparts. Their successes arguably sustained the print circulation of newspapers in this period. Ogola notes that his was also the era when the gutter press – illegal pamphlets often supported by opposition politicians that were vocally critical of the state – thrived.[16] The gutter press was catering to a niche audience, and while none of these papers transformed into a credible news source, they did much to expand the space for political criticism.

Wary of losing circulation numbers to these highly popular, informal presses, the two major newspapers – now fully fledged media groups with developing radio and television presences – shifted from a state-centred model to a market-based model. Consequently, Ogola notes, their relationship with the state became more adversarial. They were more critical of state officials, except perhaps the president, who was spared the brunt. Regional expansion through acquisitions in neighbouring countries and on the backs of increased economic cooperation in East Africa also boosted their income and standing. The state retained a significant measure of control over both outlets because it remained the major revenue stream through their advertising, necessarily placing limits on their ability to capitalise on the nascent freedom in the arena.

The *Standard* in particular failed to truly capitalise on the shifting space. Whereas the *Nation* almost immediately began challenging the government, the *Standard* seemed stuck in developmental journalism. Ogola argues that this is because the paper was directly owned by the president and his proxies, unlike the *Nation* that was only influenced indirectly. To make up for lost revenue, the paper experimented with various formats, including the tabloid format – focusing on personal and sexual scandals – but recovery was slow in coming. The lack of independence was all too apparent to an increasingly savvy public, and the *Nation* capitalised by continuing to push the boundaries of criticism.

Under President Kibaki (2002–12), both major newspapers suffered a significant identity crisis. The first four years of Kibaki were arguably the best years for press freedom in Kenya's history. Although the *Standard* floundered in the early days it managed to successfully poach several senior staff members from its competitor and began to recover. Meanwhile, the *Nation* under Moi became closely aligned with opposition politics and then with Kibaki once Moi left. Over time, the newspaper seemed reluctant to criticise the Kibaki administration directly. Speculation by those who study this period is that the newspaper's leadership was in some ways privy to the political compromises that led to the selection of Kibaki as the official candidate of the opposition. Either way, the newspaper did not know how to approach the Kibaki administration and left it alone.

Over time, the *Standard* took up the mantle of critic in chief, earning a reputation for relative objectivity as the Kibaki regime began to lose its varnish. This culminated in one of the nastiest ever acts of intimidation against the Kenyan press. In March 2006 the offices of the Standard group were raided by a group of masked men who destroyed expensive equipment, intimidated journalists and ended up setting much of the building on fire. Surprisingly, the government admitted that the masked men were police officers and that the attack was retaliation for the *Standard*'s unfavourable coverage of the government.[17] Then Minister for Internal Security, John Michuki, famously said in an interview about the incident, 'if you rattle a snake, you can expect to get bitten'.[18] That day, thousands of copies of newspapers were burnt and journalists' computers and camera equipment seized.

Another high-profile incident during this time involved the former first lady, Lucy Kibaki. In December 2007, Mrs Kibaki stormed the offices of the *Nation* to confront journalists whom she accused of publishing unfavourable stories about her family. Unaware that the incident was being filmed and broadcast, Mrs Kibaki held an angry vigil in the newsroom, staring down journalists who dared to address her directly, and going as far as slapping one, Mr Clifford Omondi. Curiously, although the incident was covered by all major news outlets, almost all evidence of it has been erased from Kenyan sites – a function of the self-censorship that media houses practise and rely on for their political survival, and their hyper-sanitation of the legacies of powerful people.[19] When the journalist in question sought legal redress, the first lady allegedly slapped his attorney too.[20]

Thus, by the time the 2007/08 post-election violence occurred both major print newspapers were already at odds with the administration that had become violently intolerant of media criticism. The speed and scale of the post-election violence caught the entire country by surprise, given that for the first time since the 1982 attempted coup Nairobi was also affected. The prospect of interminable violence was real, and as a result everyone panicked and just wanted the uncertainty to go away. The media seemed to internalise criticisms from the state that any kind of critical reporting was inciting ethnic hatred. As such, at the height of the violence, rather than continue to publish objective reports, the papers struck a conciliatory note, beginning with a single editorial that was published in all the newspapers under the headline 'Save Our Beloved Country'. It would be a watershed moment in which the nascent free press in Kenya signed its own death warrant.

The first years of Kibaki's second term were characterised by a steady retreat from the new space for press freedom created in the 1990s. For the first time in history, the government was able to exercise coercive power over both major newspapers, and the newspapers played along. It was during this period that the newspapers began openly taking meetings with state officials at State House. Inflation soared, at one point hitting an eye-watering high of 31.5%,[21] with food markets especially hard hit; but while Kenyans starved the newspapers refrained from publishing explicitly critical stories. Blind items – stories in which events are narrated but no characters are named – and 'unnamed officials' became the preferred method of writing stories about Kenya.

This essentially returned the country to the nation-building era, and developmental journalism was again on trend. The bland, unsatisfying coverage drove more and more Kenyans – particularly educated, urban elites who were more critical of state-crafted narratives on illusory national unity than their predecessors – to seek information elsewhere. Many built their own sites using software like Blogger or Wordpress. But at the time blogging and building news websites was an expensive and time-consuming process. Many of the better blogs of this era did not survive.

The advent of microblogging and instant publishing sites like Twitter and Facebook came at the tail-end of this. The first few Kenyan accounts opened in 2010 and became popular because they allowed the user to have the experience of publishing their own content without the hassle of building and maintaining their own platform. This confluence of circumstances was the perfect storm of factors that led to the emergence of social media and blogging as key sources of information, especially for the small but economically powerful and politically visible middle class.

Initially, online spaces that mimicked print media became the go-to spaces for news about what was happening in Kenya. Bloggers became the archivists of Kenya's post-election violence; comment sections on blogs and other websites were electric spaces for searing commentary but also for virulent tribalism and sexism. It was as if after 44 years of masquerading, the internet was finally allowing Kenyans to be true to who they were, and the results were not always positive.

During this time bloggers also inserted themselves into the national discourse, increasing internet traffic in the country. Their profile was only increased when the ban on live broadcasting was lifted and mainstream media continued to use or reference bloggers[22] in their broadcasts. As a way of demonstrating their connections to the zeitgeist, television and radio stations began to read tweets and Facebook posts as live reactions to the broadcast in lieu of text messaging or calls.

The intentions of bloggers in this period were not always benign – for every blogger using their influence to preach peace and reconciliation a good number used their sites to encourage ethnic hatred and deepen existing cultural divides.[23] The post-election violence created a space where a nation that had been characterised by passivity and disengagement – proudly defined by the mediocre mantra 'at least we have peace' – began the slow process of becoming more alert, more aware and more engaged.

In 2017, the Kenyan press remained compromised if not entirely captured. The second Kenyatta administration (2012–) made courting the media a priority, and one of its first actions after the transition was inviting all major media houses and practitioners to State House 'for tea'.[24] Unfortunately, in Kenya 'tea' as a colloquialism has a negative connotation – often used as a euphemism for a bribe and the association would inevitably taint reports of the meeting. Some journalists who attended told me that the whole thing felt uncomfortable even though nothing specifically ominous was said. It just felt like something important had shifted in the relationship between the media and the state. Suddenly, State House had all the cards.

The link between State House and the media has never been stronger. A change of guard at the *Nation* left journalists particularly vulnerable, as for the first time in the history of the paper the CEO was not a journalist. Insiders claim he was more committed to the fiscal survival of the paper than publishing good journalism. In 2016, the *Nation* did not renew editorial cartoonist Gado's contract after 23 years of service, a move he argues was demanded by the government:

> It is no secret that there were many in government who did not like my cartoons over the years. But we had grown used to that and the *Nation* thankfully consistently pushed back. Things changed in 2013 after a new government came into place and the pressure became far more intense. I have no doubt that the *Nation* crumbled, which is quite sad and should be seen in the broader context of efforts by those in government to control the press.[25]

Similarly, the newspaper fired *Saturday Nation* managing editor Dennis Galava after he published an editorial that was directly critical of the president.[26] The New Year's editorial itself was mild and in some places even complimentary, but it was the first time since the 2007/08 period that one of the major newspapers directly criticised the head of state.[27] Like Gado, Galava believes that his firing was instigated by State House, saying: 'My view is that the editor is taking instructions from State House [the seat of the president], and is now hiding behind procedure'.[28]

While none of the actions that the Uhuru administration have undertaken to date amount to the outright violence of previous regimes, the administration has demonstrated a worrying inclination to repeatedly censor or coerce silence that is in some ways more dangerous. Recall that the newspapers had already taken a giant leap backwards. These moves would be a threat to a robust media anywhere but they are particularly threatening to a weakened and compromised fourth estate.

At the same time, according to the Committee to Project Journalists, there was only one case of assassination of a media figure at this time. John Kituyi was an investigative journalist for the *Weekly Mirror*, a small independent newspaper in Eldoret.[29] Kituyi had been investigating the death and disappearance of witnesses connected to the indictments of President Kenyatta and the deputy president at the ICC. Kituyi submitted two highly critical pieces to the paper towards the end of April but never lived to see the second published. He was killed on 29 April 2015. Aside from this, human rights organisations report that more common have been incidents of intimidation and arrest. For example, Walter Menya, a journalist with the *Nation*, was arrested some days before the 2017 election allegedly for taking a bribe.[30] He argued his arrest was due to a story he published on public officials donating to the ruling party's electoral campaign.

That said, the Kenyan press has shown a tremendous knack for excessive self-censorship even where there is seemingly little to be gained. Following the death of former First Lady Lucy Kibaki in 2016, all unflattering references to her were deleted from the websites of both major media houses. Politicians who have been accused of sexual assault, drug trafficking or even murder are referred to simply as politicians or private developers, even while facing criminal charges for their violence. It is common for stories previously covered in the press to disappear from the archives later because the politician died or became president.

Another concerning pattern of behaviour became evident during the 2017 election. The Kenyan media began to parrot state-constructed narratives without interrogating them. This was particularly evident when it came to the announcement of official results, when the media broadcast state-produced results that the state itself later disowned in court. Insiders told me that this was because the Cabinet Secretary for the Interior at the time issued a directive that anyone who published or broadcast unofficial election results would be subject to fines or prosecution. In 2007, there had been vast contra-dictions between election results announced by different media houses, as well as those announced by the ECK. As such, in 2011 the law on announcing results was amended. The new electoral law held that the IEBC was the only entity allowed to announce election results in Kenya, even though all media houses and indeed political parties were allowed to generate their own tallies.

The unintended outcome of this history is that Kenyans do not trust the media as the first draft of history or the creators of its archive. An archive is not simply a collection of disparate pieces of information, but a political act of memorialisation, in which a society decides what about itself is worth preserving and why. Sanya and Lutomia argue regarding the modern archive that: 'Cultural production through visual and digital devices ... have the potential to advance various forms of democratisation by broadening the knowledge base'.[31]

The process of archiving tells us who we are and how we came to be, and if the person who controls the archive editorialises it to such an extent that it no longer represents how people see themselves or the journey that led them to their current moment, then that archive essentially writes its own obsolescence. This is creeping up on tradi-tional media in Kenya. The level of mistrust that the general public has on what is covered there isn't just about outright lying. It's about telling a story that doesn't resonate with what people know to be their truth.

This partly explains why new media as a source of informa-tion in Kenya has thrived.[32] In the context of growing mistrust of traditional media, new media has become a space where narratives can be challenged and evidence presented directly to the public to contradict officialdom. An archive of Kenyan history is being built on these platforms that challenges traditional media's monopoly on the national identity. These spaces allow individuals to prior-itise the news and perspective that they feel is interesting even if the press ignores it. The rise of new media has shifted the balance of agenda-setting power in the news back to the public, and every major outlet in Kenya today has been forced to direct its energies towards courting and sustaining this audience.

Significantly, new media archives, because they are somewhat beyond the control of the state are seen as more trustworthy than those that belong to the traditional media even if they are more transient. Unlike the traditional media archive that is curated by power and often for power, the new media archive is seen as a collaborative effort that democratises knowledge-making. This makes new media particularly attractive to those who think of themselves as resisting power. Statements can be challenged instantly and those challenges recorded for posterity. Screenshots allow people to keep an inventory of statements that the declarants might want to erase from their history. In countries like Kenya, this is essentially curating an alternative history that allows the public to redefine the political spaces. Participants are saying no to the official narrative and proposing alternatives, and then working together to delete, save, reject or accept what will go into the final story of a specific event.

Still, as mentioned, it's very easy for new media to function as an echo chamber – where people are only talking to people they already agree with and therefore having their biases reaffirmed rather than constantly challenged and critiqued. Although they were already compromised by rampant layoffs and cost-cutting measures, important functions in traditional media like fact-checking and citation are almost completely absent on new media. This can be particularly dangerous in societies like Kenya where rumours can quickly lead to widespread destruction, as was the case in 2007. Moreover, as experienced during the research for this book, these archives are transient, as individuals can easily delete content that they no longer want on their pages. Most importantly, social media platforms are commercial entities like their traditional media counterparts, but with less incentive to favour the public good over private interests. This leaves those who rely on them for news vulnerable to unprecedented forms of manipulation, as will be highlighted in the following chapters.

All of these factors conspire to increase the significance of social networks in 'partially free' states like Kenya, while also raising the risks. These new spaces have allowed people to feel they have a little more control over their personal and national narratives. They have reclaimed territory that the traditional media abandoned. And the more they feel the sense of agency, the more people are likely to use it, leading to a virtuous/vicious cycle that reinforces the prominence of these spaces – at least until the next best thing comes along. Digital platforms and new media have created a captive audience for broad-ranging social and political manipulation, with deep consequences for the user and the societies they live in. The advent of multiparty democracy in Kenya in 1991 was supposed to stop at the opening up of the political space: with the country meant to get a host of new political parties, have a couple of elections and stop at that. Instead, as soon as the political space eased open the entire society exhaled and began reaching for freedom. Individuals and groups immediately took to the streets demanding more rights – freedom for political detainees, protection of parks and forests, fair wages in the public sector. The art and music scene exploded with new, edgy political themes. That first taste of freedom triggered a deep yearning for more.

Institutions that had held the one-party political and economic system together also unravelled. Some of this was in response to pressure from competition in the newly vibrant private sector, as when the national broadcaster Kenya Broadcasting Corporation (KBC) balked at the ascendance of the Kenya Television Network (KTN). But some of it was imposed from outside as part of the Washington Consensus and the push for privatisation in the post-Cold War era.[33] With the end of balance-of-power macro-economics, Western neoliberal economic institutions found new power to reorganise politics and economics in the global south, and privatisation was at the centre of their efforts.

Kenya after Moi was a major victim of the Washington Consensus.[34] For one thing, the push for privatisation broke up the state conglomerates that had dominated cultural spaces. Second the push to reduce public sector spending resulted in many cutbacks and state-supported cultural production was one of the first sectors to feel the heat. Yet at the same time there was agency and there was negotiation. As much as the state retreated and abandoned culture, individuals developed new ways of reviving it. This was the era of Kenya's cultural renaissance as new ways of thinking about what it meant to be Kenyan, away from state control, took off.

Of course power never concedes space willingly. These forces – an externally forced retreat as well as internally driven occupation of territory previously reserved for the state – set the public and the state on a collision course. The next section considers three of these points of collision that pertain to digital spaces. First, the collision between new and old media. Second, the collision between a shrinking state and its growing hunger for data from the public. Third, the collision that is captured by the word 'disruption' – where a new technology completely changes the ways in which people experience an aspect of their lives.

In Kenya, home of m-Pesa, the third collision is possibly the easiest to discuss. Mobile money in general and m-Pesa as the largest company are providing a service that has completely changed how Kenyans interact with money. In the 1980s Kenya was one of the first countries to sign up to the disastrous Structural Adjustment policies that many blame for eventual economic collapse of the 1990s.[35] The subsequent push for privatisation in the 1990s led to a great deal of unemployment and the Kenyan currency depreciated considerably. New bills in high denominations of 1,000 and 500 shillings became common as inflation soared. But at this time banks were also unwilling to extend services to much of the public. By 2006, for example, only 27.4% of Kenya's adult population was using formal financial services.[36] Paper and metal money was heavy, cumbersome and dangerous to carry around, but with the high interest rates they were able to charge, banks were not in a hurry to provide Kenyan customers with alternatives.

As part of the Washington Consensus push for privatisation, in 1999 Kenya's state monopoly on communication devices – the Kenya Posts and Telecommunications Corporation (KPTC) – was dismembered into three separate entities. The tools for actual tele-communications went to Telecoms Kenya, postal services became Postal Corporation of Kenya, and licensing and regulation went to the Communications Commission of Kenya (CCK). The government also incorporated what had previously been a department of the behemoth as a private–public corporation that provided mobile phone communications. This was Safaricom. When the various corporations split, Safaricom found room to exist as an independent entity and in 2002 was listed as a public corporation in Kenya.

In 2007, Safaricom launched a ground-breaking service known as m-Pesa.[37] This is a mobile-based platform that allows subscribers to send and receive money on their mobile phones. After registering an account with the company, a customer can send money directly to another customer or pay directly for goods and services through their phone. They can also visit a physical Safaricom agent to receive cash. Over time several functions have been added to the platforms, including a savings system (m-Akiba), access to small loans and cash advances, and the ability to bank money directly on the phone rather than have to go to an agent to receive it.

The platform is immensely popular in Kenya, where physical banks often refused to provide any of these services even to people who might otherwise be considered middle class. In the first year of its launch, nearly 2 million people subscribed to the service, rising to 10 million within the first three years.[38] There are far more Kenyans who own a mobile phone (and thus can use mobile money) than those who have bank accounts.[39] At the time it was developed, many banks in Kenya would not allow consumers to hold less than

50,000 Kenya shillings in deposits when the minimum wage was approximately 3,000 shillings per month. Realising the potential, other mobile companies in Kenya and around the world have launched similar services. By 2017, mobile money transactions amounted to the equivalent of 50% of Kenya's GDP, with m-Pesa transactions alone amounting to 3.572 trillion Kenya shillings (about US$35.72 billion) or the equivalent of 30% of GDP.[40] Mobile money has captured the business of Kenya's millions of unbanked in a country where the informal sector does large volumes of small transactions. During its ten years, m-Pesa has been revolutionary.

Safaricom's principal shareholder, UK mobile phone operator Vodafone, has been unable to replicate the success in other parts of the world, however.[41] This is because m-Pesa's success in Kenya reflects the unique characteristics of the society in which it was launched. For one thing, sending and receiving mobile money depends on literacy, as m-Pesa is a text-based system. As mentioned, Kenya has an unusually high literacy rate in English for a developing country.

m-Pesa's success can also be attributed to its relationship with the Kenyan government, a major shareholder. In 2002 when the company was floated, the state held 40% of the company's shares. In 2016 some of these shares were sold so that in 2017 the government holds 35% of the company.[42] This is significant because due to the digitisation process, many government agencies made m-Pesa the only method through which citizens can pay for key services. As part of their anti-corruption initiatives, cash offices in various government offices do not accept cash as a payment system. However, most Kenyans don't have credit cards and government offices don't run point-of-sale (POS) systems with which to process them. This means that citizens are forced to get m-Pesa accounts or to use m-Pesa stalls – to give their business to a corporation in which the government is a major shareholder – in order to access government services.

Another aspect of m-Pesa's success is a reflection of the moment at which it was born. Today, many Kenyans who would be ideal customers for the service are captured in microfinance, which offers far better rates than m-Pesa. Kenyans also have what researchers call a 'dual system' – a significant urban population that retains strong links with a rural community.[43] Rural–urban migration is high and rising, and one way of maintaining these connections is through the ability to send money in a hurry. Many people are sending money to communities that don't have any kind of banking system; nor will banks invest in those regions anytime soon. Add to this refugee diasporas from Somalia, South Sudan, Ethiopia, Burundi and other countries in the region who do not have the documentation to access bank accounts, and Kenya presents the perfect conditions for the success of a financial service that users until recently only needed a phone number to access.

Another element of the disruptive collision between technology and politics in Kenya is the case of Ushahidi. The crisis-mapping platform was also born in 2007. More than Safaricom, Ushahidi owes its existence to the 2007/08 post-election violence and the culture of blogging that was born around it. The history of Ushahidi was captured by Joshua Goldstein and Juliana Rotich – a co-founder of the platform – in a 2008 paper for the Berkman Klein Center for the Internet at Harvard University.[44] The paper recalls that a week into the post-election violence, a group of Kenyans in the diaspora launched a campaign to raise awareness of the ongoing violence in the country and to propose concrete steps for help. This group engaged in a variety of projects, including fundraising through m-Pesa and other mobile money platforms to support the Kenya Society of the Red Cross.

On 2 January, Ory Okolloh, the blogger behind kenyanpundit.com triggered the conversation that would become Ushahidi when she observed that Google Earth made it possible to monitor damage being done in Kenya in some detail.[45] The initial idea was to document the damage for archival purposes but Okolloh invited any developers who wanted to build mapping software to do so for the good of the country. David Kobia and Erik Hersman, based in Kenya, took up the challenge and launched Ushahidi on 9 January. The site used SMS (short messaging service) data to map information about attacks across the country and create an aggregate picture. Users could report incidents that would populate the map, and those overseas especially could zoom in to various points and see the damage for themselves. Developers built the platform, but Ushahidi only worked because people were using it – the more data was sent to the platform the more meaningful the site became.

Once again, Ushahidi was a tremendous success for reasons unique to Kenya's situation at the time. For one thing, it was warmly welcomed by Kenya's diaspora as an important way of staying connected with what was happening at home. At the time, Google Maps and Google Earth consumed a great deal of internet bandwidth – too much for Kenyans in Kenya using the country's nascent internet infrastructure. However, Kenyans abroad with better internet connections were able to use the platform cheaply and often. Similarly, at the time the government had a very weak grasp of what was being done on these platforms. Ushahidi was able to develop with minimal state support but also with minimal state interference. There was no regulatory framework on data collection and dissemination to work around. Developers could just build.

Today, Ushahidi exists as open source software that anyone monitoring a crisis can use to build their own context-specific platform.[46] It has been used to map crises in Haiti, Nepal and other parts of the world. The Ushahidi team has also incubated a number of related initiatives like the iHub space in Nairobi or the BRCK box, which is a self-powered router that allows internet connectivity in remote areas.[47]

Ushahidi is not without its critics, however. The website 'Dead Ushahidi' argues that mapping without a goal and a strategy inevitably leads to 'dead maps' – collecting examples on the site.[48] Tech founders may try to stay morally ambivalent but proliferation of data collection without a specific intention eventually starves the maps of purpose and they become irrelevant. This perhaps explains why some founders of Ushahidi like Ory Okolloh left to form Mzalendo, a website that collects data on the national legislature with the explicit intention of increasing accountability.[49] In the same breath, some Kenyan scholars have also raised concerns about the near-universal praise for the site that fails to reckon with glaring intellectual queries, including the questionable possibility that so many individuals in the midst of an unprecedented crisis could stop to upload data on the site.

Eventually the government did catch on to what was happening online and used Ushahidi's success as the premise of what would later be dubbed 'Silicon Savannah'.[50] Launched to great fanfare after Ushahidi went global, this was the government's attempt to impose itself on the nascent tech scene in the country. In exchange for increased oversight in the sector, the government promised to invest in giving ICT experts the infrastructure they needed to make their programmes work. And to their credit, some of these have been delivered. For example, investments in the fibre-optic network have dramatically improved internet speeds in the country and brought more Kenyans online.[51]

In a 2015 paper, former Kenyan Minister for ICT, Bitange Ndemo outlines the government's contribution to creating an enabling environment for ICT in the country.[52] He argues that Kenya's overall embrace of ICTs was in part because of deliberate policy decisions that he and his team undertook beginning with his 2005 appointment as Permanent Secretary for ICT at the Ministry of Information and Communications. As Permanent Secretary, Ndemo prioritised liberalisation of the sector and the privatisation of Telkom Kenya. Given that then President Mwai Kibaki had pushed capitalist ideology in Kenya during his tenure as Minister of Finance and Vice President, Ndemo's message was well received. It was Ndemo's single-minded focus on opening up Kenya to international information and communications technology (ICT) traffic that saw the development of the fibre-optic network despite the challenges of the 2007/08 PEV. He also oversaw the creation of the Kenya Open Data Portal, which centralises government data in easily accessible formats.[53]

However, once Ndemo left government in 2013 it became clear that the absence of ideology that he celebrated as creating room for innovation in the ICT sector was also a problem. Many of the projects launched to much fanfare turned out to be white elephants. The much-lauded Konza Tech City that was supposed to provide a physical site for tech to take off was still in 2017 a large empty field.[54] Ndemo himself acknowledges that the rural ICT project, which was supposed to give loans of $50,000 to rural entrepreneurs to build rural ICT hubs, was a failure because of poor planning and research.

Late entrants to Kenya's tech scene will not benefit from the relatively free reign that early entrants Ushahidi and m-Pesa enjoyed. For example, in 2016 the leader of government business in parliament Aden Duale proposed the Information Communication and Technology Bill which was supposed to increase government oversight on who gets to present themselves as an ICT professional.[55] Under this law, all ICT professionals would have to register with a state agency. To be eligible for registration, the bill proposed that the person would need a degree or diploma in ICT or at least three years' work experience. There was also a vague requirement of 'good moral standing' and the need to renew the licence yearly. The bill would have crushed Kenya's nascent ICT sector. Perhaps sensing this, Cabinet Secretary for ICT Joe Mucheru refused to provide his ministry's support for the bill and it was rejected.[56]

Overall, home-grown innovations like Ushahidi and m-Pesa did successfully disrupt Kenya's society and politics. They put considerable power in the hands of Kenyan consumers at a key time. M-Pesa allowed Kenyans to access financial services that established banks refused to provide to them. This allowed them to invest and grow their businesses tremendously. In 2017, a viral article captured how m-pesa loans had transformed the lives of petty traders in Nairobi markets, who were able to borrow money in the morning, trade with it all day and then repay their loans the same evening at low interest rates.[57] Meanwhile, Ushahidi allowed Kenyans to curate the composite story of a period that the government was forcing local media to paper over and significantly changed the conversation on what was possible in the country with regard to technology. Technology shifted power towards citizens. But the government hasn't quite relinquished its power.

The second way in which tech and society have collided in Kenya is in the ways the state is increasingly using digital platforms to collect, process and store information. Many states argue that collecting more information about citizens will go some way towards improving governance. In many parts of the world, this can sometimes happen through the creation of platforms that gauge public opinion or allow individuals to share their own. Examples of this are the petitions.gov.uk website in the UK, where any citizen can create a petition to the government, and after garnering a certain amount of signatures, parliament is obligated to debate the petition. Indeed, in a 2010 book on overcoming digital divides, Brendan Burke defines a digital democracy as 'the use of the Internet and other computer technologies to enhance governance processes such as voting or participation in public hearings'.[58]

Today, the advantages of such state-centred data collection are unclear. In the ideal situation, the state, possessing disproportionate resources and capacities, should be compelled to be more open with citizens, while citizens' rights of privacy should be enhanced. However, more often than not, the vast data collection systems built by states resemble Bentham's panopticon – a large surveillance system that is more interested in siphoning citizen data while keeping the state opaque, making civilians toe the line than in improving the services that states provide to citizens. Very few African governments have initiated bidirectional data systems. They argue that it's expensive and requires higher levels of input, but more likely the government isn't interested in hearing what people have to say.

Kenya is an example of a country that has been building a vast panopticon even though it has an extremely ambiguous relationship with technology for enhancing governance. On one hand, both the Kibaki (2002–12) and Kenyatta (2012–present) administrations went to great pains to present themselves as 'digital governments'. In its election manifesto, Kenyatta's Jubilee coalition had an entire chapter dedicated to ICT.[59] The manifesto promised that the administration would turn Kenya into a hub for technological developments and incorporate technology into efforts to fight corruption, illiteracy and poor coordination between various agencies.

Some of these promises have been fulfilled. As mentioned, several government services – registration of births or deaths, acquisition of driver's licences, passports, visas, voter registration and other key documents are today conducted on digital platforms like the e-Citizen platform. This has made it easier for the government to maintain records of key transactions as well as to generate aggregate statistics for the entire country. Arguably the country has leapfrogged many developments to get there – recall that by 2017, only 12% of Kenyans had access to a computer in the home. The government is today better at collecting citizen's data than it was ten years ago.

But the government is not better at allowing citizens to hold it accountable, and certainly not at managing citizen data. Several ICT tools that have been put in place in order to increase accountability – e.g. the Integrated Financial Management Information System (IFMIS) for government tenders or the Biometric Voter Registration (BVR) system of the IEBC – have been deliberately sabotaged. Instead of enhancing the participation of the public in the process of governance they have discouraged it.

The case of IFMIS is instructive. IFMIS is a system developed and promoted by the United States Agency for International Development (USAID) in various countries around the world to 'computerise and automate key aspects of budget execution and accounting operations across the institutions of government'.[60] The idea is basically that automation fosters transparency – that human beings are the core obstacle to increased accountability for corruption and reducing the ability for individuals to insert themselves into the budget's execution makes everything more accountable. With the support of USAID and other institutions, IFMIS systems have been deployed in Kosovo, the Slovak Republic, Kazakhstan, Uganda and other countries.

In Kenya, IFMIS was introduced by Ann Waiguru while she was the director of the IFMIS team and the head of governance at the National Treasury as a revolution in government accountability.[61] It soon became a flagship project for the ruling party. According to the Jubilee Manifesto, IFMIS would 'tackle corruption at the Central and County government levels ... [and] allow the public to walk with the Government through every step of the tendering process and to track every tax shilling spent through the county governments and the national government'.[62] IFMIS was the cornerstone of the government's plans to bring the public into the process of government budgeting and accounting.

Instead, those who implemented the system found that it was cumbersome and ineffective. In March 2016, the Auditor General Edward Ouko, who had previously outed corruption and financial mismanagement scandals, declared that the system did not make his work any easier and in fact made it harder to track finances 'once it gets off the main road'.[63] The chairperson of the Public Accounts Committee declared that the system is 'neither integrated nor can it manage anything' especially because so many of the accounts staff in the various ministries did not even know how to use it.[64]

Moreover, in Kenya IFMIS has become inseparable from the vast government corruption scandals in the country, notably the 791 million shilling (approximately US$8 million) National Youth Service (NYS) scandal. The NYS is a revival of one of the first President Kenyatta's programmes to get young people to perform public service. Young people are recruited and provided with practical and paramilitary training for six months at various centres across the country before being deployed to various service sites. Many work as security guards in government buildings, for instance, or provide manual labour in sectors like construction.

In a report tabled to the National Assembly in June 2016, Auditor General (AG) Ouko blamed a combination of 'manipulation of the government's financial management software, outright forgery and neglect of duty' for the theft of 1.8 billion shillings (approximately $18 million) meant for the NYS.[65] Ouko's report revealed forgery of key documents, inflation of figures by a factor of ten to increase the value of payments, failure to inspect goods and irregular access to the system, which allowed the thefts to happen. Significantly, the AG found that IFMIS passwords were shared in breach of protocol and remained unchanged so that even after access was denied, individuals could still access it – some up to five months later, sometimes after government offices were officially closed. At the time of writing, no one has been held responsible for the NYS–IFMIS scandal even though Waiguru and others were under investigation.

The fact IFMIS was not only pioneered but also effectively championed by politicians suggests that digitisation will increasingly become inevitable. Both the ruling party and the civil service embraced digital democracy as a policy position and made many tangible efforts to incorporate its principles. The appointment of a head of IFMIS at a senior level in the treasury affirms this.

However, the system was undone by the same government, underscoring its schizophrenia regarding greater accountability and public participation, and IFMIS is another example of an all-talk system where the government launches policies for publicity and then undermines them.[66] IFMIS had been a constant government talking point since 2013, but there has been very little by way of public awareness campaigns to help the public to understand exactly how the system works. Even the officials who work with the system daily – the AG and the chairpersons of both the Public Accounts Committee and the Public Investment Committee – affirm that the system is completely unworkable in the Kenyan context and that they don't really understand what it's supposed to do. Some analysts

in Kenya have argued that the country only had partial implementation of the IFMIS model: the version operating in the country is
neither fully integrated nor allows for the efficient management of
public money.[67]

This is a reminder that, such as it exists, digital democracy
doesn't happen in a vacuum. The efficacy of digital systems is highly
dependent on the intentions of those who develop and implement
them. In Kenya, IFMIS was a major project of the post-Washington
Consensus good governance drift of the 1990s – a push for broader
systemic changes rather than dramatic cuts to public services or
hyper-privatisation. Theoretically, changing the ethos of governance institutions is a good step forward, but practically, it's too
much to expect abstract institutions to deliver good governance
without tackling the values of those who will run those systems.

Significantly, without public confidence even the best-designed
systems will be seen to be ineffective, even if they aren't. It doesn't
matter how loudly the government touts the successes of IFMIS –
the public simply cannot trust it when it has been so publicly linked
to corruption scandals. And without that trust from the public there
can be no participation, which undercuts the 'democracy' element
of 'digital democracy'. All this is in the context of a country that
does not, at the time of writing, have a data protection law.

In fact, Kenya's panopticon keeps growing even while it lacks a
robust framework for the protection of citizen data. The Communications Commission of Kenya, rebranded as the Communications
Authority, one of KPTC's offshoots, has announced a system to
monitor incoming and outgoing digital communications.[68] The
Communications Authority has also announced a social media
monitoring initiative. Data collection at the borders including
fingerprinting and photography is now mandatory.

In the same breath, Safaricom built a network of surveillance
cameras for Nairobi and Mombasa that have had no palpable
impact on the levels of crime in the country.[69] To use m-Pesa individuals must hand over private details to an m-Pesa agent who often

simply records them in a notebook.[70] Many of these notebooks are not kept securely even though they contain information that could easily be used for identity theft. Researchers also confirm that Safaricom operates a 'middle box' device which is either used to enhance connectivity, or to manipulate traffic and for surveillance.[71] Ingenious spouses are using m-Pesa's reporting features to investigate cheating spouses because the service responds with the full details of everyone who receives money from it.[72] At the time of writing, apart from a broad right to privacy in the constitution, Kenya still has no law to regulate what any of these agencies does with customer information once they have it.[73]

This is the current condition of the digital democracy project in Kenya. The government continues to push digital initiatives as solutions to various public sector problems and comes up short, even if the systems themselves are world class. The government is also stuck between two contradictory impulses – on one hand to appear progressive and forward-looking, on the other to sabotage itself to keep the old gravy trains running. And in all this, citizen data keeps disappearing into an unregulated black hole.

The third way that digital platforms collide with society in Kenya is with social media as a surrogate for traditional media, the focus of this book. With an estimated literacy rate of 82% the written word in Kenya has significant influence on shaping the national public sphere. Newspapers are read on television and on radio as well, giving them disproportionate influence over the public agenda. Where the main print media outlets are owned and operated by the country's elite, the public sphere is very directly and tangibly shaped by the aspirations and perversions of this clique. This is why social media has come to matter so much.

As mentioned, Benkler notes that the networked public sphere triggers a 'shift from a hub-and-spoke architecture', with information flowing from the central agency out to people, to a 'distributed architecture with multidirectional connections'.[74] Consumers are now creating and generating their own content and feeding it back to the centre, or sometimes circumventing the centre altogether and communicating to each other directly. Secondly, we are not only communicating more efficiently but also much more cheaply, and anyone with enough passion and commitment to the process can be a content creator.

The state of Kenya's offline democracy shapes the ways in which these global changes play out. According to most rankings on democracy around the world, Kenya is a middling country. In its most recent annual Freedom in the World Ranking, Freedom House suggests that Kenya is 'partly free', a rank that has remained unchanged from preceding years. Those who live in Kenya will concur. It's not that Kenya is the worst place in the world for democratic participation but the country could do better. Kenyans vote and their votes matter more than in fully autocratic countries; but with the impact of corruption, their votes certainly do not matter enough that elections can be considered 'free and fair'. There is general access to public discourse – if one is rich, male, from a major ethnic group and not disabled. The press is robust – sort of.

Many of the new technologies have not developed with partly free countries in mind and they have unpredictable effects in those countries. Twitter did not set out to play a starring role in the Egyptian revolution, nor did Facebook have in is growth plan a goal to trigger conversations about class-consciousness in India. These things happened despite these platforms constricting spaces available in more liberal societies. It's like salt. When mixed with water, salt can seem like a neutral substance, but when mixed with sulfuric acid it triggers a powerful, unforgettable reaction.

In the early days of social networks, the presumption was that digital spaces were somehow separate from the reality of political action offline. Many people saw them as spaces for teenagers and narcissists to post pictures of their food or share too many details of their personal lives. While this may have been consistent with the ways in which digital spaces were deployed in the countries where they were developed, for individuals in the partly free world, they represented an opportunity to reinvent their societies and finally give voice to previously unheard voices. Thus in many societies where analogue or offline spaces have been compromised by power and are impossible to penetrate if one is not of the right social, economic or political affiliation, digital spaces – with those inherent characteristics that make it hard to control or censor – become incredibly politically significant. When people in the partly free world fight for digital access they're not simply fighting for the right to post selfies: often they are fighting for the right to be seen and heard in nations that will not see or hear them any other way.

Human beings everywhere want to live in inclusive societies where they will at least be heard, if not represented, and will use whatever means are available to achieve that. When a historical moment emerges in which the possibility of greater freedom is within reach, whatever tools survive authoritarianism become the most important means at hand to allow individuals to participate in public life. Some of the successes that we attribute to digital platforms don't belong to those platforms but to the people that use them – as do many of the failures. This mix of preexisting offline conditions and online opportunities is in part what makes new media such a potent site for redefining politics in countries like Kenya.

Chapter 4

RATTLING THE SNAKE WITHOUT GETTING BITTEN: NEW MEDIA USURPING TRADITIONAL MEDIA IN KENYA[1]

To understand how digital spaces are impacting democracy in Kenya it is necessary to first understand how these spaces work, and then how they interact with what already exists in the country. The conversation on social media and politics in Africa generally exists in what de Sousa Santos calls the 'sociology of absence': that is, that the ideas that shape how social media works in countries outside the West is designed to not see the developing world as places where these ideas have relevance.[2] As such, this chapter reconstructs some of the research around social media and politics but with a focus on seeing Kenya.

Social media platforms are not neutral spaces but rather commercial platforms that reflect the developer's fundamental interest in making profit, allowing individuals and corporations to exert unprecedented agenda-setting and preference-shaping power over the electorate. And while this impact in Kenya is currently moderated by the relatively small population of voters using the platforms in this way, that number is growing rapidly by the day given developments in both technology and in media.

Democracy is rooted in the idea of belonging, which can be defined as a 'close or intimate relationship'.[3] Belonging is really the sense of peace that results from having unchallenged access to the rights and privileges that are given to members of a certain community, and so democracy is in part about giving people space to make those demands. As previously discussed, Kenya has struggled to give all its citizens a sense of belonging and traditional media especially is notorious for flattening or ignoring identities that don't align with what is viewed as 'tradition'. The swing towards social and new media as a surrogate for or extension of the analogue public sphere is therefore fuelled in part by a thirst for belonging in a country that routinely 'unsees' the Other. As such, some of the most vocal, best organised and most organic groups on social media are those that struggled to find space in traditional media. But that doesn't mean that social media doesn't have its own rules of belonging – the internet doesn't compensate for the inequalities that exist offline. In fact it creates new methods of exclusion or exacerbates them. The subsequent discussion not only highlights the ambiguity of key features of new media, and social media especially, and the impact they are having on political discourse in Kenya.

In 2011, the UN Special Rapporteur on the Right to Freedom of Opinion and Expression wrote: 'by vastly expanding the capacity of individuals to enjoy their right to freedom of opinion and expression ... ensuring universal access to the Internet should be a priority for all states'.[4] In contemporary public policy, the link between extensive internet access and development is almost unchallenged. Research (like that presented by Stork, Callandro and Gillward at the 2012 Annual International Telecommunications Society (ITS)) commonly says that mobile phones: 'have a positive impact on economic welfare and GDP ... generates employment opportunities and improves productivity of other sectors, as it contributes to business expansion, to entrepreneurship, to banking the unbanked and to reduced transaction costs'.[5] The economic benefits of increased connectivity are well researched, its democratic benefits less so.

In Africa, the Arab Spring stimulated interest in whether digital spaces, and particularly social media, were good or bad for democracy. At first there was broad consensus that internet access, and social media especially, was good for democracy on the continent. The speed with which the Ben Ali regime in Tunisia fell after nearly 30 years of authoritarianism was startling. And soon many people tried to replicate the effect across the Middle East – young people armed with mobile phones and courage gathering in public spaces in Cairo, Tripoli or Damascus to demand political change. In late 2015 as social media-supported revolutions in Burkina Faso and the Gambia overthrew long-standing regimes, there was increasing talk of the possibility of an 'African Spring'. Meanwhile the new media companies basked in the idea that these sites that were initially dismissed as trivial were at the centre of the most significant political developments of the decade.

The gloss quickly wore off. After Tunis, there was Cairo and a greater awareness of how tweets and Facebook posts transform into a resistance movement. Unlike Ben Ali, who calmly left the country, the Egyptian government pushed back – and is continuing to push back as many who participated in the Tahrir Square protests are still in jail. Amir Hatem Ali argues, based on the Egyptian experience, that you have to measure what people are using mobile phones or the internet for in order to deal properly with the 'digital divide' – understood as the difference in access particularly between developing and developed countries.[6] To properly integrate digital spaces into democracy, we have to go beyond simply giving people access to the internet. Individuals have to see that the internet adds value to some facet of their lives and subsequently invest time and effort into making it work. Hatem Ali calls this value 'meaningful use'.

Hatem Ali is arguing that simply giving people more internet is counterproductive where the state still retains final authority on who can access the internet and when. The misguided idea that social media is a benign place where young people can talk about trends or popular culture is the very reason why it was insulated from scrutiny for so long. Once policy wonks and the media started using social media as a place to get and disseminate information, to monitor and amplify political unrest, governments took notice. Today countries around the world routinely shut down the internet to stifle political dissent. Hatem Ali argues that it is critical to break down the power dynamics that surround the use of social media in order to understand its political currency.

Kenya, constantly hovering at the margins of authoritarianism, has repeatedly tried to pass laws to curb political organisation on social media, hinting at the increasing political potency of these spaces. The now repealed and ambiguously formulated Kenya Information and Communication Act permitted arrest following the 'misuse of a communication device'.[7] During its lifetime, the law was repeatedly and punitively used against bloggers and individuals active on social media to stifle criticism amongst other seemingly petty civil violations easily covered by other laws.[8] The courts repealed this law as unconstitutional, only for the government to pass another law in 2018 – the Cybercrimes Act – that regurgitated many of these provisions under the guise of fighting 'fake news'. To date, the law has mainly been used to threaten bloggers and netizens who are seen as too critical of the state.

These desperate attempts at regulation underscore that social media has the Kenya government rattled, and it is important to understand how these spaces function in order to understand why.

Figure 3 highlights the popularity of social media platforms in Kenya. Social media is a collective term for different platforms that work differently but are presumed to serve an identical public function. Communications researchers Boyd and Ellison define social media – social networking sites – as:

web-based services that allow individuals to (1) construct a public or semi-public profile within a bounded system, (2) articulate a list of other users with whom they share a connection, and (3) view and traverse their list of connections and those made by others within the system.[9]

A social networking site or a social media platform is unique because it allows us make our networks public. So a group listserve – an email mailing list – isn't a social media site because the connections are only visible to those who manage the platform. This is also why messaging apps like WhatsApp or Signal, known as the 'Dark Web', exist at the margins of what we consider social media – the connections that exist on that platform are known only to the users, even if more people can be invited to participate in conversations than in traditional text messaging or email.

In their history of social media platforms, Boyd and Ellison point to SixDegreees.com launched in 1997 as the first social media.[10] SixDegrees was arguably the first true social networking

Figure 3 Social media accounts in Kenya

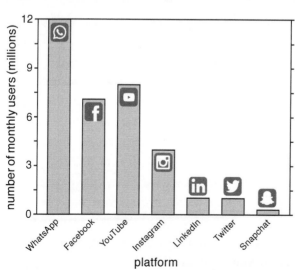

site because it added the visibility of social networks to features of existing platforms like AIM. As more and more people got online, the second wave of sites added specific interests to this basic model – Ryze.com and LinkedIn focused on business networks and platforms like Friendster and Tribe.com focused on friendships and personal relationships. Of these, only LinkedIn survived, Boyd and Ellison arguing this is because it was the only one that was truly responsive to the needs of users.[11] Finally, the third wave of social networking systems (SNS) sites doubled down on courting niche audiences like Care2, focusing on activists, and Couchsurfing.com, which courts travellers.[12]

MySpace, the first truly global social media platform, was the first fourth-wave site. MySpace deliberately set out to attract disappointed Friendster users by focusing on usability.[13] A significant boost came when notable public figures – musicians especially – began setting up MySpace pages to connect directly with audiences. MySpace also allowed personalisation of individual pages, giving users more control over how the network portrayed them in public. Mainstream media widely ignored the expansion of MySpace until it was bought by Rupert Murdoch's News Corporation for a whopping $580 million.[14] This hinted at the potential profitability of such sites even though the site was very quickly plagued by security issues, especially for the millions of underage users, some of whom were targeted for grooming by sexual predators.[15]

The next big thing was Facebook, which started in 2004 as a Harvard-only social media site. When they realised how popular the site was, the creators decided to allow university students from all over the world to join using valid university email addresses. This allowed the site to remain relatively closed, creating a 'cool factor' by excluding older and younger users who may be seen as out of touch. Facebook in the early years had a feeling of insulation that encouraged users to be more forthcoming in what they posted.

Facebook is the second most popular social media platform in Kenya (after WhatsApp). The earliest study of Facebook use in

Kenya by Wyche et al. found that between March and September 2012, the number of Facebook users in Kenya grew from just over 1.3 million to nearly 1.6 million.[16] The same study at a cybercafé in an informal settlement in Nairobi found that 80% of those who were using the facilities came to start Facebook accounts, which the owner charged 60 shillings to open for users.[17] By 2017, there were an estimated 7.1 million Facebook users in Kenya.

Facebook did eventually open to all users, but this shift brought along all the security concerns that had plagued its predecessors and eventually the company decided to give users more autonomy on what elements of their profile they chose to make public.[18] Similarly, while initially Facebook restricted audiences to those you consider 'friends', over the years it has allowed media personalities to count strangers as friends, or to have fans 'follow' them so that they can mimic the intimacy of friendship without actually having to be friends. This paradox is central to the role that Facebook has played in political discourse – it creates an illusion of privacy because people have some control over their privacy settings but the site allows advertisers to circumvent these settings by permitting sales of niche advertising.

Facebook constantly changes the way users interact with its platform. Today's platform 'curates' what content it thinks you want to read rather than letting you organically sift through the material yourself. You now have to subscribe to pages curated by your preferred public figures in addition to liking them on Facebook in order to view them on their home page. These features make it difficult to expand the reach of one's community, which is important for people who use it as an alternative publishing platform. In Kenya, with the exception of a few high-profile figures like activist Boniface Mwangi, who says he likes that Facebook allows him to publish article-length posts for free, Facebook doesn't organically permit conversations between strangers.

In recent years there has also been increasing concern about Facebook's corporate culture. Beyond its role as a space to allow people to connect, Facebook has increasingly ventured into spaces like education and the providing of internet connectivity. None of these has been without controversy. In the developing world, Facebook introduced a controversial platform known as Free Basics. Unlike its much hyped but failed launch in India, in Africa the Facebook Free Basics app was rolled out so quietly that most people in targeted countries probably don't realise it was available until Facebook shut it down. Free Basics was available in 22 countries in Africa – together accounting for nearly 50% of the continent's population – and used Facebook's infrastructure to make a selection of websites available to users. As a result, today Facebook and its wholly owned subsidiary WhatsApp are available without data charges in many countries in Africa.

Free Basics seemed like the answer to many interconnected prayers. It makes the internet available to more people. Secondly, as more and more states are digitising key public services it meant more people should have been able to access services like the e-Citizen platform in Kenya. But as the Special Rapporteur observed, the objective is getting people connected in a way that enhances their freedoms, particularly of opinion and expression.[19] Essentially, while there will always be disparities of access to the tools we use to connect, the system itself cannot have these disparities built into it. We should all ideally be consuming the same information and making social and political decisions based on it in order for the internet to enhance democracy.

At the same time Facebook also has a history of aligning itself with power rather than with citizens. The firm has, for example, facilitated government agencies accessing user data to target activists and protesters. On 12 October 2016 the American Civil Liberties Union (ACLU) accused Facebook and Instagram (owned by Facebook) of handing over information to location-based social media service the Geofeedia website, which in turn used the information in partnership with law enforcement agencies like the Baltimore Police Department to target protestors in the Black Lives

Matter movement. Luckily for these activists there are organisations like the ACLU in the US that will defend the rights of protestors against such punitive law enforcement. Similar organisations don't exist in countries like Kenya. Instead the government has repeatedly pressured private corporations to hand over information about users. For example, in 2017 Privacy International provided substantial evidence that Safaricom regularly either provides or permits government agencies access to user data.[20]

Another vulnerability inherent in the site as pertains to democracy is that Facebook allows third-party developers to build apps like games, quizzes or even dating sites through a piece of code called the API. This code allows these developers to access and mine user data in order to run their apps. Although Facebook promises that it does not sell user data, the 2018 Cambridge Analytica scandal confirmed that until 2014 this was simply untrue. In 2014, a researcher at the University of Cambridge paid 270,000 Facebook users about $20 each to take a personality quiz online.[21] These users voluntarily participated in the study, but the developers of the quiz also collected data on their friends who had not consented. Despite its public denials, this was all perfectly legitimate until 2014 when Facebook changed its API after realising how many developers were doing this.[22] Through this quiz alone, Cambridge Analytica collected data on up to 50 million Facebook users worldwide, and investigators argue that they used this data to influence voter behaviour during both the 2016 US election and the UK vote to leave the European Union (Brexit). The details of this scandal and its impact on Kenya will be discussed in Chapter 9.

Twitter joined the social media fray in 2006, two years after Facebook. Its main distinguishing feature is that it is a microblogging site where until November 2017 users posts were restricted to 140 characters or less[23] (since then this has been increased to 280 characters or less). Unlike Facebook, Twitter by default makes everyone's content public and searchable, even by people who don't use the platform, unless the user opts out by locking their account. Twitter therefore allows individuals to form connections with people outside their immediate social network. This makes it a particularly potent place for building networks around shared interests and for effectively sharing information. Using Twitter feels like broadcasting – passing a message out into the world – as opposed to using Facebook which feels like communicating to a much smaller group.

For political groups and movements around the world, Twitter has become almost indispensable. In her 2017 book, *Twitter and Teargas*, Zeynep Tufekci outlines the significance of the platform (and other social networking sites) to political organisation in the Middle East and Turkey.[24] She argues that the networked public sphere has fundamentally changed how movements connect, organise and evolve, and Twitter's particular operational quirks lend it particularly well to political organising in authoritarian and semi-authoritarian contexts. She observes that in many of these movements, Twitter allows like-minded people to find each other much faster than on other platforms and to coordinate with strangers much more effectively than in Facebook's closed network.

Twitter's pioneering use of the hashtag is integral to its role in community-building. A hashtag is a topical marker – a string of characters preceded by the hash (#) character.[25] It is something that gives a tweet context, ties it to a broader core idea, or connects various people commenting on a specific subject. A hashtag can also convey subtext or irony, which allows the user to infuse the main text with humour or sarcasm. Hashtags are then adopted by other people contributing similar content or to express a related idea.[26] Practically, a hashtag on Twitter sets the words attached to it off from the rest of the tweet as the colour of the words changes to a brighter highlight colour. It makes the user's words publicly searchable: by simply clicking on a hashtag, a user can see all other instances of the use of the hashtag on the website.

Hashtags are also part of the basis on which trending – the total number of instances in which a specific subject is mentioned – is measured. Twitter automatically collates the most popular hashtags in a specific location to determine what is 'trending', and every day ranks the top 20 trending topics in that region on the home pages of everyone who uses the site. Trending is therefore a very quick and easy way of taking the temperature on a subject. Trending is also a way to gauge the extent to which a specific story or news item or event has captured the attention of the general public, especially because hashtags can be filtered either geographically or by other metrics. Where individuals do not have the location service switched on, they are shown the global trending topics – the 20 most popular hashtags in the world. Because of this, trending on Twitter has become a core goal for individuals and brands using the site.

With an estimated 1 million users by 2018, Twitter is the one of the most popular social media platforms in Kenya, after Facebook and Instagram, and the preferred space for political discourse online.[27] Reinforcing the urban/rural divide of social media use in Kenya, most Kenyans are tweeting in English, with 81% of the tweets recorded in the 2014 École Polytechnique Fédérale de Lausanne (EPFL) study in English and only 5% in Swahili.[28] Most people who did tweet in other languages combined this with English, whereas it is not uncommon for people to write Facebook posts in Swahili or other local languages.

Kenyans using Twitter initially coalesced around the hashtag #KOT or 'Kenyans on Twitter'. In a 2015 video, some of the most prominent Twitter users in the country called #KOT 'the most important thing in Kenya right now'.[29] For many Kenyans, the hashtag has come to encapsulate the identity of the country, the diversity of the country and the wit and humour with which Kenyans approach daily life. #KOT is a force and a phenomenon, able to move and act as a unit, while still remaining deeply divided within itself. A quick Twitter search for use of the hashtag in the first quarter of 2016 revealed the following uses:

1. A group of activists under the banner #ThirdwayKE used it to promote engagement with issues of domestic and political violence, and the marginalisation of women as political candidates.

2. User @wacuka used it to recall one of the original incidents of the use of the hashtag.[30]

3. Several organisations used it to promote tweetchats or online conversations on issues they were advocating for, particularly International Women's Day campaigns on 8 March and the #SaveKaruraForest campaign by the Wangari Maathai Foundation.[31]

4. Users used it to congratulate sports teams and people – Kiprop winning the Tokyo marathon, the rugby sevens team beating New Zealand at the Las Vegas Sevens tournament.

5. Musicians used it to promote new music.

6. Advertisers used it to promote travel and tour packages to a Kenyan audience, while another used it to promote a job advertisement.

7. Several users used it to urge peace and sobriety following political tensions in the build-up to the March by-elections in Kericho and Malindi.

8. Others used it to flag incidences of political malpractice in relation to these elections, including pictures showing irregularities, violence against voters and letters showing malpractice.

9. User @erikooh simply used it to affirm 'Even with our flaws and cyberbully tendencies, I thank God I'm a #KOT'.[32]

This cursory analysis suggests that the dynamics of the hashtag are complicated and highly malleable. A hashtag can be used to mobilise political awareness but interference by brands and marketers is strong. #KOT is no longer a purely political or social tool, and this makes it less and less useful for political tweets, whose impact (retweets) is weaker than branded tweets. It's best to think of #KOT as a reliable base from which other tweets can flow in order to capture the attention of a specific subset of people. Using a series of hashtags is like creating a network of Venn diagrams so that you are only talking to those who are most interested in the confluence of the subjects you're highlighting. This increases the levels of engagement a user can trigger.

A hashtag's popularity is not independent of the number of followers that a specific Twitter personality has, and the number of 'real users' that make up that following. A hashtag relies very heavily on a multiplier effect from superusers – those with thousands or even millions of followers, in order to establish its popularity. A person with 50 followers could tweet a hilarious tweet with a key hashtag but without that multiplier effect – no one will see it or respond to what it says. Sometimes this means that a tweet can lie 'dormant' for many months only to resurface after a superuser sees it while scrolling through a hashtag, or when a specific subject resurfaces. This makes superusers highly attractive to brands, institutions and the general public as lighthouses around which the national digital narrative flows. In Kenya, superusers can earn an extremely attractive income not just from promoting brands (some users are known to charge upwards of half a million shillings, approximately US$5,000, per tweet) but also where they parlay their status into offline engagement.

One key way of becoming a superuser that has had significant political import in Kenya is the use of bots, or fake accounts that inflate the number of followers one has and automatically amplify content created by them. Programmers around the world earn a significant income from creating bots and then selling them to individuals or brands that wish to establish themselves as 'popular'. Until 2018, the Kenyan government's Presidential Strategic Communications Unit (PSCU) was essentially a collective of online personalities that was hired by the president precisely to manage his reputation online and periodically uses bots to amplify tweets from the President's Office. PSCU has been repeatedly shamed by #KOT because these bots often promote tone-deaf hashtags in order to counteract strong criticism of the president online.[33] The hashtags #Kenya-IsMe and #MyPresidentMyChoice created to drum up patriotic support for the president failed when superuser @Insecurity KE noticed that most of those who were using it were bots.[34] On that day, identical tweets were shared at exactly the same time by 'different people'. For these and other fumbles, PSCU executive Dennis Itumbi and those who use the office's hashtags have earned the moniker 'Itumbots'.

The use of bots in this way is known as creating a smokescreen: that is, popularising banal or unrelated content in order to distract from heightened criticism, as such bots make it difficult – but not impossible – to determine what matters in the digital public sphere. It is a form of manipulation that dilutes the real impact of Twitter as a digital public sphere, and critics are increasingly calling for the site to develop methods of verifying that all accounts that exist are affiliated with a living human.

As with the digital space in general, Kenya's Twitter community is overwhelmingly urban, educated and highly localised. Perhaps a more accurate hashtag would be 'Nairobians on Twitter' as the capital city dominates Kenya's Twitter presence. It is a collection of citizens who appeal to a sense of community to draw attention to or to stimulate engagement with issues, ideas or products that they deem to be useful. This Twitter identity is also malleable and used for everything from political mobilisation to fundraising. It is a space to start and sustain some kind of activism in a space that permits stronger criticism of institutions than in a society defined by its deference to seniority. Kenya's Twitter community is the middle class of a developing country finding its political voice – perhaps to the detriment of their offline political engagement, perhaps to its advantage – and in the process attracting the fear of the elite ruling class.

A 2016 survey, 'How Africa Tweets', found that Kenyans on Twitter are more political than their counterparts in other parts of the world.[35] This has everything to do with the way the features of the site interact with the characteristics of the society at large. Because of the possibility of anonymity, Twitter allows people to operate outside their offline communities – particularly of ethnicity and gender – and constitute new online communities with more inclusive rules of belonging. Twitter also allows the content creator significant latitude to control the amount of personal information that they put on the site and for activists in particular Twitter allows a significant amount of protection from government retribution.

Twitter also allows for instant responses/reactions to unfolding events, circumventing the long delays in news production on traditional media. On the use of Twitter during the Westgate terrorist attack in Nairobi in September 2013 (discussed in more detail in the next chapter), Simon et al. found that people felt social media contributed to better emergency response management in Kenya.[36] During the attack, and a four-day siege in a shopping mall in an affluent district in Nairobi, 67 people were killed and 175 wounded. Emergency services set up camp around the mall during the siege to provide medical, psychosocial and other forms of support to those trapped inside, as well as first responders. Emergency services in Kenya often used multiple Twitter accounts to speak to each other, privately and publicly, quickly and fairly reliably. It made coordination of services like blood and food donations easier. Although official handles struggled to direct traffic solely to their websites, they did see a significant uptick in traffic. (It's also worth noting that the group that claimed responsibility for the attack did so on Twitter.)

These characteristics allow users to directly confront government, particularly with regard to the manipulation and propaganda that is common on traditional media where the government exerts more control. This was evident during the Garissa University attack. On 2 April 2015 a group of heavily armed terrorists laid siege to the largest university in Kenya's north-eastern region.[37] They entered the dormitories at around 5:00 a.m. and rounded up students, forcing them to lie on their stomachs before opening fire into the group; 147 students were killed in the massacre – the second most deadly terrorist attack in independent Kenya. Almost as soon as news of the attack broke, the government spin machine swung into action. But soon Twitter users began challenging the government narrative, arguing that the rescue operation was severely hamstrung by inefficiencies caused by corruption. For example, a photo shared on Instagram that went viral revealed that at the time of the attack the main police chopper was flying the daughter of a senior police official to Mombasa for a holiday. Stories like these embarrassed the government considerably but also put a great deal of agency into the hands of the public.

That's the good news. Twitter is making it possible for Kenyans to have more and better conversations about their country. The bad news is that not everyone in the country is participating in the conversations happening there. A 2014 study found that the majority of tweets in Kenya are concentrated between the Central Business District, along major thoroughfares and in middle and upper class suburbs around the city – people who are commuting and people who are rich.[38] There are also small but active Twitter communities at the Coast, in Garissa and several towns in the Rift Valley, the growth of online political activism triggering Twitter hubs in these areas that are otherwise ignored in national politics. Kenyan academic and analyst Duncan Omanga has highlighted how a rural chief from the outskirts of Nakuru – the fifth largest town in Kenya – uses Twitter to transform public dialogue in his village.[39]

Many Kenyans on Twitter are also passive consumers of the medium. As stated, only about 250,000 Twitter accounts in Kenya are regularly active. Many are bots. The EPFL research found that most conversations on Kenyan Twitter are 'idle chit-chat' which is arguably still important, particularly with regard to undoing prejudice and constructing new forms of belonging.[40] Moreover, Twitter is optimised for written English but most of Kenya's multilingual public are oral and more comfortable in languages other than English. This leads to some disconnect between how people engage. Binyavanga Wainaina writes beautifully about how language creates separate worlds which trilingual Kenyans move between, never fully inhabiting any.[41] He says that to understand how Nairobi especially works, you have to be able to move fluidly between the languages and capture the nuances of identity with which people might not be able to cross linguistic borders. Language is not just words. It's a constructed self, an orientation towards the world, an attempt to make sense of external phenomena. Language is the hands with which our minds reach into the world and try to make sense of it.

Some Twitter users have tried to address Twitter's language gap. For example, Sheng'Nation (@shengnation) is a popular handle that promotes *sheng'*, a patois common in all urban centres in Kenya. The handle engages with the same issues that have captured the zeitgeist in the mainstream and translates them into sheng', therefore taking them to a bigger audience. The offline impact of such activity is difficult to measure but with 5,856 followers at the time of writing this is a fairly popular, non-commercial Twitter presence.

Figure 4 shows that Facebook followers interact primarily with people that they know personally and those they may know through their friends, but rarely interact with people they don't know personally. In contrast, Twitter users are predominantly interacting with people that they don't know personally. This means that a purely Twitter user is far more likely to encounter a person who

Figure 4 Who is talking to who on social media

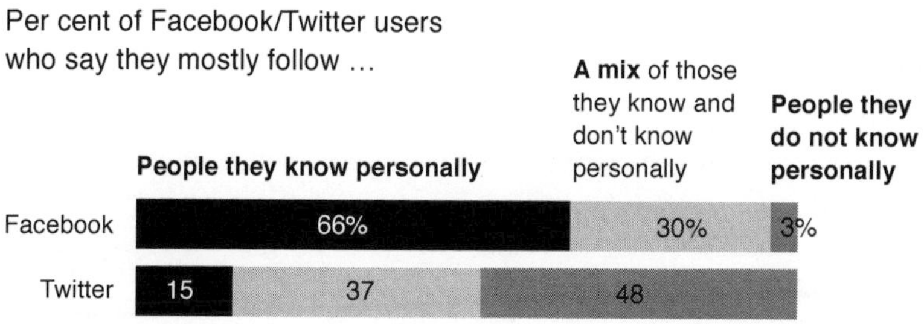

Per cent of Facebook/Twitter users
who say they mostly follow …

	People they know personally	A mix of those they know and don't know personally	People they do not know personally
Facebook	66%	30%	3%
Twitter	15	37	48

Source: Pew Centre study on social media platforms

holds an opinion they disagree with than a purely Facebook user, and by extension that a Twitter user is far more likely to engage with a conflicting opinion than a Facebook user. This finding is important for understanding why the different platforms lend themselves to certain types of political engagement and not others. For one thing, conversations on Facebook are more likely to remain insular than those on Twitter, which, as discussed in subsequent chapters, had major consequences for global politics in 2016, and this has major implications for the way in which political information – and especially hate speech – travels within the population.

As far as other social media platforms go, many have retained the niche audience approach while still trying to be open to many. WhatsApp is the most popular social media platform in Kenya, but it exists in an ill-defined space between social media and purely messaging that is known as dark social, which includes apps like Telegram and Signal. These platforms are technically social media although they act more as substitutes for text messaging than for news media. They are called 'Dark Social'[42] because they are private communication channels that generate internet traffic.[43] Unlike platforms like Twitter or Facebook, where networks are public, dark social relies on private networks to spread content, and this content cannot be measured using traditional analytics, so it is almost impossible to measure how far and fast it spreads.

In politics, dark social matters a great deal – possibly more than public facing sites. Alexis C. Madrigal found that in 2012 more than 56% of all internet traffic to the Atlantic was coming from these platforms.[44] Dark social is the preferred platform for social and political organising but also for organising violence and crime. In Singapore 63% of respondents to a survey about political information said they got their information from WhatsApp and similar platforms.[45] With more than 1 billion registered users by 2017, WhatsApp – wholly owned by Facebook – is by far the favourite.[46] WhatsApp has been used to plan parliamentary coups in the UK and university students in Sudan have also used it to plan protests.[47]

In Syria, Telegram, which is a messaging platform that can automatically delete messages after a set period of time, has been used to buy and sell weapons.[48] There are an estimated 10 million WhatsApp users in Kenya, and while studies on their behaviour are still rare, there is increasing concern that the platform has been integral to the creation and dissemination of dangerous political propaganda in the country.[49]

When the late C.S. Michuki threatened the media that if they rattled a snake they might get bitten, he could not have foreseen so many people reaching into these new spaces as a means of escaping the snake's bite. The numbers of people using social media in Kenya for political conversations is significant and growing, and the main lesson from the UK and the US is that this could have significant political import. Similarly, the relatively strong connections between social media and traditional media in Kenya create a multiplier effect for political discourse generated there. Trending is not just about popularity – it is also about agenda-setting. At the intersection between social media and traditional media is the ability to influence information generated and shared on traditional media that is making social media such a potent force. Moreover, those who use social media for political action in Kenya demonstrate a heightened level of political awareness, organisation and engagement that has made them a powerful, political constituency. Their numbers are significant enough that the government has taken notice, whether through attempting to regulate the space or through responding to criticisms published there.

Tied with the changes that it is triggering in the ways people define and express belonging, social media is slowly but surely changing the way politics is conducted in Kenya in more complicated ways than those who developed it may have expected.

Part II

DIGITAL
DEMOCRACY?

Chapter 5

AN AFRICAN COUNTRY IN THE DIGITAL AGE: THE MAKING AND USES OF #KOT

After several heady years of relative freedom, states around the world are beginning to catch up with the impact of new media and digital spaces on politics, and are responding in diverse ways. The result has been a fascinating cat-and-mouse game of negotiation and adaptation. For instance, when the Ugandan government shut down social media during a hotly contested election in 2016 people simply adapted to the restrictions by staying a step ahead of the authorities. Once the government shut down Facebook and WhatsApp, thousands of Ugandans downloaded Virtual Private Networks (VPNs) that allowed them to continue using the platform to show instances of voter fraud and electoral malpractice.[1] This is consistent with young people in other countries, including Egypt, where in fact social media became even more popular and more critical after a similar ban was lifted.[2]

Still, with regard to digital spaces, negotiation around power is highly dependent on offline dynamics of access. Social media remains a relatively niche product in Kenya. As stated earlier, those who are making politics online are a subset of a subset of yet another subset – those who have access to electricity, those who have access to the internet, and finally those who have accounts on social media.

Digging deeper into the use of Twitter in Kenya underscores the dynamics of this negotiation.

The statistics below were generated from private communication with researchers from the Social Computing Group at IDIAP research institute in Switzerland based on a 2013 study that they conducted of how Kenyans use Twitter, and show the number of times the hashtag #KOT was used between August 2013 and April 2014 (out of a total number of 801,237 Tweets sent by Kenyans during this period).

Behind the numbers is a story of how between 2013 and 2017 digital spaces claimed their place at the core of political action in Kenya, prying significant power away from traditional media especially. In March 2013, Uhuru Kenyatta was officially declared president of the country even while he and his running mate were facing charges of crimes against humanity at the ICC. Some in the country celebrated what they saw as a victory over imperialism but a significant number of people felt that it signalled the beginning of an era of impunity. Hundreds of thousands who had been displaced during the post-election violence remained displaced. Civil society especially was deeply troubled by what this government would mean for Kenya. The mood in the country was decidedly mixed.

Kenyatta's Jubilee administration presented itself as a digital government and made online engagement a priority. It would later emerge that it engaged data analytics firm Cambridge Analytica in 2013 to help manage the online reputation and communication of the campaign.[3] At the time, the deal didn't draw specific attention, but would become a sensational revelation during the 2017 election because the same firm had in 2016 supported the Trump presidential campaign and the successful Brexit campaign.

The ambivalent mood in the country shifted dramatically on 21 September 2013 when militants allegedly affiliated with Somali terrorist organisation Al-Shabaab raided the upscale Westgate shopping mall in Nairobi.[4] The official tally said 67 people were

Figure 5: Usage of the hashtag #KOT during the period of research (number of tweets per month)

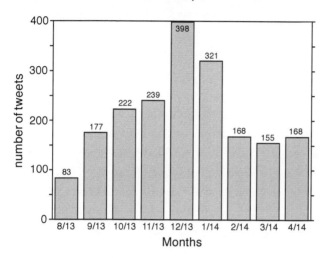

killed and 175 injured during the four-day siege. The most dramatic moments of the siege played out on television and in the press, as photographs of young children forced to play dead by their parents in the blood of other victims, and of plainclothes policemen heroically carrying babies out in one arm while brandishing firearms in the other, filled the airwaves. For a brief time, the country was united in wishing safety for those trapped in the mall.

However, even before the siege was over there were cracks in the facade. First, there were questions around the professionalism of the security forces.[5] Twitter users quickly began to circulate photographs and videos allegedly showing members of the security forces raiding shops in the mall even while the siege was underway. Second, there were concerns regarding the length of time it took to end the siege and amount of damage done in the process. This was followed by accusations that some of the suspects had escaped despite all the bluster. Overall there was frustration with how poorly the entire situation was handled, much of which played out on social media and quickly undid the state-sanctioned, nationalist narrative being pushed in the traditional press.

The hashtag #WeAreOne was started by seven young people who wanted to encourage other Kenyans to rally for the cause. It was quickly adopted by corporations and entities like the Kenya Society for the Red Cross to raise resources to support victims and first responders.[6] It was meant to be a celebration of national unity that emerged in the days of the attack, particularly from the country's community of South Asian descent which had been largely absent from the public sphere since the 1982 attempted coup. But a rival hashtag #WeAreDone soon overshadowed it, debating the uncritical patriotism and stealthy censorship of the traditional media.

Until this point, anyone who dared dispute the official narrative was accused of everything from lack of patriotism to abetting terrorism. It is no coincidence that the archive on Westgate is dominated by foreign journalists. Mohammed Ali and John-Allan Namu, the only Kenyan journalists who attempted to investigate the numerous security failures leading up to and following the event were accused by the Ministry of the Interior of abetting terrorism and threatened with arrest.[7] The only critical pieces of long-form journalism were by foreign journalists, some of whom received awards for their work.[8] As a result, most of the critical, intellectual labour by Kenyans on the Westgate attack was done online, which had everything to do with the characteristics of these platforms.

Reading across the two hashtags – #WeAreOne and #KOT – two conflicting narratives of citizenship and belonging emerge. Within the period captured by Figure 4, both these conflicting ideas of what it means to be patriotic battled for the public imagination. There are the blind believers who agree that criticism of the state at such a vulnerable moment is unpatriotic and inappropriate; and there are the critics for whom patriotism requires reciprocity from the state in the form of transparency and truth. Critics dominated the narrative due to sheer doggedness. Supplementing their criticisms with CCTV footage, long-form journalism from international journalists and survivor narratives that were ignored by the press, they made sure that even though the press was ignoring their criticisms their observations would live on online.

It's not a coincidence that #KOT peaked in December 2013. On 12 December 2013, Kenya turned 50. On social media, there was heated discussion on what this really meant. While the government tried to focus on celebrating the moment – again aiming for patriotic fervour – their thunder was stolen by numerous politically damaging incidents.[9] By 12 December, the cloud of Westgate still hung over the country while an outbreak of violence in neighbouring South Sudan led to the clumsy, haphazard repatriation of thousands of Kenyans who worked there.[10] Further, cross-border incursions from Somalia by Al-Shabaab led to the death of eight, including five policemen.[11]

Meanwhile, early in December the president signed into law the 2013 Media Act – a contentious bill that practitioners and opposition leaders argued amounted to a gagging of the press and a return to authoritarianism.[12] Healthcare workers – doctors and nurses – at two of the largest hospitals in the country went on strike owing to unpaid salaries.[13] The president and the vice-president were still facing criminal prosecution at the ICC. A high number of road accident fatalities during the holiday season prompted a patronising ban on night-time driving. Finally there was the appointment of many older individuals who had served in previous governments to key positions in state-owned corporations – an insult in a country where by 2016 more than a quarter (26%) the country's population was below the age of 18.

By the end of the year, even the newspapers could no longer put a gloss on the government's performance. Two articles captured the melancholy of the year's end. One headline blared 'Kenya Moving in the Wrong Direction',[14] while another screamed 'Jubilee on the Spot over the Unfulfilled Promises', citing a survey that showed that the majority of Kenyans – up to 70% – did not believe that their lives would improve under the Uhuru administration.[15]

Kenyans jumped on the two hashtags – #KOT and #KenyaAt50 – to debate the issues. Once again a sharp division emerged between those who wanted to celebrate what they saw as major political achievements in the country's history and those who felt that the touted gains were illusory. Significantly, there was a contingent that was upset about the amount of money that was spent on the Kenya At 50 celebration event in the shadow of a struggling economy, Westgate and a looming teacher's strike over unpaid salaries.[16] The hashtags were also used alongside the #KenyaAt50 hashtag to poke fun at the numerous organisational failures of the celebration event which was broadcast live across all television and radio outlets. The gaffes fuelled the idea that the supposed gains of the previous 50 years were illusory.[17]

The hashtag #KOT thus joined critics and supporters of the government in a spirited debate over what it meant to be patriotic in Kenya in 2013. The government spent money – on bots, paid bloggers and other forms of stealth marketing – to wrest control of the narrative from its critics. This is a critical difference from the developmental narratives that were being processed by the traditional media. Stage-managed patriotism was simply not good enough anymore. Online spaces gave Kenyans agency over their stories.

Not only is social media changing the way Kenyans communicate with their governments, it is also changing the way they communicate with the world. Much of this was shaped by the #SomeoneTellCNN moment in the build-up to the 2013 election, originally slated for December 2012 but moved forward under the new constitution. Foreign journalists, many of whom had never worked in the region before, used social media as a starting point to learn how Kenyans worked. As both a participant and an observer, I can say that it felt like being under anthropological observation. The 2013 Kenyan election was expected to be more of the same politics as in previous years. Instead, it was a defining moment for #KOT to define itself as a community and exercise its agency, inserting itself into the narrative of the country oriented towards an international audience.

The election was hotly contested. On the one hand there was the Jubilee coalition fronted by Uhuru Kenyatta and William Ruto, both facing indictment at the ICC for crimes against humanity during the violent 2007/08 elections. On the other hand there was the Coalition for Reforms and Democracy (CORD) coalition, fronted by Raila Odinga, who saw this as his best chance to ascend to the presidency after losing out in 1997, 2002 and 2007. The stakes were high and all available tools, including strong social media presence from all the major candidates, were used. There were great expectations but also frustration with how electoral politics was conducted in the region. Kenya had been expected to be a beacon of progress towards this end, but the shadow of the 2007 violence still hung heavily over the country. Victims had still not received any justice. Many loose threads were still unresolved.

Still, pessimism was higher outside the country than within. There was a sense that the global media fraternity was anticipating a blood-bath of Rwandan proportions. Many stories around the election were therefore framed as if the aborted genocide in 2007 would somehow be completed in 2013, but those invested in the country resisted the alarmist reporting. Five years earlier, in December 2007, Kenyans had been paralysed and helpless as alarmist reports often inaccurately depicted the country as another failed African states. In 2013, there was resistance.

This was not an outright denial of the prospect of violence. The point was that the violence needed to be placed in context, the argument being that it was important to explore the political dimensions of the crisis, and also shed light on what individuals were doing to mitigate or ideally end such violence. It was about agency – about not condemning a place without giving those who lived there a chance to defend it somehow.

It was into this tension that CNN sent a journalist to cover the alleged mobilisation of militia groups in the Rift Valley in the lead-up to the August 2013 vote. On 28 February 2013, on its international website, CNN screened a short video by journalist Nima Elbagir titled 'Armed and Ready to Vote'.[18] The video opens with woebegone-looking young men wearing washed-out camouflage wear, crouching in the underbrush of a forest, brandishing homemade guns and stopping just shy of grunting unintelligibly at each other. Some of the men are wearing threadbare wigs and are covered in chalk. Between the exaggerated application of the chalk and the caricature-like dress, they look more like extras on a low-budget Nollywood films than highly trained militias.

It doesn't help that Elbagir seemingly mis-translates what one victim she interviews is saying. The audio cuts out once her narration resumes, but one of the things he says is 'sioni kama ninaweza kurudi', which is more accurately translated as 'I don't see myself returning' rather than 'I will never ever live here again. I have nothing worth fighting for', as Elbagir narrates. Both the tone and the context of the video is highly alarming and unsettling.

In fact, CNN has been a repeat offender in misreading Kenya. During the 2007 elections I personally recall a CNN journalist completely mistranslating the cries of a protester waving a white flag in the streets of Nairobi in 2007 – he was crying for peace, the journalist translated this as a cry for support of his ethnic group. I wrote emails complaining to CNN that were ignored. This, though, was before Twitter had become the political space that it is today, and there was really nothing more to do than write op-eds.

By 2013, the Kenyan presence on the internet had expanded dramatically and it was becoming harder to get away with such statements. Elbagir's report did in fact go viral but not in the way she might have hoped. By the end of the week, it would become one of the definitive rallying points for the #KOT community as the hashtag #SomeoneTellCNN trended. CNN was soon the butt of all kinds of jokes from #KOT. The makers of the report probably assumed three things when putting it together. One: that Kenyans wouldn't see it. Two: that if they did see it, they wouldn't react to it.

Three: that if they did react, such reactions could be ignored. None of these were true.

Is it possible that the Elbagir was right about some people preparing for violence? Absolutely. That wasn't the point of contention. Rather, it was the presumption that this was the norm rather than the exception, and the failure to acknowledge the great efforts that people made to prevent violence during and after the election. It was also in part, judging from many of the tweets, the low production values of the video.

From a political perspective, the video completely missed the true nature of political violence in Kenya. Tribal clashes, ethnic clashes, or whatever one chooses to call political violence, are not the product of ragtag militia groups taking the law into their own hands. They are systematically financed and orchestrated by powerful individuals to displace communities occupying certain disputed areas of the country. If there is anything that 2007/08 taught those who watch Kenya keenly it is that those who unleash the dogs of war do have some say in where they are unleashed, how and for how long. Fighters in militia groups are primarily young, unemployed men but they do not start violence for free. They are funded, armed, supported and organised by political actors. This is partly why Elbagir's report looked more like a joke or a bad film than actual serious reporting. Political violence in Kenya is an industry that is very much tied to the political ambitions of powerful people.

The backlash on Twitter under the hashtag #someonetellCNN exemplifies the role of digital spaces in creating a networked public sphere that permits the creation of a locally driven counter-narrative. One can only make such a video if one presumes that the subjects of the video will never see it. But at only 2 minutes and 50 seconds long the video was very easy to share, particularly on Twitter, and given the number of Kenyans who use the medium on their phones, it was easy to disseminate the indignation. This malleability made it straightforward to rebut Elbagir's claims with evidence – including pictures of opposing political candidates' supporters linking arms, dancing in the streets together and generally avoiding trouble.

It made it easy to set up jokes too, which would come in handy when the hashtag trended in Kenya a second time around. This time, it was around the 2015 visits of US President Barack Obama and Pope Francis. In 2015 then US President Barack Obama was flying to Kenya for his first visit to his father's homeland since becoming president. At this time, Obama was arguably the most popular political leader in the country – more than any other politician in Kenya and perhaps only rivalled by the Pope, who was visiting a few weeks later. In Kenya, the visit was billed as a homecoming of sorts. For the Jubilee administration it was a signal bringing them back in from the cold after the frosty international reception triggered by the ICC indictments. The atmosphere in Nairobi was electric. A few weeks later, the air would sizzle again with the visit of Pope Francis.

The challenge for CNN this time had nothing to do with a specific journalist but with the chyron – the scrolling text at the bottom of a television screen that summarises for a viewer what the current story is about. In the lead-up to both these visits, CNN ran a chyron during its news broadcast that made Kenya seem like one of the most violent places on earth. For Obama, the chyron was a 'Hotbed of Terror'. For the Pope's visit it said 'Pope visits Wartorn Africa'. They probably didn't expect Kenyans to see it, but they did.

The hashtag #SomeoneTellCNN once again became a way for #KOT to unite in anger against a news outlet. The hashtag was flooded with tweets rejecting this framing – some angry, others funny. Superuser Cyprian Nyakundi tweeted '#SomeoneTellCNN It is obnoxious, cantankerous, belligerent [to] besmirch [Kenya]. This has caused consternation, discomposure and discomfiture of spirits' (edited for clarity).[19] Some played on words to flip the criticism back on CNN. Patrick Sampao tweeted 'Good morning Kenyans. Our hospitals are ready to receive those of you who suffered burns from their #hotbeds last night. #SomeoneTellCNN'.[20] Superuser Chris Kirubi tweeted, alongside a screenshot of the chyron in use: 'unless you are the one bringing the terror, we are a hotbed of investment opportunities and great people'.[21] In the 24 hours after the CNN news story on President Obama surfaced, the hashtag was used over 75,000 times.

This is a useful moment to stop and note the impact of superusers on the vitality of a hashtag. A tweet goes viral when it is retweeted – shared – by hundreds or thousands of users. The most viral tweet in history has been shared 3.65 million times. A key determinant of whether a tweet will go viral is if it is retweeted by one or many superusers. Twitter users are clustered around malleable communities of interest – you only follow people who are likely to tweet about subjects that you are already interested in. Superusers therefore allow hashtags to move between these communities of interest easily. When a cluster of superusers uses a hashtag, it will inevitably trend on the site, as was the case with #someonetellCNN.

Superusers on Twitter often function as thought leaders based entirely on their online presence. In Kenya it is important to observe that Twitter has allowed several women to attain thought leader status on the basis of the work they do on the site. When you say @kenyanpundit and @RookieKE to other #KOT, almost everyone knows who you're referring to – two female superusers who rarely publish in traditional media but around whom several communities of activists and interest groups have clustered. It is impossible to think of a female Kenyan thought leader who has achieved the same status based entirely on traditional media.

Many of the #SomeoneTellCNN tweets went viral because superusers took them up. Kirubi, with 451,000 followers at the time of writing, received the most number of retweets at 4,123. Nyakundi, with 683,000 followers at the time of writing, was retweeted 801 times. Patrick Sampao, who is not a superuser with 2,439 followers, was retweeted only 235 times because of the number of superusers who shared his tweets. Although Nyakundi has more followers than Kirubi, Kirubi has a much higher profile offline as the former director of Uchumi supermarkets. Kirubi has more superusers

– particularly journalists – in his circle, who would retweet his opinions without prompting.

The virality – the speed and frequency of sharing – of #someone-tellCNN affirms that a lot of Kenyans wanted to play a more active role in writing and shaping their narratives. Narratives matter because they shape what we think is possible as political action. The emergence of the 'Africa Rising' narrative is a case in point. Many of the cited examples of 'Africa Rising' are in fact looking again at developments that international media especially chose not to pay attention to, or the reimagining of Africa as a consumer of Western manufacturing excess.[22] Facing stagnating economies in their home countries, European and North American firms need to garner support for expanded investment abroad in 'virgin' or 'emerging' markets, encouraging Western media houses – which are, in the end, part of the systems in which these corporations operate – to perpetuate the idea of a 'changed Africa' that can be 'successfully incorporated' into the global economic system. In Kenya at least, this 'Africa Rising' narrative warrants some cynicism and trepidation. Changes are visible, but questions linger about who exactly is benefiting from them. Even while nominally the economy is growing, endemic corruption means that almost none of this money is making it to civilians.[23]

Unlike opinion pieces and articles, platforms like Twitter make it possible for actors to express their frustrations publicly and in accessible language. Despite disparities in access, the gatekeeping function of media is greatly diminished and users are able to challenge narratives they disagree with somewhat directly. Moreover, because they are used by people from various social and economic backgrounds these platforms allow the powerful and the disempowered to communicate directly with each other, revealing or challenging each other's biases.

By the time Elbagir released her report, Kenyans on Twitter were already tired of the hackneyed election coverage. #SomeoneTellCNN signalled that Kenyans wanted to be included in the process of defining the narrative of the election. It wasn't a choice between pre-packaged government propaganda and lazy tropes – there was a more complex story that needed telling. Practically, #SomeoneTellCNN created momentum for #KOT and gave the amorphous group something to rally behind – it gave form and intention to what had hitherto been a loose affiliation.

In 2015, CNN escaped worse criticism because of some critical intervention. Kenya is a major advertiser on the CNN International channel, spending millions of dollars promoting 'Brand Kenya'. A critical hashtag trending for several days during the Obama visit was a deep embarrassment to the station, and the president's communication team issued a stern statement condemning the broadcast, saying it 'undermined the sacrifices made by our Kenyan troops [in Somalia] ... that's why Kenyans, as expressed by those on Twitter, were so angry. Kenya is nothing like the countries that have real war'.[24] The Kenya Tourism Board claimed that it had cancelled its advertising with the station.

In response, CNN executive Tony Maddox flew to Kenya to apologise personally for the report. 'We acknowledge', he said, 'there is a widespread feeling that the report annoyed many, which is why we pulled down the report as soon as we noticed.'[25] Note that Maddox was not apologising for the inaccuracy of the report per se, or the impact it had on Kenyan people. Rather he is apologising that people were so upset about it. This is not an ethical stance against misrepresenting Africans in Western media. It is recognition that annoying customers is bad for business. Still, it was enough for the Kenyan government. The Tourist Board reinstated its advertising. President Kenyatta was photographed with Mr Maddox, accepting his apology and laughing away the offence. A few weeks later, #SomeoneTellCNN was trending again, this time criticising the channel's claim that the Pope was visiting 'War Torn Africa [sic]'.

In 2017, and in a decidedly more toxic political environment, the criticism of foreign journalists online took a troubling turn. Foreign journalists I spoke to at the time confirmed the attacks were far more coordinated and bitter than they had been in 2013. There were also far more bots than there had been in 2013 working hard to counter any stories of clashes or potential violence around the election. The public was braced for a #SomeoneTellCNN moment, which put foreign journalists on edge.

It also created an opening for the state to silence foreign journalists. Afraid of harsh criticism online, some journalists muted direct criticism of the state. The government also held a series of briefings with the foreign press corps while denying local media the same access.[26] Between 11 and 15 August there were many notable incidents of police violence across the country, but local media did not cover any stories of violence or potential violence until the reports were too pervasive on international media to be ignored. There was indeed some coverage that was decidedly fatalistic. AJ+, the social media-facing division of Al Jazeera English published a video that gave the impression the whole country was up in arms, when in fact protests were highly localised.[27] The short clip also ignored that any killing done up to this point had been done by the police.

Still #SomeoneTellCNN established #KOT as an unforgiving but necessary force, compelling international media to reach for objectivity, and the coverage of the 2017 election – despite the chaos of the election process itself – was by many measures more objective and balanced than in previous years.

Chapter 6

REDEFINING COMMUNITY: THE POLITICS OF PUBLIC PERFORMANCES OF EMPATHY

Social media interactions are also changing how Kenyans see and relate to each other. The politics of Kenya has always been synonymous with violent ethno-nationalisms that crowd out more inclusive ways of being. Although in practice ethnic identities are far more malleable than most Kenyans concede, the dominant perception is that ethnic identities are the most important political identities in the country. By permitting unmoderated public interactions social media is urging at least its core users to reconsider entrenched biases, as well as allowing those who question the utility of these social constructions to find each other.

A key way through which this happens is by allowing people to build successful communities of interest and concern that transcend ethnic boundaries. 'Tribe' is a nebulous identity that in practical terms demands loyalty through material support, e.g. through fundraisers or providing jobs and opportunity. Building trust beyond the boundaries of ethnic identity helps to demystify and deconstruct the bonds that keep the imagined community unified.

One case that demonstrated the potency of these new communities of concern was that of #Jadudi. On 4 August 2015, Jackson Biko, one of Kenya's most popular online figures who goes by the name Bikozulu, published an unusual post on his site.[1] It was an emotional, heartbreaking but not unfamiliar story of a working class family facing tragedy because of an inadequate medical system and no real social safety net for people outside their families. A young student at the University of Nairobi, Jadudi, who had up to that point lived a normal and fairly unremarkable life, was unexpectedly diagnosed with a large tumour in his brain. Biko wrote up Jadudi's story on his blog in a post that shocked, inspired and channelled some much-needed help. The first half of the post was the story of how the discovery had disrupted the young man's life. The second half was a direct appeal: a request for 1 million shillings (about $100,000 at the time of writing) to allow Jadudi to fly to India for life-saving surgery.

There are many interesting things about Biko's blog post, but what concerns this chapter the most are the social and political factors that made #Jadudi one of the most shared, followed and dissected hashtags in the history of Kenyan social media. The story itself starts on Twitter. Bikozulu recounts that Jadudi reached out to him through the Direct Message (DM) feature to let the blogger know that he was a fan and that his posts were keeping him company during his first round of chemotherapy. Several months later, Jadudi would renew the acquaintance, telling Bikozulu over a series of messages that his cancer had returned and that without immediate treatment the prognosis was not good.

The DM feature allows Twitter users to message each other directly and privately, meaning that the content of the messaging is not part of the public archive unless one of the recipients makes it so. It allows for more private communication between Twitter users. When the site first launched, only individuals who followed each other or who were followed by other users could DM, but in 2015 the site changed the settings so that individuals who opted in could receive DMs from anyone who uses Twitter. It also removed character limits on DMs. This new approach has advantages for those who prefer private conversations. Many women report being harassed and threatened even on the public tweets – given that DMs are psychologically a safe and private space the feeling of violation can be extreme.

DMs allow for lengthy, private communications. The privacy allows people to be more like their offline selves but with the knowledge that contact can be terminated through blocking the offending party, and therefore people can be more flirtatious, edgier or just a different version of themselves. Basically, DMs allow for somewhat more normal human interactions. Thus it's important that Jadudi and Bikozulu's initial conversations occurred in DM space, because they lack the performative elements of open communication and are shielded from public scrutiny and perhaps each of the users believes they are getting a more truthful version of the other. The blog post presents Biko and Jadudi's communications as a blossoming friendship across which major intimacies are shared: Jadudi's fears that his cancer has returned, his concern for his family's financial situation, his open admiration for Bikozulu as a writer. The DM space allowed for this connection, and perhaps this connection inspired Biko to launch an online appeal to raise funds for Jadudi's latest round of treatment – he felt as if he was doing it for a person he knows, maybe even a friend.

What happened next was staggering. Five hours after the initial blog post was shared, through his network of followers Biko had managed to raise the requested 1 million shillings over m-Pesa; 24 hours later they had managed to raise 6.4 million shillings. By the end of the 48-hour project window, the project had raised 7.6 million shillings to be administered on Jadudi's behalf by a coalition of social media followers. Jadudi went to India for his treatment later that week, but left in his wake many questions that kept #KOT enthralled for months.

The Africa Cancer Foundation (ACF), which received and is administering contributions on behalf of Jadudi, analysed the social media impact of the campaign and concluded that it was the most successful social media fundraising campaign in Kenya's history.[2] During the period of the campaign, the hashtag #Jadudi was mentioned 19,527 times, of which 18% were original tweets and 79% were retweets – people sharing the information into their own networks.[3] On the first day the campaign peaked at 8,000 mentions before settling at 4,000 mentions two days later. According to Twitter analytics, this means that overall the campaign made 187 million impressions, where impressions are estimates of the number of individual interactions with the hashtag by both active and passive users (including multiple interactions by the same person). These are impressive figures.

Perhaps more impressive, however, is the ability to translate this significant online presence into offline social action – to turn a hashtag into a 'harambee'. Harambee culture is an integral part of public life in Kenya in general. The etymology of the word is disputed but the popular narrative is that the word has roots in Hindi, and was an exclamation of the 'coolies' who built the railway to urge coordination in the act of moving large pieces. 'Harambee' was specifically translated as 'let's pull together' by founding President Jomo Kenyatta, who used it to imply figurative heavy lifting to get large projects moving. The first Kenyatta was given to shouting 'Harambee' at the end of his speeches while waving his flywhisk, a practice extended by the second president, Moi, who used it to invite listeners to respond 'Nyayo!' – his nickname.

Harambee is also a noun referring to either an event or a process of collecting money to complete a specific financial task that may be too heavy for an individual or family to bear alone. Initially, harambees were reserved for major institutional projects like construction of new church premises or a new hospital wing, or for unforeseen circumstances like death (which in Kenya means an expensive funeral). As the Kenyan economy collapsed, the practice became more pervasive and today Kenyans have harambees for everything from tuition fees to weddings to a simple visit to a church by a local politician.

Pervasive harambee culture has shifted public life in Kenya significantly. First, it has created an expectation of largesse, which

some argue fuels the culture of corruption in the country. Politicians have argued that the expectation that they attend and give the
largest contributions at harambees justifies their disproportionately
large and ever-increasing salaries. A harambee is also a political
moment – it allows the biggest donor to show off their generosity
and unabashedly receive the adulation of those witnessing it. Politicians love harambees as they provide a context in which they can
feel adored in a country often publicly and devastatingly contemp-
tuous of politicians. This is also why government announcements
are often made at harambees.

Secondly, harambee culture has desensitised Kenyans to
requests for assistance, and has strained many normal relationship
or social ties. On any given weekend there are hundreds of harambees happening in Kenya, and the wealthiest politicians or business
figures are expected to attend all of those in their district, bearing
substantial gifts. For many high-profile figures, the decision to
attend or not to attend a harambee is a difficult calculation between
'loyalty points' or adulation, and feeling put upon by a vast network
of distant relatives.

This is part of what makes the success of the Jadudi campaign so
remarkable. Recall that most of #KOT is relatively middle class, at
least in relation to the rest of the country. These are the people who
receive an invitation to harambee once or twice a month. Many have
been invited to join wedding parties in exchange for fundraising
towards the cost of the wedding. Raising 1 million shillings in five
hours would be remarkable anyway: that the 1 million was raised
by a somewhat jaded Kenyan public with no politician associated
makes it even more remarkable.

No one involved with the campaign doubts that social media was
a necessary condition for the enormous success of the campaign.
Both Biko and Zawadi Nyong'o, the CEO of the Africa Cancer
Foundation, who was an integral part of the campaign in both her
official and unofficial roles, say without a doubt that Twitter allowed
them to accelerate the scale of the outreach. A solid campaign is

only one part of the equation, with the multiplier effect of a few superusers needed so the campaign can go viral.

As one of Kenya's most visible superusers, Biko has a massive online and social media presence. His blog generally shies away from the heavy political discourse that characterises many other popular blogs, but is not niche enough to exclude curious visitors (as is the case with blogs dealing with sex, women's rights issues or finances). He has a more diverse audience than most other blogs with a specific focus. In fact, most of his blog posts are best described as extended diary entries recounting specific experiences, interactions or even dreams.

By engaging regularly with readers of his blog he had already built a community, and a direct and personalised request from the centre of the community is likely to be treated with more deference than a random request in the comments section, for example. The audience is captive and emotionally unguarded in the cognitive safety of the context, and therefore more receptive to messages from the blogger than those, for instance, reading a newspaper. But this is still a relatively closed network. Like an offline community, an online community has its own codes and shorthands and callbacks (references to past events), which an outsider might find intimidating and therefore choose not to engage with the space.

Yet the blog alone does not account for the campaign's success. In fact, it can be attributed to the mix of a well-crafted piece, the pre-existing social latticework and the unseen network of social media orchestration. The call to action embedded in the campaign was that people give whatever balance they had in their m-Pesa accounts and the success of the campaign speaks to the pervasiveness of mobile money in Kenya. m-Pesa allows a transaction to happen in minutes – before the sender can have second thoughts about giving money to a stranger.

So the success of the #Jadudi campaign is about online–offline synergies rather than the pure magic of social media. Most people in Kenya didn't know that Jadudi's campaign involved not one but two superusers, the other being Zawadi Nyong'o, herself an active social media user in addition to her role as the chairperson of the ACF. In the official report on the campaign, Nyong'o suggests that it was in fact the ACF that put Jadudi in touch with Biko rather than spontaneous outreach on the part of the young man.[4] It was the ACF, the report suggests, that developed the hashtags that would become associated with the campaign – #Jadudi and #1MilliforJadudi. It was the ACF that did most of the heavy offline lifting required to make the hashtags go beyond the relatively closed network of Biko's followers.

The facts of this report are today the subject of heated debate between the two fundraisers, but that will be discussed later. For now, presuming that they are true, this affirms that Twitter as an ecosystem still needs regular infusions of passion and direction from offline spaces in order to thrive as a space for political action. The success of the Jadudi campaign was not spontaneous – it was a well-coordinated effort supported by substantial offline organising to draw attention to the online campaign. It affirms that social media is simply a tool, and its efficacy depends greatly on the user and their ability to link online visibility with offline action.

Using Twitter for harambees is not uniquely Kenyan. The major difference is that in other countries, individuals then have to go to a separate crowdfunding site, set up an account, hand over their account details and then finally give a small amount to a campaign of their choice. In Kenya, all the user needs is a five-digit mobile money shortcode. It makes it infinitely easier to share and implement the request, and in this way makes it much easier to raise significant amounts of money over a short period of time.

The scale of the contributions in the Jadudi case also highlights that Kenyans want to care, and when given a well-crafted and focused call to action, they will respond favourably. The Jadudi campaign not only featured a highly sympathetic central character but was orchestrated by a social media superuser who has built his brand out of spinning yarns from incidents that other people might find banal, and another superuser who is a professional fundraiser with significant online skills herself. Jadudi had a fantastic team on his side, but more importantly, the team was able to tap into that altruistic instinct that keeps Kenyans going to harambees without needing anyone to make a high-profile single contribution.

There are other factors that may have contributed to the success of the campaign that are difficult to test for. The campaign launched on 4 August, around the time when most salaried employees would have just been paid. This may seem like a frivolous point, but anyone who has driven in Nairobi will tell you that proximity to payday can have a significant impact on individual behaviour. The fact that traffic is almost always lighter the week before payday is anecdotally attributed to the fact that many city residents fill their petrol tanks on a week by week basis, and when there is no money for petrol, people use public transport or walk. Arguably, the campaign was launched at a time when participants were 'feeling rich' and there-fore comfortable giving what they may have felt was a small amount.

It may also be the fact that health can be a fairly neutral subject in a space that is often deeply divided by other political and social issues. As stated, Jadudi cuts a benign figure whose personal trajec-tory mimics the ideal many Kenyans envision for themselves. The image crafted by Biko depicts a young man of modest means who has defied significant odds to attend university; who has chipped away at a difficult programme before receiving this dire prog-nosis; whose family has borne significant economic and emotional hardship as a result. Many Kenyan families have also felt loss at the hands of a crumbling healthcare system, further fuelling any impetus to give. Almost none of the traditional barriers to concern in Kenya – ethnicity especially – came up during the campaign, which was optimised for the young, urban, cosmopolitan set that makes up #KOT.

The sheer volume of individual contributors to the #Jadudi campaign and the conversations it triggered online suggest that it transcended many of the boundaries of ethnic solidarity. Commu-nities of solidarity like #Jadudi built on Kenyan social media are able to do this in ways that are difficult to replicate offline. They directly challenge the idea that ethnicity is an insurmountable social barrier in Kenya, which is perhaps why so many social rights activists in the country see social media as a potent space to push for new forms of politics in the country. But they are susceptible to other complexities.

The backlash to the campaign began about two weeks after it ended. In part it was triggered by the participation of major Kenyan brands in the process of getting Jadudi to India for treatment and back. The Sarova Stanely provided him with free accommodation. Kenya Airways flew him both ways for free. Kiko Romeo provided him with free clothing to wear on his return. Almost perversely, by succeeding in getting the attention of major brands in support of the cause, the campaign lost public trust. On 9 September, one user with over 6,000 followers tweeted 'this Jadudi thing is fast becoming a showbiz and celebrity moment for some people'.[5]

As harambees have become more intertwined with the political culture they have also become increasingly objects of suspicion. People have called harambees to request funding for university studies, only to use the money to buy a second home or to take holidays abroad. The success of a harambee offline relies greatly on trust and social networks for accountability – the idea that you wouldn't call your family and friends together just to rip them off (even though people do). Online harambees amongst strangers do not have these structures of accountability, and so predictably, once the euphoria subsided, many people began to ask questions, and not just about how much money was raised but for whose benefit the money was raised.

Some users began to speculate that those involved were using the campaign to further their personal brand rather than to actually help a young man fighting for his life – a difficult criticism to defend against because promoting personal brands is precisely the reason why a brand would associate itself with such an activity. Kenya Airways did not give Jadudi a free flight simply because they were feeling charitable. They did it – and took numerous photographs showing that they were doing it – because it associates their brand with a sympathetic cause and ideally leads to more sales. The question in the doubter's minds is: are the individuals driving the campaign driven by the same instincts?

Rumours of hidden agendas escalated quickly, and the tension was exacerbated by a newspaper article in which Biko appeared to focus only on his contribution to the campaign while ignoring Nyong'o's contribution.[6] This erasure was particularly visible to Kenya's active feminist social media community, who called Biko out. They argued that it was part of a recurring pattern of misogyny that pervades Kenya's public sphere, in which women's contributions to important issues are often written out of historical accounts. In October, Biko issued a statement on his blog apologising, clarifying and responding to the backlash against him.[7] #KOT is a fickle space, and the same forces that make a reputation can easily unmake it, with only the usually reliable collective national amnesia over controversial issues acting as a fall-back.

Yet Biko was also responding to a deeply damaging rumour. On 21 October 2015 Nairobi News, an online tabloid, ran a story asserting that the entire Jadudi campaign had been a financial scam.[8] The clickbait title actually overstates the content of the article. Essentially, the National Health Insurance Fund (NHIF) is the national safety net mechanism into which all Kenyans pay contributions and from which they expect to get support for medical expenses. According to several Twitter users cited by the article, Jadudi's family had received significant financial support from NHIF and therefore did not need the money raised through the campaign. According to Nyong'o, however, the family had repeatedly tried to get support from NHIF and failed, and it was only the shame of such a highly visible campaign that spurred them into action. In a country where official information is scarce and rumours are often more legitimate than official news sources, these kinds of rumours can be highly damaging. This was perhaps why both Nyong'o and Biko reacted swiftly, independently issuing statements on their Twitter handles and blogs respectively, clarifying their involvement in the campaign.

Questions around the campaign have lingered, especially as other similarly situated individuals have tried and failed to raise even a fraction of the public concern that Jadudi raised. Yet the successes of the campaign cannot be overstated. #Jadudi represented the perfect confluence of old and new media, as well as existing social systems and mobile technology to demonstrate that Kenyans are interested in building communities of concern that transcend offline divisions. A cursory review of the tweets at the hashtag shows that Jadudi's supporters were drawn from various ethnic groups and age categories, undercutting the myth of the tribe as the only institution in Kenya on which a person can rely for help in times of need.

This is extremely important, because, as some tweeters noted, it is the starting point for the post-ethnic discourse on belonging in Kenya. To understand this, we have to understand what the 'tribe' is for. Kenya is characterised as a low-trust society: that is, one where citizens believe that most people in the society are dishonest. A 2007 survey found that Kenya had the lowest rate of public trust of ten African countries surveyed – below countries like Nigeria, Ethiopia or Egypt.[9] Research on trust distinguishes between political trust and social trust to acknowledge that while trust is an absolutely necessary factor for a functional democracy, it operates through different channels in different societies. In Kenya, the 'tribe' is the main conduit through which those who are unrelated and otherwise disconnected can manifest trust. The 'tribe' therefore functions as the main social safety net, particularly as formal institutions like the NHIF and the National Social Security Fund (NSSF) crumble and lose public confidence.

Ethnic politics works in Kenya because ethnic groups are able to demand and repay trust in a way that other institutions don't. There are material benefits to appealing to this loyalty that are not evident in other ways of belonging. And this is why the ability to deliver material benefits beyond the 'tribe' is a crucial way of ameliorating the political import of ethnicity. Communities of concern like those built around Jadudi matter because people are able to see that political action not predicated on ethnic groups works.

Still, the campaign hinted at some of the limits of these new possibilities, particularly in reinforcing troubling patterns about gender relations in the country. The fact that so many tweeters so quickly questioned the ethics around the campaign once Nyong'o came forward as its main orchestrator either speaks to a natural suspicion against famous people (Nyong'o's father is a prominent politician and her younger sister is a world-famous actress) or against women. It's hard to tell, but the fact is that Nyong'o received significant online harassment from her detractors whereas Biko did not.[10] This suggests that when push comes to shove, the digital public sphere is as likely as the analogue to come after women – personally and virulently – in a way that they would never come after a man. Digital platforms are giving Kenyans a space to define new ways of belonging, yes, but who is welcome to be a part of these communities and on what terms?

Chapter 7

WOMEN AT WORK: KENYAN FEMINIST ORGANISING ON SOCIAL MEDIA[1]

Perhaps no other group has capitalised as much on the new spaces that social media has created in Kenyan society than young, radical feminists. Online spaces have amplified women's voices and lived experiences in a way that traditional media still struggles with, allowing them to create communities of safety and of action. Particularly by providing young women a space to publicly articulate their radical politics to a large audience, social media has reinvigorated feminist discourse in Kenya.

That's the good news. The bad news is that self-identifying as a feminist in Kenya can be a dangerous proposition, where the belief that feminists are angry, unhappy and looking to destroy everyone else's happiness is pervasive. One popular *Daily Nation* columnist built her entire fan base out of insulting other women, including one particularly bitter and rancid article that referred to 'Twitter feminists' as 'the scum of the earth'.[2] Once you factor in the derision stemming from the belief that feminism on social media has no impact offline, publicly identifying as a feminist on Twitter seems like insanity.

Thankfully, feminists are resilient. At many key periods, Kenyan feminists have used new media to give women's political organising in Kenya a much-needed shot in the arm after decades of stagnation under an autocratic regime. The case of the #MyDressMyChoice hashtag demonstrates how strong and effective this organising can be, provided that those who wish to use it as a tool for organising remain focused and united.

As usual, the story begins offline. On any day, downtown Nairobi is a chaotic and frenetic place. The Central Business District (CBD) is the heart of the city and all of the residential neighbourhoods are oriented around it. Most public transit in the city is also directed towards the CBD, so that individuals crossing from one part of the city often have to change buses or *matatus* there. At the same time, these *matatus* and buses operate hectic schedules. The owners often set ambitious fare targets for the drivers that, after paying bribes to police officers who deliberately target *matatus*, either have to put in long hours or overload their vehicles to meet them. These layers of tensions make *matatu* stage and bus stops unpredictable places. Even on a good day, between fear of being pick-pocketed or prices being raised at the last minute, people are at their edgiest. Yet the crush of people in a hurry makes bus stops perfect sites for petty traders, especially those selling snacks.

On 7 November 2014 Wairimu,[3] a female trader in Nairobi, was one of many women selling boiled eggs at a bus stop in downtown Nairobi. Earlier in the day, she had sold one of the *matatu* conductors three boiled eggs and some *kachumbari* salad. He then boarded his *matatu* and went back to work, as did she. Given that the man was a regular customer, Wairimu had allowed him a few hours to pay for the snack, although she was determined to recover the money by the end of the business day.

When she approached the man and asked him to pay up so she could close up shop, instead of paying for the food the customer responded by calling Wairimu a 'whore' – one of the most offensive insults you can spit in Swahili. He also threatened to rape her in her home later that night. Undeterred, Wairimu pressed her claim. Shockingly, the customer then turned on her, beating Wairimu until she passed out. He then pulled at her clothes and tried to strip her. Rather than helping Wairimu, several men in the area joined in. Wairimu came to at the hospital several hours later with only her sister, also a trader at the market, having intervened on her behalf. This sister was also attacked herself. The attack was partially captured on film, and the instigator was eventually arrested in part due to pressure generated online.

If terrorism is violence perpetrated with the intent of spreading fear, then by many measures, Kenyan women have been terrorised. In November 2014, four different stripping attacks were recorded across the country – three in the capital Nairobi, and one in the coastal city of Mombasa. These attacks are random and often based on nothing more than the attacker's sense that the woman in question has violated his own standard on what amounts to 'decency'. He could be infuriated by the sight of the back of a woman's knees. He might be angry that she dared speak up to him. Generally they betray a frustration that women exist in public on their own terms.

The #MyDressMyChoice movement was a social media movement designed to reclaim women's right to a public life on their own terms, and a riposte to the notion that men – strangers at that – have the right to determine what counts as acceptable public dress for women. It recognised that in many ways women in Kenya were still being treated as second-class citizens, and was a push for agency. #MyDressMyChoice wanted to render this seemingly simple facet of the women's rights struggle visible. #MyDressMyChoice worked – an online demand had a tangible, offline impact that made the lives of women in Nairobi better – for specific reasons that had to do with the cause and the ways in which advocates presented and executed it.

Around the world, men often use public violence to shame and terrorise women into hiding, but social media networks are increasingly integral to pushing back against these attacks. In Kenya, a schoolgirl was once attacked on board a *matatu* by a number of men, one of whom turned out to be a police officer. The attack was filmed on a camera phone and went viral on social media.

Eventually, the officer and the *matatu* were both positively identified – not through formal investigation channels but through persistent action from a group of feminists on Twitter and Facebook. The entire incident encapsulates all that is good and bad about these spaces. On the one hand, someone filmed a violent attack and uploaded it for titillation and public consumption. On the other, concerned users turned the video around and used it to find and punish the attackers, who were eventually arrested. Although the video has since been taken down by YouTube for violating its harassment and bullying policies, stills from the distressing clip are still available online,[4] underscoring the extent to which the suffering of women is not taken seriously enough.

The #MyDressMyChoice movement started on the Facebook page of Kilimani Moms, a coalition of mothers from one of Nairobi's more affluent suburbs that has quickly morphed into a mixture of neighbourhood association and political advocacy platform.[5] It was the Kilimani Moms who began mobilising people around the hashtag, calling for a protest in the days after the video was released to support the right of women to dress as they would like. In these first days, the movement was almost entirely started, coordinated and disseminated over social media, culminating in the street protest on 16 November.

In the days leading up to the offline protest, participants flooded Kenyan social media with the hashtag, and #MyDressMyChoice became one of the key trending topics in Kenya. But it wasn't only being used by protesters. A quick review of the hashtag on that day points to the deep disagreement in the general public on the issue of women's dress. The hashtag triggered a potent debate on the concept of 'decency'. What does it mean to be decent? Who has an obligation to be decent? Who has a responsibility to preserve decency? What does it all entail?

The core feminist group that propagated the hashtag was an unambiguous defence of the absolute right for women to dress however they want to, wherever they want to, including miniskirts, shorts, hijabs or niqabs in the Central Business District where the attacks happened. 'Decency' to this group is respecting individual agency and giving room for freedom of expression, particularly when it comes to clothing. One user tweeted '#MyDressMyChoice Men unless [you] are supporting women's rights, shut up about their bodies! #WomenForFeminism'. The right is vested in the woman: the obligation in the society around her is to respect her exercise of this right.

However, there was a group that was advocating a less categorical stance. This group claimed to respect the right of a woman to dress however she wanted while at the same time vesting an obligation in her to respect others in the way that she dresses. 'Decency' for this group is a code word for social mores or norms. It implies that a woman has an obligation to protect others – men especially – from sexual thoughts inspired by her choice of clothing.

Another user tweeted: 'Your are (sic) free to wear whatever you want, but ask yourself the question, is the society ready for what you have put on? #MyDressMyChoice'. Interestingly, many women embraced this position. For example, user @MawakMary tweeted 'ladies lets dress decently, stripping one naked is not the solution men zip your [trousers] plus eyes. #MyDressMyChoice'. The intent behind this is to reconcile both condemnation of the violence of stripping and public shaming but also to preserve the status quo by discouraging women from pushing society's boundaries. This formulation suggests that everyone has the right not to be offended and that the woman in question has the obligation not to cause offence.

Others still opposed the idea that women have a fundamental right to decide how they dress. These were people who believe that a woman's choice of dress is directly related to whether or not she is a victim of violence. 'Decency' in this formulation is not simply protecting men from sexual thoughts, but is tied to the idea of women's public sexuality as provocation. A woman can only permissibly exist public if she is completely asexual to a standard determined by men. The underlying philosophy is a return to purity that distorts the reality of Kenyan history in favour of a puritanical, Victorian – and thus colonial – perspective on women's sexuality. These users tend to appeal to 'African culture' as rejecting indecency, overlooking the fact that there are still many communities in Kenya today where women don't wear shirts. Many members of this group created their own hashtag, #NudityIsNotMyChoice, on which one user tweeted 'Time to reserve our African culture and morals #NudityIsNotMyChoice to hell with #MyDressMyChoice'.

Interestingly enough, #NudityIsNotMyChoice was a hashtag used primarily by men even though it ostensibly speaks in a female voice. Often their gambit was linking 'decency' to the idea of desirability. Another user tweeted, 'It is a man's job to respect a woman but a woman has to give the man something to respect #NudityIsNotMyChoice'. Secondly, in the months following the campaign, tweets with the hashtag have become inundated with nude pictures of men showing off their genitals. (Seriously, don't search this hashtag at work.) Many Twitter hashtags tend to descend into pornography as those selling the product try to hijack the momentum to promote their product, so this in itself isn't rare or unusual. But the irony is remarkable – showing how women's public sexuality can court such controversy but men's public sexuality is either celebrated or ignored.

So, this formulation of the decency debate does interesting cognitive work. Not only does it vest a right not to be offended in men, but it also suggests that the default setting for a man is 'violent attacker'. Much like a starving beast tethered by a flimsy chain, it suggests that the slightest provocation – the back of a knee peeking from under a knee-length skirt, the faint outline of a panty line under a pair of tights or really any kind of clothing that celebrates the female form – might push the beast to violence. It debases the humanity of Kenyan men by showing them as rabid, violent beasts with no ability to rise above whatever baser instincts they purportedly have. In essence, it says that Kenyan men are by nature weak and violent, and Kenyan women have an obligation not to poke the beast.

It's worth pointing out that what was presented as 'indecently dressed' in Kenya would barely register in other societies, even in Africa. Unlike in Madagascar or Togo for instance, where women regularly wear hotpants around town, Kenyan women have been exposed to systematic violence for wearing knee-length skirts or sleeveless shirts. Pictures taken during the #MyDressMyChoice protest, where women were asked to wear miniskirts in protest, affirmed that women weren't fighting for the right to march through the streets in bikinis – they were having to fight for the right to wear what would ordinarily pass for acceptable businesswear. This has everything to do with Kenya's history as a settler colony of Victorian Britain.

Indeed one of the most interesting pushbacks to the #NudityIsNotMyChoice campaign was people posting pictures of their mothers and grandmothers wearing miniskirts in the 1960s or traditional outfits – even in the contemporary age – that would be considered indecent by the #NudityIsNotMyChoice brigade. This underscores that the conservative standards of 'decency' being advocated for are not 'African' but rather imposed upon African women in order to manage their sexuality.

Furthermore, the idea of managing African sexuality itself stems from a racist colonial fear of the same. Fear of black men was a cornerstone of anthropological texts of the time, painting Africans as sexually deviant and unable to control their baser instincts as evidenced by their prolific reproduction.[6] The idea that sex was dirty and shameful is not 'African'. Indeed, there are several examples of Kenyan communities having what would be considered a positive approach to sexuality today – where for instance the Agikuyu encouraged couples to have premarital sex in order to ascertain fertility and compatibility.[7] 'Hide yourself and don't provoke me' is the same as saying 'hide yourself because I cannot control myself' and Kenyan men should be offended by this presumption, not propagate it.

To understand just how radical the #MyDressMyChoice movement was in the context of Kenya's – and indeed Nairobi's –

history, it's important to chart the evolution of the CBD as a public space through a historical arc that predates even independence. The idea of public sexuality as provocation cannot be separated from the broader discussion on colonisation and physical space. It's not a coincidence that so many of these attacks on women happen in the CBD.

From its founding in 1899 until independence in 1963, Nairobi was de jure a racially segregated city. African men who lived and worked in Nairobi were not legally allowed to live with their families and so most of the African inhabitants of the city – even those who worked in colonialists' homes – were men. At the same time, Africans were not allowed to move within the CBD without wearing a *kipande* – a metal 'pass' bearing their name and details about their ethnic origin – around their necks. Any European had the right to stop a man and demand that he show his pass. Any African found without a pass could be summarily arrested, detained, often tortured and then returned to the reserves (rural area).[8]

The CBD in Nairobi is therefore the historical epicentre of the racial and gender violence of colonial Kenya: a physical manifestation of the subjugation of colonisation and, in this context, black Kenyans and men especially were conditioned through violence into approaching the CBD with a certain reverence. This corresponds to Ekeh's conception of the two publics – the experience of colonialism forces people to present different versions of themselves in different physical or intellectual environments.[9] This multiplicity of identities didn't change after independence. 'Going to Town' retains an air of mystique for many Nairobi residents, who are expected to dress up before entering this hallowed space. So, for instance, unlike in many other capital cities where women will wear running shoes while commuting and change into heels once they arrive in the office, until recently Kenyan women would rarely be seen in anything that wouldn't pass for office footwear in the CBD.

So the idea of men as beasts with no impulse control is inherent to the physical space of the Nairobi CBD. It is the most cosmopolitan place in Kenya but this cosmopolitan identity is founded on apartheid and the violent exercise of power, as well as repression of any kind of self-expression. The system persists in some form because it continues to benefit some people, just as Kenya's decolonisation is incomplete because those who succeeded the colonial administration continue to benefit. Spatial repression persists because it facilitates control, and keeping the CBD 'pure' is integral to preventing its use as a site for earnest political mobilisation.

The ongoing experience of South Africa underscores that spatial repression is often the most difficult form of repression to undo because it necessarily involves material dispossession – we cannot decolonise neighbourhoods without challenging the property and succession rights of those who took it by force.[10] Similarly, we cannot reclaim public spaces for everyone if we don't challenge and undo the dominance of one group over another, a process of dispossession that has only happened in small increments in Kenya.

In the post-independence euphoria, there was some reclaiming of the CBD and other public spaces, and women in miniskirts – even police officers – were not uncommon. But one effect of the repressive 1970s and 1980s was that women lost some of the territory they had won. These were the years when the Maendeleo Ya Wanawake (progress for women) movement was annexed by the ruling party KANU and ceased functioning as an independent organisation advocating for the rights of women.[11] Concrete policy discussions on women's rights issues were sidelined in favour of mealy-mouthed discourse on individual morality and heteronormative values. There was pushback but the more autocratic the government became the more it needed easy wins, and controlling women was an easy win in a patriarchal society. Novelist Toni Morrison has argued that the purpose of racism is distraction.[12] Here, the purpose of this sexism was to distract women from the bigger fight for political autonomy.

This system of control and silencing peaked during the pro-democracy era in the paradoxical 1990s. On one hand, women like Wangari Maathai used the shame culture against itself, operationalising public nudity and the hang-up with decency as a form of protest. When threatened with arrest for protesting the detention of political prisoners in Nyayo House in Kenya, Maathai and the mothers of the political prisoners stripped, shaming the young men who were sent to arrest them into capitulation.[13]

On the other hand, these were the years when violently stripping women seen as 'indecently dressed' became common, even though it frequency ebbed and flowed with the state of broader political tension. Women were the canary in the coalmine of political violence in Kenya. When political tensions ran high, the risks for women were high, perhaps because they were seen as easy targets in the context of generalised violence. Regardless, the public reaction to these attacks was not condemnation, but involved shifting the burden of obligations onto women, arguing that if they wanted to stay safe in the CBD, they couldn't go out 'indecently dressed'.

For women in Kenya today, their scope for self-expression in the CBD is intimately connected to the status of patriarchy in the society as a whole. Patriarchy wants women to remain unseen in the public sphere; and women's issues to remain subordinate to the concerns of men. In many ways, therefore, the scope or space for women to move around the CBD dressed in the way they choose is indicative of the broader ability of women to be present, visible and active agents in the national political discourse. The #MyDressMyChoice conversation suggests they recognise their right to self-expression, that they are confident that the law will protect this right, and that at least some men have recognised their own obligation to respect these rights.

Social media allowed like-minded women and their allies working towards these goals to find each other relatively easily, which increased the reach of the protest and gave it permanence beyond the day's activities. It prioritised the conversation, allowing it for the first time to be articulated as a public safety issue rather than a question of decency or morality. It therefore finally allowed women's rights issues in Nairobi to be articulated in women's own terms for a wide audience, even if a lot of the audience disagreed.

The backlash to #MyDressMyChoice suggests that in a country fragmented across lines of ethnicity ('tribe'), class and age, one thing that cuts across divisions is the interest in policing women and their bodies. This in turn points to the fact that women's rights issues are perhaps the only truly national issue in Kenya, which in turn suggests that a politics predicated on women's rights issues offers a way forward in building new and less violent political organisation in Kenya.

The direction of the rights and obligations in these formulations are important because they give a basis for actions or remedies. If a person has a right that is violated then the person who has infringed upon that right owes them some kind of remedy. If a woman has the right to dress however she wants then a society has an obligation to defend her and give her remedies where she endures even verbal harassment as a result. This is the formulation that exists in Kenyan law, where the bill of rights guarantees freedom of expression for the society.[14] If, on the other hand, the woman has an obligation to dress decently, then she isn't owed any remedies if she is punished, legally or extrajudicially, for violating this obligation. This is the case for example in countries like Sudan that have a public morality code. Kenya's social position veers towards the latter, in which women have an obligation to preserve the morality of the society and men especially argue they have a right not to be offended and scandalised.

What this means is that legal remedies for violence or harassment endured by women dressed in ways that are seen to offend public morality are rarely enforced, leaving women vulnerable to violence and harassment in person and online. One prominent male blogger who otherwise positions himself as a 'champion of the people' tweeted during the height of the #MyDressMyChoice movement 'Make no mistake about it, if you are indecently dressed, I will be the first to strip you'. Not only was this now-deleted tweet supported by many of his followers: it earned him even more followers and did nothing to damage his standing as a public figure.

#MyDressMyChoice is not significant just because of what it did online. It was a notable victory because it led to significant political changes offline. Quite soon after the protest the judiciary responded by prosecuting those caught molesting the woman, the first time there had been a prosecution for this kind of behaviour in recent memory. The outcome emboldened women, signalling decreasing tolerance for this kind of public violence. Today, women feel safer dressing less austerely in the CBD, and it is not uncommon to see women in knee-length skirts or sleeveless tops.

In this case social media activism worked, because the demand was specific, well-articulated, grounded in law and reason, and supported by a broad coalition of women's and human rights organisations. If the state in the form of the judiciary had not responded it would have undermined its own legitimacy. An online demand had a tangible, offline impact that made the lives of women in Nairobi better. This dynamic – using public shame on social media to push state actors to work – has become an integral part of advocacy and activism in Kenya, although it doesn't always work.

Today, digital platforms are integral to the radical feminist resurgence in Kenya. Digital platforms have been used to advocate for more women commentators on television and in print (#SayNoToManels). Women have organised around advocacy for the implementation of gender quotas contained in the constitution (#WeAre52Pc). Over the last ten years, new media has become a space for voices the mainstream would rather not hear to be able to loudly voice discontent over the country's patriarchal public sphere and to recast women as more than just mothers or mothers in waiting. Where traditional media resists expanding women's identities beyond their reproductive capacities – sexualising news readers, denying women airtime save for instances where they are speaking about their roles as women or mothers – social media has allowed women who want it to cultivate public identities that are relatively autonomous from their biological gender. New media has offered a space where women can be funny, witty, creative, political or whatever they choose to be in public.

Women's private and public lives are multifaceted. In Kenya, women's labour has been exploited both in and outside the home while keeping them underpaid and unprotected. Most of Kenya's massive domestic labour force is women who are often subject to sexual assault and abuse from their employers. Kenyan women are significantly underrepresented in politics, and work less in formal wage employment even though most of Kenya's small businesses are owned by women.[15] The government itself has taken advantage of women's entrepreneurial interests to encourage them to work in Gulf States with deplorable human rights records.[16]

Deeply embedded ideas of identity and belonging can doubly marginalise women. Ethnic identities especially can reinforce the patriarchy while erasing women's human right to determine how they choose to identify. Women bear the burden of their ethnic identities in the obligation to expand the family through childbirth only to have their own ethnic identities erased almost completely through marriage. Kenyan women are often told that they are born a visitor– a woman's family home is a merely a transit point before she gets to her 'true home' with her husband. This alienating consciousness has created vulnerabilities for women, including in relation to domestic violence, where it is not uncommon for abused women to be returned to abusive partners because they 'no longer have a home' with their birth families.

The offline women's rights movement in Kenya has floundered when it comes to pushing back against these challenges. Even recognising that women's struggles are disparate and that different ethnic or racial groups have different ways of understanding the role of women in public life, there are enough cross-cutting themes and issues for a coordinated women's movement to emerge. It hasn't. Issues like female genital mutilation have managed to build signifi-cant momentum, but these practices are not universal across ethnic groups. In the public sphere they are often discussed as niche subjects that only affect specific groups. Meanwhile, issues like domestic violence or political marginalisation – alarmingly common for all women, all ages, all tribes, all races – that could be the focal point of a national women's rights movement are routinely overlooked.

As the institutionalised women's rights movement has focused its attention on politely requesting space, those who feel shut out of the space – lesbians, young feminists, anti-capitalists – have resorted to new ways of raising their voices. Social media is a big part of this. In a study on the relationship between mobile phones and feminism, Sanya theorises that technology is a new site where the agency of the user complicates oversimplified depictions of Kenyan women.[17] Social media is allowing women to challenge presumptions about female identity in Kenya, allowing non-mainstream voices to expand their reach and to articulate often uncomfortable truths about the situation facing women in Kenya today. It has allowed radical feminists to find each other. Social media is hosting some majorly transformative conversations on women's rights issues – from the Maslaha conversation against a practice in which Somali families pay a small fine for domestic violence cases in order to avoid criminal proceedings, to conversations on the choices that women have in the ways they present themselves in public. These are conversations that traditional media cannot host because they are still bound by patriarchal norms of 'decorum'.

The idea of being accepted as 'good women' keeps institutional activism shackled and unable to push for the very necessary radical and transformative dialogue that is needed to bring Kenyan women's rights into the twenty-first century: to defend the idea of women as complete persons and not just men's accessories. In contrast, social media is allowing women in Kenya to move beyond the burden of 'goodness' and be as combative, opinionated and uncompromising as is needed in order to create a more just society. As institutional women's rights groups have struggled with purpose and/or funding, women's rights organising online has racked up some major victories for individual women as well as the cause. This has led to striking contrasts of strategy, messaging and even impact between what traditional, offline organising has been able to accomplish in the last decade in Kenya and what social media advocacy is accomplishing.

Three high-profile cases underscore these discrepancies. The first and perhaps the most definitive was #JusticeForLiz. On 26 June 2013, a 16-year-old girl – Liz (not her real name) – was walking home alone from her grandfather's funeral in Butula County, a rural part of Western Kenya. While en route, she was dragged into the nearby scrub by six men, who proceeded to beat and gang-rape for her several hours.[18] Liz passed out at some point during her ordeal because of the violence of the attack. Likely afraid that they had committed murder, her attackers threw her into a pit latrine and fled. She was found early next morning, still alive but deeply physically and emotionally damaged. The well-wishers who found her rushed her to hospital for treatment but, tragically, Liz endured major spinal injuries and developed an obstetric fistula – an abnormal passage that develops between two organs when hollow organs are punctured – as a result of her attack.

This story was first reported on 7 October in Kenya as a small article in the newspaper. However, the online version quickly went viral in Kenya and overseas. It was a brutal indictment both of women's security but also the cavalier and spiteful reaction of the local police. When details emerged of the crime, the local community frogmarched the suspects to the police station demanding that the police take action. Instead of holding them in custody while awaiting a judicial decision, the policemen in charge offered the suspects a deal – rather than facing criminal proceedings the suspects would perform manual labour at the station in return for their freedom. The police sentenced them to cutting the long grass around the police station before releasing them. It was this derisory punishment that triggered a subsequent protest in Nairobi after the story broke. A petition of over 1.2 million signatures gathered online was also delivered to the Attorney General's office and finally the police were compelled to review and re-prosecute the case.[19]

Two years later, #JusticeForKhadija rolled out after an attack against a teenager in Mandera county. Mandera is the north-east corner of Kenya – more than 500km away from Nairobi and more remote still because of the lack of infrastructure in the area. This is an area that has been routinely ignored by the central state since independence, and residents are accustomed to organising on their own terms. In 2015, a 16-year-old girl in Mandera town was delivered to the county hospital badly burnt and fighting for her life. She had allegedly been brutally burnt by her 40-year-old husband, who, instead of rushing her to hospital, locked her in the house for two weeks. She quickly began to waste away with neglect and her husband panicked.[20] He finally rushed her to hospital, where he abandoned her.

Eight months following the Khadija account, there was #Justice-ForFatuma in Wajir County. Wajir is just south of Mandera and shares a border with Somalia. In late 2015, a man in Wajir arrived at the county referral hospital with his wife. Much of the hospital staff was in Nairobi for a medical conference so it is unlikely that people paid much attention to the strange duo. What is clear is that he left her in the hospital alone, frail and with a 10-inch blade sticking out of her cheek. He had stabbed her six times before a seventh strike that left the blade wedged right through one cheek, buried into the opposite cheekbone. She was found by activists in the understaffed and under-resourced hospital.

Each of these campaigns led to significant offline activity on behalf of the women. Their husbands were prosecuted for domestic violence, which in North Eastern Kenya is rarely prosecuted but regularly resolved through a traditional conflict resolution system known as 'maslaha'.[21] Liz's attackers and the policemen who allowed them to go free were punished. Khadija received medical treatment and a divorce. Fatuma also received medical treatment and her husband was jailed for assaulting her. The perpetrators were arrested and charged with serious felonies like grievous bodily harm and assault. None of this would have happened without the significant organising that happened online, but, more importantly, much of the rest of the country wouldn't have been awakened to the resource crisis facing women's rights organisations in Kenya.

The three cases are united by more than the hashtag format. First they hint at the scale and devastation of violence against women in Kenya. According to official statistics, this is perhaps the most pervasive human rights issue in the country, with 42% of women over the age of 40 reporting sexual or physical violence from a partner.[22] In fact, according to the same dataset, violence against women is an issue that cuts across all other social or economic cleavages – age, gender, class, rural versus urban, etc. The behaviour is not only prevalent but broadly normalised, where young women might hear from older women during bridal showers that it is normal for men to be violent, that they must adapt to their partners' violence, or that it is merely another predictable expression of masculinity. This is perhaps why when the governor of Nairobi slapped a female nominated member of Parliament in full view of cameras, or when a member of Parliament threatened to insert a glass bottle into a female member's vagina, the reaction of a major section the public was to laugh.

Kenyan women are, statistically and for a developing country, relatively more educated, more represented in private enterprise and certainly enjoy more freedoms, at least in urban areas, than their counterparts even in neighbouring countries. Yet these freedoms cannot protect against unchallenged beliefs about the inherent superiority of men, especially where men are socialised to protect their entitlements with violence. Thus, while Kenyan women do enjoy a significant amount of latitude given that their progress adds to the combined financial success of a marriage relationship, they often find such freedoms violently challenged where only the progress of women is on the cards.

Moreover, considering the physical distance between the site of the above cases and the capital, without social media they would arguably have disappeared into the abyss of a hamstrung judicial system that struggles to deliver justice for victims of all crime, let alone gender-based violence, which isn't taken seriously. Mandera, Wajir and Butula exist at the periphery of Kenya's imagined geography that centres on Nairobi. Busia is closer to Kampala than it is to Nairobi, and Wajir is closer to Mogadishu. Traditional media does not have a permanent presence in Busia or Wajir and coverage of these areas is minimal, often consisting of no more than two or three lines from each county. Moreover, given that most of the stringers in these outlying towns are men, women's rights issues are often de-prioritised. With the exception of the #JusticeForLiz story, which was in fact first carried by the press, without a sensational political hook it is difficult for such stories to find space in the press. Without the intervention of social media personalities, it is unlikely that people – especially those in the capital – would have known enough to care about what happened to Liz or Khadija.

Beyond drawing attention to these cases, the online mobilisation created a tangible call to action that concerned members of the public could respond to. Altruism is a difficult instinct to cultivate in a low-trust society like Kenya, where it is common, for instance, for drivers to rush past the scene of an accident because of the countless stories of robberies and kidnappings of those who stop. But this doesn't mean that the instinct to assist is gone. It simply needs alternative avenues for expression. This is what social media did in these and other cases. Organisers gave the public space and direction to show concern and act. It's a low-risk, low-energy, high-reward way for those who are interested in doing right or being seen to do right to express their solidarity with victims of various struggles.

Social media also shamed and compelled public institutions to work and intervene in these cases. Individual action could never accomplish what these hashtags did in the few weeks they were up. It is normal for cases in court to take two years from indictment to the first hearing. Detention without trial can legally last up to one year. And even if your case is heard, as in the case of Liz, there is no guarantee that officials will not be bribed by opposing parties. In these circumstances, individuals have slowly given up on making institutions work.

At the same time, many of these institutions are thirsty for the easy PR wins that online spaces offer, and so are sensitive to concerns and queries raised there. Recall that even in the most dysfunctional societies, governments will rarely come out and spite citizens directly. They still want to maintain the illusion that they are governing 'for the people' because even the most powerful government cannot govern entirely through force. Some measure of public denial or acquiescence is necessary to keep a society functioning without universal violence. Spaces like social media where this illusion can be directly challenged and contradicted are especially threatening to these governments and institutions.

The Kenyan judiciary especially has tried to use social media as a space to redeem its image, with individual judges, including the two chief justices who sat between 2013 and 2017, and lawyers responding to individual questions about judicial process and individuals' relationship with the courts. This has made raising grievances in public central to the shifting dynamic between individuals and institutions in Kenya. There are enough social media users in Kenya – family members, friends, friends of friends – that public officials can no longer be insulated from well-researched and well-articulated grievances. Individuals with a basic sense of decency can't ignore such criticism, and this is part of what makes public shaming on social media such an effective tool for public policy in Kenya. It is also the main reason why online petitioning works in ways that offline advocacy will not: inviting the public to spectate on the shaming is more effective than privately seeking audience over a grievance.

This culture of publicly appealing to leaders and institutions is not new to Kenya. 'Naomba serekali' is a Kiswahili phrase that translates into 'I request the government' and is a common refrain at political rallies, harambees and other public gatherings. Despairing of institutional responses, members of the public often appeal directly to individual government officials to resolve their issues. But the dynamic of shaming on social media versus these appeals is obvious. When shaming public officials into action the citizen acts from a position of power and demands fair and equal treatment before the law. When appealing to the benevolence of an individual state employee the citizen is seeking the indulgence of the state. State officials in Kenya are not accustomed to the former power dynamic and have allowed it to gain currency in the meantime.

To defend the rights of these women, the online women's rights movement has harnessed the power of public shame effectively. It has allowed young women especially, who struggle in a society where age is sacrosanct, to insert themselves directly into conversations on how they want to be perceived and treated in the public sphere. In the cases of Liz, Khadija and Fatuma, it was primarily young women who took advantage of the hashtag to loudly and powerfully demand public safety for women, and directly from the authorities whose job it is to provide this security.

Prior to the advent of online activism, women who were seen as brash and confrontational, as many young feminist activists are on Kenyan social media, would find themselves isolated. Today they are able to build communities online where they can find strength in numbers. Prior to the new media moment, a woman breaking with traditional public roles for women would find her status as a 'woman' challenged, being accused of behaving mannishly. New media allows such women to basically take on that rejection and use it to create a stronger platform for advocacy. 'Go ahead and consider me angry, bitter, or unmarriageable', they insist, 'but you will not ignore me, and I never wanted to marry you in the first place.'

This increasing visibility has been met with resistance, particularly in the form of violence. In December 2016, Millie Mabona, MP from Mbita, was caught on a hot mic allegedly making disparaging comments about the president. For her comments she received various forms of chastisement from all quarters, including many women politicians who demanded that she apologise.[23] In contrast, a few days earlier, Gatundu South MP Moses Kuria posted on Facebook that he would insert a broken glass bottle into Mabona's vagina after she spoke out against the electoral laws that were being pushed through by the Uhuru administration. At least online, he received little censure, no demand for an apology and no threat of prosecution. Women's rights activists are routinely threatened with violence and death by men who feel that they are being too vocal or too visible. Some women have been forced to delete their social media accounts and start again; many opt for private accounts where they can have direct conversations with those they draw strength from.

Unfortunately, many women have also joined the men who focus on putting women back in what they think is their place. Especially in traditional media or institutionalised advocacy, articles have proliferated resisting these new militant women. In a 2016 piece,[24] a *Nation* columnist shared a vitriolic diatribe against 'angry Twitter feminists', disparaging the work that online advocacy does despite ample evidence that this space is making a difference. Embracing the patriarchal idea of opinionated women as 'hysterical', the author branded Twitter feminists as 'the madwomen of the village'. And yet, instead of actively engaging with the subject matter of online feminist action, she focused her attack on her own perception or ideas rather than on any person she knew.

The author got her 15 minutes of fame at the expense of a movement that was fighting for her right to be safe in her own country. Her piece was celebrated and shared – primarily by men. In my own personal conversations, I have had that piece brought up as a 'counterargument' to issues that I try to raise on behalf of women in Kenya. The argument that anger or being confrontational is 'unfeminine' is often used against social media organising unless it is the spectacle of women berating each other, and the piece is brought up to substantiate the claim because 'it is written by a woman'.

It's important to note that online organising of the women's rights movement in Kenya has highlighted cleavages, particularly generational gaps. In October 2017, the chair of the Maendeleo ya Wanawake organisation (Progress for Women) gave an interview on primetime television to discuss women's rights in the country. At its height, Maendeleo ya Wanawake was the largest women's rights organisation in the country, with hundreds of thousands of fee-paying members. It was, however, co-opted by the ruling party in the 1980s and quickly became a mouthpiece for patriarchal politics that conspired to keep women out of public life.[25]

During the interview on KTN, the national chair of the organisation was asked about the state of domestic violence shelters and support for victims in the country.[26] Surprising even the interviewer, the chairperson responded that while a woman should never accept a beating that lands her in hospital, she felt that women had taken the idea of empowerment 'too far'. She insisted that her role as the leading women's rights activist in the country ended at her doorstep. For her, men were created inherently superior to women and women are required to recognise and submit to that dynamic. The chair argued that marriage was the best institution 'created by god ... to be nurtured and protected ... and women who get beaten by men are probably asking to be beaten'. She essentially argued that women have to submit themselves to potential violence in order to remain married because that's how men are.

Young feminists of all social and economic backgrounds were deeply offended by the clip. But beyond being justifiably angry at the idea that domestic violence is an inherent part of a marriage, the subsequent debate demonstrated a yawning age gap. Underpinning the chair's comments was the idea that marriage is the ultimate achievement for a women in Kenya. Many young urban Kenyan women would disagree.

The gender gap is also apparent in the debate on the two-thirds constitutional principle, which provides that no arm of the government should be dominated by either gender by more than two-thirds.[27] If this law was followed to the letter, the National Assembly and the Cabinet in Kenya would as of 2016 be unconstitutional. And yet there has been no mass public mobilisation by institutional women's rights groups on this. Institutional women's rights advocacy has championed the cause and lost publicly as men in parliament refuse to abide by the principle and continue to seek ways of undermining it.

Meanwhile, young feminists who have repeatedly demonstrated willingness, ability and agility in articulating such causes to a non-specialist audience have been left out of the movement and the conversation. Where the institutional women's rights movement requires numbers in order to force a referendum to protect the cause, they have neither inspired nor sought the support of the new, primarily online, feminists. There has been little coalition-building outside formal institutions, and no attempt to translate the provisions into Kiswahili and other local languages so that people could understand why this principle was so important. Galvanising around the hashtag #WeAre52pc, young feminists organised to place the issue on the agenda on television and media, as well as raising it with the United Nations during the annual Convention for the Elimination of All Forms of Discrimination Against Women (CEDAW) meeting.

And so the conversation has stalled. Young feminists have scored several major victories for individual cases but are struggling to insert themselves into policy-level conversations on women's rights. Those who do control such platforms have decided not to engage online feminism directly, even though it is their very expertise that could muster the numbers needed to defend the two-thirds principle. Women at policy level insist that they must remain conciliatory 'because we have to work with men', while online activists insist that there is nothing within the status quo that is worth salvaging. The traditionalists hold fast to the label 'angry twitter feminist' and men encourage them to do so, while a key opportunity to expand conversations on women's rights in the country is lost.

For 'angry twitter feminists' there are no invitations to conferences, panels or television appearances. In some ways this is good because it means that a doctrine of Kenyan feminism is developing on its own terms, but in other ways it keeps their work marginal.

This restricts the ability of online feminists to translate their work into offline action. Without the offline platforms it is difficult to push through policy-level change. A key part of why all the campaigns highlighted in this chapter worked was that there were one or more activists or advocates in the background who went to the hospital to procure pictures, who met the victims at the airport and escorted them to a safe house, who made sure that the victim was available for court appearances. Because of the limitations of online advocacy, these advocates are mostly operating at great personal cost outside the framework of the underfunded agencies that are supposed to respond to such cases. They are overworked, underpaid and underappreciated.

During the #JusticeForKhadija case, I personally worked alongside Wanjeri Nderu, the online activist who first drew attention to her case. While attempting to find a safe house for Khadija, I remember scrambling to find a caseworker in one of the institutional women's rights movements and failing. We were repeatedly told that the caseworker had been fired because of budget cuts, and that the safe house no longer existed. The case had all the attention of the nation, but in the end we struggled to marshal the material resources that would ensure her safety. These are issues that can be mitigated with greater coordination between online advocates, who, as previously noted, have demonstrated expertise in fundraising for various causes, and the institutional women's rights movement that have structures in place to respond to such cases.

Yet despite all these challenges, online activism has managed to deliver for individual women in astonishing ways. It has really been the difference between an anonymous death in a remote part of the country and justice before the law. The onus is on the two branches of the women's rights movement to find more points of synergy and compromise in order to consolidate these wins and turn them into a sustainable movement for justice.

Feminist theory has embraced digital platforms as a new, exciting frontier for political action. A 2013 special edition of the leading feminist journal on the continent, *Feminist Africa*, mapped the various opportunities that online organising offered African women.[28] But the efficacy of organising online in Kenya is debated. For every successful fundraising effort there are several that fail; for every attempt at hashtag activism there are many more that never take off. And for every woman who stands up to speak, there are tens if not hundreds of detractors demanding that she sit down and shut up.

The most obvious determining factor is the person at the receiving end of the campaign. Where government officials like Deputy Public Prosecutor Duncan Ondimo are not only present on the platform but also engage with it constantly, one can be assured of relatively swift and thorough responses to complaints. It is Ondimo that people turn to when they find cases of overly enthusiastic sentencing or miscarriages of justice by judges. It was to Ondimo that women's rights activists sought relief in the cases of Fatima, Liz and Khadija.

However, many of the country's best-known public figures, including the president, use the platform unilaterally, sharing pictures or messages but rarely reacting to information they are sent. In such cases, people generally stop petitioning these public figures to respond and instead resort to blanket shaming tactics that target entire departments. One could argue that some positions are more 'front facing' than others, and therefore require a higher degree of responsiveness. The president (who is probably not tweeting on his own behalf) cannot be expected to respond to each tweet that is sent to him.

Especially when the object of a campaign is a state official, the efficacy of a social media campaign is very unpredictable. The core philosophy behind the campaigns is that people or institutions can be publicly shamed into action. Sometimes shame works because these departments or institutions are headed up by people who are sensitive to it. Sometimes it works because they are sensitive to censure from their superiors – they don't want to look bad. The latter only works if the superior in question is on the platform or if the story is adequately amplified offline.

Shame also works if the state officer is interested in upholding the veneer of functionality. As long as enough people believe the system works, the general population will remain complacent. Once it emerges that the system –at an individual, manageable level as opposed to the generic level – doesn't work then questions about culpability will arise. It's easy to fire one person when there are complaints about that person whereas it is impossible to reorganise a whole nation based on the complaints of a few people in a niche space. So shame works as a method of online activism in Kenya because it allows people to aggregate their grievances, and government officials or heads of institutions have an interest in avoiding being singled out for criticism. Meanwhile government officials need to respond to such criticism to avoiding personalised consequences. Fear of public shaming and individualised consequences is what makes social media such an effective platform for political organising.

In 'partially free' societies like Kenya, where there is enough of a glimmer of democracy to keep individuals engaged, social media will continue to be important as spaces where individuals can keep pushing towards the society they want. As long as it is easier to get the electoral commission to respond to claims of bribery online than by filing a petition in their office, these digital spaces will continue to set the tone for analogue engagement with political institutions and with the public in general.

Perhaps based on feminist successes online, social networking platforms play a disproportionate role in shaping conversations about how citizens of African countries want their 'partially free' societies to function. Online activism is pervasive around the world.

However, the major underlying reason why social media has thrived in Kenya and in other parts of the developing world is because the state has not understood it. But as Zeynep Tufecki outlines in her book, governments are learning.[29] At first, there simply weren't enough people on the platform for it to be worth paying attention to. Then it became apparent that it was a cheap and easy way to do some public relations work. Now, as it's becoming clearer that there is political potency in the space, the state is paying more and more attention, and this creates personal and collective risk for those who are organising online.

Techniques for online monitoring and censorship have grown increasingly elaborate. In the US, the police have software that uses social media data to monitor the online relationships and behaviour of Black Lives Matter activists.[30] The internet companies did block this kind of access once the link was discovered but by that time police had profiled and violated the rights of many activists of colour. Facebook has also shut down an anti-government Facebook page in Ethiopia at the request of the government.[31]

In other countries in Africa, social media users calling for political change have been arrested and persecuted. In Zimbabwe, Pastor Evan Mawarire was forced into exile for calling for political protests on Twitter. In the Democratic Republic of Congo (DRC), youth activists using the #Telema hashtag have been rounded up and arrested. In Kenya, as stated, many bloggers and social media personalities have used the platforms to create constituencies, but have also been subject to legal action for things they have said on that platform. Activist Boniface Mwangi was sued by the Deputy President William Ruto for defamation in a tweet in which he linked the deputy president to the death of another Twitter superuser and businessman, Jacob Juma.[32] The state – big, burly and lackadaisical as it is – will not remain unaware of the power of the space forever, and the repercussions for activists may be severe.

In the same breath, social media platforms are businesses. Where their business interests collide with the interests of the state, there has been a tendency for the state's interests to win, underscoring the dangers of shifting to an entirely online strategy. Facebook and Google, for example, have offered to alter their business models in order to operate in China, which has stringent censorship requirements.[33]

An easy way to plug these vulnerabilities is to approach social media activism as an important tool in the toolkit of social change, but not an end in itself. It is important not to dismiss the important work of rallying support and drawing attention to causes rarely championed through other platforms, but without parallel offline activity many initiatives die. Organising effectively requires sustained offline action – a lot of it dull and repetitive. Door knocking, public forums, producing printed materials – so much needs to go hand in hand with the process of raising consciousness online. It requires confrontation – physical if not necessarily violent – to raise awareness of the issues being contested. That means protest, marches, petitions, sit-ins and any of the other tools that bring issues to the attention of political actors.

Social media has been significant in allowing individual activists – many of whom do lonely, challenging and sometimes traumatising work – to create networks of support and dialogue. It has allowed individuals to reach beyond their immediate community, which may not fully understand what it is they do and why they do it, to find similarly situated individuals who are keen on collaborating. Still, there remains a significant gap between online and offline activism, particularly because aggregate statistics can give the illusion of enthusiasm, whereas in real life they only represent the least possible amount of work that can be done to address an ongoing situation.

Traditional media has played a major role in conflating these ideas. Today in Kenya, all of the major stations now dedicate significant portions of their airtime to analysing what's trending on Twitter, and who is saying what. It's a perverse self-reifying argument in which the media – cash- and vision-strapped – stops going out of the newsroom to find stories and instead chooses to follow trends established by social media, which in turn uses content created by traditional media to perpetuate the trends.

Trends are not movements.

Bring Back Our Girls is a great example of this contradiction. In April 2014, the Boko Haram militia group kidnapped nearly 200 girls from their schools in the Northern Nigerian city of Chibok.[34] The story sent shockwaves worldwide, particularly when the group released pictures of the girls huddled together, terrified. The visual impact was intense. The online social media campaign prompted the Nigerian government to develop an effective military strategy to return the girls to their families. It was one of the most effective global social media strategies, drawing in many actors, actresses and notable public figures like the then first lady of the US, Michelle Obama.

The campaign drew attention to the Nigerian government's lacklustre response to the kidnapping. It created a moment of unity and cooperation between different feminist movements around the world, something that those of us who engage with the movement regularly will tell you is not an easy thing to achieve. It created space for conversations around ownership and steering within women's rights movements in the global south, by highlighting the moments at which the movement was almost hijacked by outsiders to the detriment of the girls in Nigeria.

What it did *not* do was bring back anyone. Quite the opposite – kidnappings in Northern Nigeria continue practically unchecked despite promises from politicians and military and policing assistance provided by third-party states.

Non-profit and other social organisations are also guilty of conflating the metrics of online trends with actual impact. Lowering the bar on what is considered 'action' to a retweet or a share makes the specific organisation look good online but it doesn't fix the larger problems they are supposed to address. Organisations then become more reluctant to engage with more difficult issues even if that's their raison d'être. The easy question of 'raising awareness' has itself become an end goal, rather than dealing with the harder questions of addressing complex social and political issues. What should people do with that awareness once they have raised it? Most organisations today don't offer a programme of action or an agenda, considering raising awareness to be sufficient. Instead of thinking about how to craft sustainable solutions, they develop catchy phrases or engage in hashtag battles. Meanwhile, the real work of organising for social change remains underfunded and underappreciated.

The experience of Kenya's feminists underscores that social media presents a unique opportunity to articulate a political message to a novel audience. It is a chance to reinvigorate a stalling conversation. But social media alone does not represent a 'movement' and to call it that is dangerous conflation of the medium and the message that is allowing popularity and stridency to overrun the hard work and skill that actually goes into building a movement for social change. Kenya's young feminists are learning that a movement has to have independent momentum to actually enact change, money has to be put to a cause, people have to turn up to protests, victims need to speak up and press charges, letters have to be sent to representatives. A hashtag is no more a movement than a pencil was prior to the digital age: an online movement without an offline component can often stop at just noise.

Chapter 8

POLITICS, PREDATORS AND PROFIT: ETHNICITY, HATE SPEECH AND DIGITAL COLONIALISM

On 2 November 2017, US multimillionaire Robert 'Bob' Mercer sent a letter to all the staff at Renaissance Technologies, a hedge fund where he was joint CEO.[1] In the letter, Mercer categorically distanced himself from Breitbart News, a right-wing online website that he had personally funded for several years. He also distanced himself from Milo Yiannopoulos, a former editor at the site and the self-appointed public face of America's ascendant far right. Mercer wrote that he had only supported Yiannopoulos because he wanted to encourage a culture of free speech among the American public and to promote healthy debate, not necessarily because he agreed with the politics of the right.

For many, Mercer's actions and statements were far too little, far too late. After all, he was only selling his stake in Breitbart to his daughters. And by the time he drew a curtain on his decade of toying with the alt-right, Bob Mercer had bankrolled racist platforms enabling everything from the Trump presidency to the return of pro-Ku Klux Klan and Nazi rallies across America. The Buzzfeed exposé that arguably triggered Mercer's retirement explained in stark terms how his financing underwrote much of the modern, racist right-wing.[2] Without Mercer's funding, platforms like Breitbart and their ideas would arguably have remained on the fringes of mainstream politics.

Bob Mercer was also the main shareholder in Cambridge Analytica (CA), a now-defunct secretive firm that billed itself as a data analytics firm. In 2015, investigative journalist Jane Mayer found that Mercer had invested over $5 million in the firm, a wholly owned US subsidiary of the UK company Strategic Communications Laboratories, London.[3] According to its website, CA specialises in 'psychographic profiling', an elaborate way of saying it mines social media's public platforms for information which it then aggregates into large datasets used to create personality profiles of voters.[4]

Data analytics tied to social media is one of those industries that wouldn't exist if it weren't for the millions of people who use social media every day to catalogue almost every facet of their lives. Firms like CA take the millions of terabytes of personal information freely given by individuals and weaponise it for political interests. They harvest publicly available information from our social media accounts and build programmes and algorithms that allow them to sort individuals according to their interests and profiles. They then give their paying customers a summary of how different people behave online and make it easier for these customers to develop content that will influence users. The more information we put about ourselves online, the more information these firms have; and the more information they have, the more subtle the content that targets you as a user becomes.

Cambridge Analytica has been repeatedly named as a decisive factor behind Donald Trump's surprising 2016 victory. Mayer argues that after losing to Barack Obama in 2012, the Republican Party in the US invested millions of dollars in building its own data analytics operation. CA essentially used its profiling information to game the advertising and content that was pushed towards voters, based on their political persuasion. The firm would produce up to 40–50,000 varieties of a single ad and learn by the frequency with which users interacted with them what kind of content would most likely trigger a response from the user.[5] It also 'colonised' hashtags in support of Democratic candidate Hillary Clinton – flooding them with negative content so the hashtag eventually became useless to those who developed it. Moreover, it was also able to support its candidate with campaign material in real time. The company tested the reception to certain subject matter on a small audience – a county where the candidate was scheduled to speak for example – through its adverts and then advised the candidate which subjects would be best received in a specific place.

Cambridge Analytica argues that its model is only disparaged because most of the media would have preferred it if Hillary Clinton had won the US election over Donald Trump, or if British voters hadn't voted to leave the European Union in 2016. In an in-depth interview with online tech magazine *Tech Crunch*, CA CEO Alexander Nix argued that the media was 'lashing out and trying to destroy every single person and every company that contributed to [Hillary Clinton's] defeat'.[6] He also hit out at critics who doubted the efficacy of his company's work. Some analysts think that CA is overstating the usefulness of its model. Jonathan Albright, a professor and researcher in data analytics, has called CA a 'propaganda machine'.[7] But Nix says these critics are merely competitors who are capitalising on the opportunity to take down their business rival. For him, psychographics is the future of political mobilisation.

In October 2017, Albright published a piece on the self-publishing site Medium claiming that he showed how CA mined Twitter users' emotions even in real time, to 'create test phrases, establish control groups and apparently provide sets of future terms around keywords related to political campaign issues'.[8] It is claims like these that have raised red flags about what CA is doing. It's one thing to shift people's preferences when trying to sell them jeans, it's another thing altogether when you are trying to get them to choose a political leader.

By November 2017, the accusations against CA had escalated. A Congressional probe was allegedly looking into possible collusion between CA and the Russian government. Although the firm maintained that it was not under investigation, Sean Illing reported in October 2017 that the US Congress suspected that it was possibly connected to the broader accusation of Russian interference in the 2016 US presidential election.[9] The firm insisted that it was cooperating with the Congressional investigation as far as was possible, but by this time its reputation had already been tarnished by the Buzzfeed exposé.

By the time Mercer announced his resignation from Renaissance, the reputation of a company that specialised in optimising political reputations was at rock bottom.

It's easy to think that these stories have nothing to do with politics in Kenya. This again goes back to de Sousa Santos' 'sociology of absence' and resisting the urge to ignore things that are 'not recognised or legitimised by the canon'[10] – that because the story of CA is playing out in Western media it has nothing to do with Kenya.

In fact, Kenya is an important part of the story. In August 2017, just before the Kenyan general election, the *Star* revealed that CA was working with the ruling Jubilee coalition.[11] The global privacy protection charity Privacy International told the BBC some days before the election that the company was paid $6 million for the contract.[12] For election watchers this was a surprising turn of events. Why would a company associated with major global events like a US presidential election or a vote on the future of the European Union be involved in a general election in an African country?

As it happened, it wasn't the first time that CA had been involved in Kenya. Indeed, Nix's interview with *Tech Crunch* revealed that the company has been active in South Africa and Nigeria as well. The firm's website confirmed that it had created a profile of the Kenyan electorate in 2013 and developed a campaign strategy 'based on the electorate's needs (jobs) and fears (tribal violence)'.[13] The exact details of the company's methodology are unclear, but by early 2018, more disclosures would come to light.

In March 2018, the *Guardian,* in collaboration with Channel 4 and the *New York Times,* launched an explosive dossier dubbed 'The Cambridge Analytica Files'. The articles and documentaries were based on a year-long investigation led by Carole Cadwalldr, a freelance journalist supported by the *Guardian,* which also fuelled public animosity between her and the company. Notably, on 27 February, Nix testified before the House of Commons that CA's work was legitimate and above-board. Less than a month later, the secret videos affirmed that this was not the case.

The exact details of CA's work in Kenya are the subject of dispute but it is safe to assume that Kenya in 2013 was the testing ground for at least some of the methodology later used in the Brexit and Trump campaigns. The firm boasts on its website that it conducted a survey of over 47,000 Kenyans prior to the 2013 election to create a profile of the Kenyan voter.[14] It identified the issues that resonated most with each group, assessed their levels of trust, their voting behaviour and how they consumed political information. Using this data, the firm advised the campaign to focus on the youth as a segment that 'could be highly influential if mobilised'.[15] The focus therefore was on an online social media campaign to 'generate a hugely active following'.[16]

In one of the Channel 4 videos, Mark Turnbull, Managing Director for Political Consulting at CA, confirms that the company did more than just surveys and data collection in Kenya:

The two fundamental human drivers when it comes to taking information on board effectively are hopes and fears, and many of those are unspoken and unconscious, you didn't know that was a fear until you saw it ... and our job is to drop the bucket further down the well than anyone else to understand what are those really deep seated fears ... it's no good fighting an election on the facts because actually it's just about emotion.[17]

Christopher Wylie, a whistle-blower and former employee who explained the depths of the crisis to the House of Commons about a week later, confirmed that the firm was not in the business of winning elections but 'to capture governments and then corruptly sell that influence to corporations'.[18]

Part of the ambiguity about the firm's work is because it was deliberately obtuse about its engagements, rarely commenting on its work publicly. But in the Channel 4 video, Turnbull alleges that, in Kenya, 'we have rebranded the entire [Jubilee] party twice, written their manifesto, done two rounds of 50,000 surveys … we'd write all the speeches, and we'd stage the whole thing, so just about every element of the campaign'.[19] The veracity of this claim is doubtful, given that another PR firm, BTP Partners, asserts that it was the one that did the PR work for the Kenya campaign. What is certain is that there was unprecedented social media mobilisation in Kenya in the lead-up to the 2013 election.[20] More importantly, it is certain that the climate was poisoned by heightened ethno-nationalist discourse.

Turnbull also says in the video: 'we put information in the bloodstream of the Internet and then watch it grow'.[21] In Kenya, this information could have been any of the numerous inflammatory, ethno-nationalist videos and memes that proliferated across social media, particularly on WhatsApp and Facebook. It could have been the partial coverage given by mainstream media houses in the context of outsize influence by government on content, as outlined in previous chapter. And growth in this sense would mean the heightened rhetoric that left those dissatisfied with the lack of transparency and blatant manipulation of the 2017 election clamouring for secession.

The central contradiction of the CA revelations in relation to the 2013 Jubilee presidential campaign was that it was built on the idea of Kenyan sovereignty and the ICC as a threat to that sovereignty.[22] The Jubilee campaign spun the Kenya general election as a referendum against the ICC, and in the face of a 'society afraid of its own capacity for violence' this was a narrative not challenged in domestic media.[23] Analysts noted that the Kenyan case at The Hague was accompanied by a torrent of abuse against the judges and the prosecutor at the court, linking them to a broader unspecified effort to colonise the country.[24] The campaign worked – the Jubilee coalition won the election by a narrow margin, destroying the reputation of the ICC in Kenya in the process.

Yet the CA disclosures confirm that the entire campaign was developed and managed by a British PR firm. Both CA and BTP partners publicly asserted that the Kenyatta election would not have been possible but for their intervention. This completely undercuts the premises of Jubilee's campaigning and raises the question of the extent to which foreign companies should be allowed to interfere in elections in which they have no stake but the financial. Arguably, CA's work in Kenya was a new frontier of neo-colonialism in Africa.

By 2013, observers of Kenyan politics were more aware of the potential impact of the internet on political behaviour than in 2007. There were, for example, efforts to monitor political conversation online as a broader effort to curb hate speech. Much of this work has its roots in the realisation that hate speech was poisoning political discourse in the country, but the culprit in the 2007 election was radio. As Kenya's technology ecosystem grew, so too did concerns that when the tactics used on radio were paired with the speed and relatively low cost of social media, Kenya would have a major problem on its hands. Indeed, social media and text messaging had been mentioned in passing as one of the culprits behind the 2007/08 post-election violence.

Combined with the shift towards digital reporting of results, 2013 was in many ways Kenya's first digital election.[25] Some of the efforts made to understand this new frontier better included an Ushahidi initiative called 'Umati' – Swahili for crowd – to monitor social media channels for any kind of hate speech and alert authorities before it escalated.[26] According to this study, social media platforms were indeed used to disseminate hate speech around the election, and – echoing patterns in other parts of the world – the most dangerous hate speech incidents online happened on Facebook.[27]

Much of this work escalated in 2017. Once again, authorities and civil society were primarily concerned with the creation and dissemination of hate speech but there was the more benign use of hashtags and viral videos to reach out to voters. Notably, attack ads in the vein of those seen in the US made their debut. There was a particularly nasty online effort that some analysts wrongly attributed to the presence of CA. The 'Real Raila' Campaign targeted social media users with social media posts, video content and links to a website that essentially argued that a vote for opposition candidate Raila Odinga would lead Kenya to the apocalypse. Curiously, no one claimed to own the website or the accompanying social media presence. Although it had almost a quarter of a million followers at the time of writing, aside from uninformative contact information (info@therealraila.com for example) it only claimed to belong to a 'group of concerned Kenyans'.[28]

In actual fact, both major political parties spent considerable sums recruiting analytics corporations to better understand and influence political behaviour online. This is a testament to the growing influence of social media on politics in the country. The NASA coalition recruited an American firm, Aristotle Inc., to oversee its analytics operations.[29] The US-registered company bills itself as a 'leading pioneer in political technology'[30] and also uses analytics to help clients segment markets, target potential voters and build effective campaigns. As proof of how much faith the government had in the company's ability to make a difference to the electoral outcome, on 6 August 2017, two days before the highly contested election, an American and a Canadian citizen consulting for the NASA coalition on behalf of the firm were taken from their homes by hooded individuals who later turned out to be police.[31] They were promptly deported, adding to the toxic cloud that was already shrouding the election.

*

The case of CA in the United States has raised significant ethical questions about the role of data analytics in political messaging, although unfortunately, to date the conversation seems to be focused on the experience of the West even though, as mentioned, many of the practices were pioneered, refined and are having major effects in other parts of the world. Significantly, it is unclear that the Kenyan government fully appreciates the risks created by parasitic corporations like CA, given that the administration benefited directly from their association. Users who make their information publicly available online do not expect or intend for it to be weaponised for political benefit, and certainly not for the vast profits of the companies that package this data for sale. Yet the underlying logic is arguably the same as the logic that underpins targeted online advertising. In order to make advertising more efficient and targeted, almost all websites track users' presence and interactions with the site. If we accept that targeted advertising is normal when the product is a soft drink or a restaurant chain, should we also accept it when the product is a political ideology?

Yet, politics is inherently different and should be shielded from such heavy-handed coercion. The new directions that data analytics and political communication have taken in recent years go beyond simple analysis and profile to manipulation. Mayer noted that the CEO of CA's holding company has publicly said that 'persuading somebody to vote a certain way is really very similar to persuading 14- to 25-year-old boys in Indonesia not to join Al Qaeda'. This suggests that the people who develop and sell these technologies recognise that what they do crosses the threshold from advertising and even political propaganda to preference-shaping and behavioural manipulation. And given that one of the core principles of a functioning democracy is a well-informed electorate, deliberate manipulation for profit in this vein is undemocratic. This particular accusation is why the House Permanent Select Committee on Intelligence investigated CA as part of a broader investigation on collusion between President Trump's campaign and Russia during the 2016 election.[32]

The use of data analytics in political advertising is preference-shaping power in action; giving those who can afford it disproportionate ability to influence political behaviour. Steven Lukes argues that to understand preference-shaping power,[33] and how political power works, we have to go beyond the material ways in which behaviour is influenced and/or the political agenda determined to the ways in which power can actually make people think they want something that they don't. It's more than just analysing people's behaviour and responding to it. It is actively skewing or manipulating political information to influence people's preferences in order to secure a specific political outcome.

Where democracy is a marketplace of ideas, the fact that this power is intimately connected to financial ability is cause for concern. In Kenya, money already has a disproportionate impact on who is able to join politics. Consider that some estimates of the average spend of a political candidate in the 2017 election was $5 million but the Jubilee administration allegedly spent $6 million on CA's services alone. This tips the balance unfairly, further increasing the influence of money over political behaviour and constricting the space available for grassroots political organisation. It also means that those who would participate do not have adequate or accurate information about the issues at hand. It compromises democracy by shifting a significant degree of power back towards those who are able to pay – an inherently undemocratic situation.

Taking a longer view of global political history, we know that political propaganda is not new. Whether or not a politician should be able to whip up segments of the population into a frenzy over contested political issues is a question as old as politics itself. And many of the techniques being used by firms like CA are built on systems that were already being used to sell products. The question is whether politics is a sacred cow. As mentioned in prior chapters, technology is not agnostic. It accelerates the rate at which propaganda travels and who is able to see it, but combined with the built-in features of these platforms these benefits are primarily reserved for those who can afford to pay for it. Filtering so much political communication through privately owned platforms that rely on corporate spending to survive privatises the public sphere. Societies will increasingly need to contend with whether this is a line that they are willing to cross.

Embedded in the CA conversation is the broader issue of 'fake news'. There are several and sometimes conflicting definitions of this concept. Although the dictionary shows that the phrase has long and deep linguistic roots, it entered the zeitgeist courtesy of US President Donald Trump, who used it to dismiss anyone – including mainstream media – who published critical, unflattering or salacious details of his political campaign and presidency.[34] Significantly, much of what he labelled fake news turned out to be true, adding to the confusion. Over time, the definition has broadened to include the various forms of technology-driven misinformation that is enabled by the data analytics industry. With the proliferation of internet-based news and the lack of journalistic integrity in much of what is produced, everything from creative editing to outright lying has been labelled fake news.

Fake news is propaganda, and propaganda is big business in Kenya. There are two ways of thinking about it. One is the proliferation of government propaganda and manipulation of mainstream media since the 2007 detente. The other is the proliferation of news and gossip sites that look like news sites but are not. Some have evolved into massive business ventures, like Mpasho news, which in recent years has converted itself into a credible – if sensationalist – entertainment and gossip site. Some, like Nairobi News, focus on publishing political content that mainstream news outlets would find too salacious. But many exist simply to generate content in favour of or against specific political groups in Kenya's highly charged political environment.

In fact, the case of Kenya underscores that 'fake news' is hardly novel. Hezron Ndunde writes that the Kenyan electorate's reliance on rumours for political information was a major reason why the 2007 election turned violent.[35] He argues that the state's attempts to control the public narrative between December 2007 and March 2008 pushed more and more people to alternative forms of expression, including offline ones like graffiti or leaflets. But as mentioned, one direct consequence is that people were now consuming raw, unprocessed and unverified information. There was a general feeling that the state was hushing or covering up the real story of the election.

Around the 2007 election Kenyans were primed to turn to unofficial news channels. Ndunde gives examples of how messages regarding alleged attacks spread throughout the internet and through text messages. Vernacular media stations with smaller budgets and less interest in verification only exacerbated the situation, often repeating what was being said in these messages without checking whether they were true. This cycle of misinformation and amplification led people to take revenge against people who turned out not to have done anything at all. One text would mention an alleged attack against a community that was an ethnic minority in one town, and a revenge attack would be organised in a separate town where that community was a majority.[36]

Moreover, rumours were already a big part of the political space in Kenya. In her book on the sensational murder of Julie Ward, a British conservationist, in one of Kenya's national parks, Grace Musila argues that rumour is a big part of how the Kenyan public reclaims truth and evidence from an oppressive state that prefers to remain shrouded in mystery.[37] Her book shows a public using rumour to circumvent state control over public narratives, as a form of expressing political agency. When the government decides not to provide the public with complete information, as has been the case around every election and every major political assassination in Kenyan history, people fill in the gaps for themselves and rumours become a particularly powerful way of taking back narratives.

The state also uses rumour to exert its control. Musila notes that the Moi administration often started and then acted on rumours in order to appear in control of a situation. For example, Moi used the rumour that Attorney General Charles Njonjo was planning a coup as an excuse to remove him from office and from public life generally.[38] In 1983, Njonjo was one of the most powerful men in Moi's cabinet but after a long rigmarole of a commission chaired by the former chief justice, he was named as the person that foreign governments were grooming to take over the presidency. The allegations were never substantiated but Njonjo lost his job and his standing in government, and Moi was able to consolidate political control.

These features mean that by 2017 there was already significant mistrust in the mainstream traditional media that was only exacerbated by failures in the 2017 election. Patrick Gathara catalogues the traditional media's litany of failures while covering the electoral race of 2017.[39] For example, traditional media deliberately refused to cover the various political protests that started up around the country immediately after the August result was announced and the police brutality that followed in opposition strongholds. Gathara also points to the use of official statistics that turned out to be false as 'exit polls', even though the media houses promised to provide independent information. The media's refusal to engage honestly with events in the country creates room for the spread of rumour as political fact, which is necessary to a thriving fake news industry.

With this background, Kenya is perhaps the African country ripest for a political strategy that relies on transmitting fake news over social media. The online community is large and engaged. Political information offline travels in such fits and starts that voters already have to rely on rumours and blind items to build a somewhat coherent political narrative. And Kenyan politics is also extremely rich. According to IEBC estimates, the 2017 election in Kenya would be the most expensive election in African history and perhaps in the world at $28 per voter.[40] And that was just spending by the state –

spending by individual candidates drives the figure much higher. Between official and covert costs, a Kenyan presidential candidate spends an average of $5 million. Adding that Kenyan politics is intensely competitive and won on the slimmest margins, any service that can provide even a marginal advantage looks highly attractive.

Yet the novelty of the speed and relative insularity with which information travels on social media raises new challenges. The 2007/08 election violence in Kenya demonstrated the risks of rumours travelling rapidly. In societies where actors still believe political violence is a legitimate form of politics, an ill-timed rumour can trigger a civil war. This partly explained why fears of political violence persisted even though several institutional changes were in place to prevent it. There was no guarantee that these mechanisms would work because the political class had crippled them.

In Kenya, the biggest mitigating factor against fake news inciting violence – effectively the biggest difference between Kenya in 2017 and Kenya in 2007 – didn't come from any online initiatives. It was a fundamental shift in the attitudes of Kenyan voters. As mentioned in prior chapters, young Kenyans are online in unprecedented numbers. Of those registered to vote in 2017, 50.63% were between the ages of 18 and 35, and one assumes a healthy number of them use their phones to access the internet. News of political developments in the US and the UK following the Trump and the Brexit votes respectively travelled in Kenya as well. The 'Stop Raila' videos on Facebook didn't trigger a widespread panic – they were mostly met with sceptical detachment.

This scepticism has to do with general fatigue after a gruelling inter-election period that saw protests against the electoral commission and legislative brinksmanship between the two main parties. The 2017 elections were also the most intensely contested elections in Kenya following the passage of the 2010 constitution which created 47 counties from the previous eight provinces. Each of these counties has its own legislature, significantly increasing the number of political seats up for grabs. Although the 2013 election was also conducted under the devolved system, in 2017 political aspirants seemed to understand what was possible within the new system. A total of 16,259 people ran for office in various levels of government, and the selection of candidates involved a bruising extended primary season.[41]

Kenyan data analysis firm Odipo Dev invested heavily in analysing data from the 2017 election.[42] Between March 2017 and April 2017 it tracked interaction with and propagation of fake news over the various social media sites used in Kenya. It found that on Facebook traditional news sites performed better than stories from fake news sites, particularly around the primary season in April. When push came to shove, people still preferred to get their news from official outlets rather than unverified ones.

A survey by GeoPoll and Portland around the same time revealed more interesting facts about Kenya's fake news ecosystem: 90% of Kenyan surveyed in the lead-up to the August poll had seen or read fake news before the election;[43] 87% of respondents also felt that the fake news was deliberately misleading. The good news in this statistic is that 90% of Kenyans *knew* that the information was fake news, and 87% *knew* that it was being produced with the intent to misinform. This speaks to the natural scepticism with which Kenyans approach information on social media. The survey also confirmed that most people preferred to get their political news from traditional media rather than from social media sites.

So although they relied more on traditional media than new media for their information, with a long experience of its limitations and foibles, the Kenyan electorate's natural scepticism towards the news was a tipping factor in protecting the country from more widespread violence. This stands in contrast to audiences in the West which are primed to believe information that comes from official sources.

At the intersection of new media, identity politics and potential violence is an interesting conversation on cause and effect. Does new media exacerbate identity politics or simply reveal what is already there? The fear that social media would enhance 'tribalism' and trigger ethnic violence is based on the fact that new media encourages people to consume information generated and targeted towards ideological silos. As mentioned, much of this is rooted in Kenya's prior experiences with vernacular language radio stations, which promote and protect cultures but also encourage insular political conversations. The expectation from a national newspaper of record is that you will get a spectrum of views from the whole country, including many that you might disagree with. But much of the news that we consume through new media is from sources we already agree with and most likely on subjects we already agree with. New media makes it harder for people to confront their biases.

Still, does social media really make us more hateful or does it simply allow our hateful instincts more space to flourish? Social media creates a guise of relative anonymity which allows individuals to display more of their 'true' personalities than they would offline. This isn't a bad thing if it allows individuals to consume information from a broad spectrum of places, backgrounds or viewpoints much like they would if they were reading a printed newspaper. The problem is that very few people are having these honest confrontations because the digital spaces they inhabit are even more closed than those they inhabit offline. And those who have developed and manage such platforms encourage people to remain in intellectual and ideological silos, arbitrarily filtering content from others based on what the computer *thinks* you want to see rather than what you actually want or need to see. This is the work of social network algorithms.

Why do social media platforms use algorithms to shape our feeds? It's a response to the problem of volume. As more and more people begin to use online platforms, the sheer volume of information being posted and shared has become overwhelming, leading some people to abandon the sites altogether as they start to feel overwhelmed.[44] For those who create these sites, this is an obvious problem – they are only valuable economically and politically if a critical mass of people are using them. For users, it becomes increasingly difficult to filter meaningful content from trash, leading to one of two outcomes. One was addiction – where people are spending inordinate amounts of time trawling through other people's content to find something that they may deem useful, and the opportunity cost of the time thus lost. The second was that people simply got too overwhelmed by the content and stopped using the sites altogether. The situation was aggravated when news outlets and corporations hopped on the bandwagon – there was simply too much information on these platforms for people to process properly.

The algorithms that all social media sites use today filter out the content on our social media networks based on past behaviour, the preferences of other people within our networks, and other pieces of information we provide, like our location, our use of third-party apps etc. An algorithm acts like it knows who you are, but in reality it only knows who you say you are based on the content you engage with and curate. The sites are then able to send you content that reinforces these preferences.

Most of the time – and especially with younger clients who are more likely to be earnest in their use of social media – the two facets of personality overlap nearly perfectly. But study after study has demonstrated that there are significant gaps between who we say we are or how we present ourselves on social media, and who we really are. Some sociologists call this 'preference falsification' – we lie about what we like in response to various pressures. In a 2005 paper, Olaf Johannson-Stenman and Peter Martinson examine the gap between actual preferences and stated or perceived preferences, identifying a number of reasons why we do this – to give a good impression, to comply with social norms, to maintain a positive self-image etc.[45] We lie about who we are and what we like because we want other people to like us. The ramifications can be significant. Where social media becomes a focal point for political discussion, it creates ideological echo chambers where one's opinions are reified rather than confronted, meaning that a person with ill-founded beliefs is rarely pushed to address them.

The stratified digital targeting of voters during the 2016 US general election demonstrated one possible end-game of preference-shaping underpinned by preference-falsification. Arguably, the winner of the election has the lowest approval rating of any US president in history and is a person whose public support is significantly lower than the numbers that voted for him. Even up to the day before the election, polling indicated that Hillary Clinton would win the election, suggesting that many people held views that they did not feel comfortable expressing openly until after the election.

Algorithms do very little for people who enjoy having friends who disagree with them. Beyond shielding you from what these people think, the algorithms also shield you from their day-to-day lives. In a way, this limits constructive engagement because we stop having a key human interaction with people we disagree with. We stop seeing the friend who supports the candidate we hate as a person who has a family that s/he cares about and start seeing them as the embodiment of an idea we detest. And while odious ideas should be rejected at every turn, without the ability to have clear but constructive dialogue, it makes us in the long run susceptible to radicalisation of our views, whatever our views may be.[46]

Ultimately, Kenya may have been saved from the trap by the fact that these sites were not built with Africa and Africans in mind. Social media sites do not see 'tribes' in the same way they see race, gender or even social class. Even offline, unless one is sufficiently educated in the nuances of last names and where they belong geographically, it's impossible to tell with 100% certainty that a Kenyan is a specific ethnic group based only on expressed preferences. Ethnic identities are often couched or correlated to other political factors. In Kenya, for instance, ethnic identities may correlate strongly with political party affiliations or places where people live. They may correlate to social associations like churches, schools or welfare associations. They may also correlate to things that are seemingly random – sports teams for example. The two best known Kenyan domestic league football teams, Gor Mahia and the AFC are both ethnically affiliated teams, drawing their fans primarily from Luo and Luhya communities respectively. But there are enough exceptions to these general rules – particularly amongst the young, urban social media networks – to render these presumptions meaningless. And the more ethnicity has been used as an excuse for political violence, the less urban Kenyans feel comfortable expressing their ethnic identities publicly, making it harder for data parasites to mine this particular vein.

If social media sites were able to segregate Kenyan users by ethnicity, would the outcome have been different? These ideological silos would create a false sense of security, possibly allowing people to be more open with their biases than they would in any other circumstances because they are more likely to gain support for these beliefs than have them challenged. And once these beliefs are supported they are reified and they become tacitly endorsed, which would make the individuals who hold these beliefs more likely to act upon them both on- and offline.

The promise of even more sophisticated data analytics mining our public data for profit should therefore be a universal concern. As political mobilisation on these platforms has grown, so too has the ethnicisation of political debate. Even simple tweets that pose a valid challenge to state policy or actions of the major opposition party are today routinely interpreted as threats to the ethnic identity of the person being criticised, and can unleash a barrage of ethnic abuse. People who have the same ethnic identity as those they are criticising often have it worst: 'betraying the tribe' has become a potent political crime.

In mainstream/US/European political science, there has been a long-standing misguided belief that 'tribalism' is an 'African problem', but the self-defeating politics of voters in the 2016 US election and the UK Brexit vote underscores that 'the tribe' is making a comeback the world over. Kenya's experience with digital elections in a highly ethnicised context therefore offers lessons that can apply in multiple contexts.

Recall that 'tribalism' – more so than racism or sexism – is a difficult thing to quantify, and is insidious in a way that would make other -isms jealous. 'Tribalism' isn't tied to an external biological marker. Rather, 'the tribe' or ethnic group is a social and political fiction based on a myth of common origin, of continuing social and economic connections and on a shared language or approach. 'Tribe' is also highly fungible. It can take on the characteristics of class-based discrimination when class is more expedient, or of racial discrimination, or of gender discrimination depending on the circumstances. 'Tribalism' is refusing to allow your child to marry a person of a certain 'tribe', offering economic or social opportunities to members of your own group, or stereotyping other groups as thieves, watchmen, witchdoctors etc. It's not as linear as exclusion based on biologically immutable characteristics like age, gender or race. Its manifestation depends entirely on what works best on that day.

Because of this, 'tribalism' is difficult to diagnose and treat. If in a choice between two well-qualified individuals from two ethnic groups, you pick the one from your own ethnic group, how is it possible to measure that as discrimination rather than simply preference? That is perhaps why every policy intervention to address tribalism in Kenya results in reifying it rather than undermining it. Increasing civil servants' and legislators' salaries in order to discourage corruption only made corruption more endemic. Devolution of state functions has only amplified inter-ethnic contestation for national funds (see e.g. #DevolutionHasFailedNEP). Demanding greater distribution of political positions based on ethnic groups has increased the political currency that ethnic groupings hold over the political process.

Social networks have created spaces where people who hold such 'tribalist' views can express them in public without the same measure of condemnation that they would face if they expressed them openly in mixed company. Again, this may seem counterintuitive, but except in situations of heightened tension, openly 'tribalist' conversations are rarely held outside private spaces – homes, weddings, private members' clubs etc. It is impossible to know what people are thinking unless you are part of that group, in which case you have a keen interest in keeping that information secret as well. So we can speculate over the nature of 'tribalism' but rarely do we ever get to hear and see its contours in public.

Thus the act of making these discussions public isn't necessarily all bad. Naming the beast is a big part of taming the beast. There are many well-intentioned Kenyans who would happily argue they are not 'tribalist', but would say or do nothing when entering a space where such views are expressed or where they stand to benefit from them. Public examples of such thinking compel such individuals to confront their own blind spots and denial. It allows us to deal with the full complex picture of identity, including this very specific, very ugly underbelly that has such tangible implications for everyone's lives. It has inspired many young social media users especially to come up with initiatives to highlight the need to move beyond these narratives (see #TribelessYouthKE).

The dangers persist, however. If everyone feels empowered to say hateful things then Facebook comments and Twitter replies quickly degenerate into name-calling, threats and psychological violence. For example, the superuser, activist and photographer Boniface Mwangi, proud of his Gikuyu heritage, routinely receives vitriolic backlash, sometimes from fellow Kikuyus who accuse him of betraying 'the tribe' every time he criticises the Kenyatta administration (President Kenyatta is also Kikuyu). For women, speaking in public about political issues often results in sexist attacks and, in some cases, rape threats.

More sinister is the ways in which social media helps those who hold such views to find, entertain and grow their constituencies. In such spaces, dog-whistle politics has thrived; that is, where the writer or user in question will frame an issue like presidential appointments or budgetary allocations in a way that looks factual and suggest that members of a certain ethnic group have been favoured in the process in question. The subtlety in dog-whistle politics can come in many forms, including simply posting a link and highlighting the names of those who have been selected. The less subtle would simply accuse an entire ethnic group of bad intentions, and conspiring against the 'national consciousness'. The most brutish of these inciters will pose the opposite party as an existential threat to the survival of the community and sometimes go as far as threatening to exterminate those they argue pose this threat.

When asked about Kenya in his interview with *Tech Crunch*, CA CEO Alexander Nix was equivocal. At first, he would not outright say that the company was in Kenya, conceding only that 'we've worked all across Africa'.[47] He shared the general fear about election violence but didn't see his company as being part of the ecosystem that created that violence. Nix's comments speak to a broader lack of concern of the moral implications of some of the technological developments that underpin his business practice, as would be confirmed by subsequent revelations. He argues that all he did was take a client's money and deliver the services required. His explanation focuses on the number of electoral points by which Kenyatta won the invalidated August election – not the political context and history in which the putative victory occurred. Not the murder of the acting head of ICT at the Electoral Commission two days before the election. Not the political history that triggered the need for an electoral election in the first place. As Cathy O'Neil notes in her book, data scientists like Nix often lose sight of the people on the other side of their transactions, and the lesson from Kenya in 2017 is that detaching political technology from social contexts can have devastating effects.[48]

Part III

HISTORY
NOT
LEARNED
FROM

Chapter 9

2017: THE MOST EXPENSIVE ELECTION IN THE WORLD

On Friday, 28 July the acting head of Information and Communications Technology at the IEBC, Chris Msando, gave a demonstration of the Kenya Integrated Election Management System (KIEMS), the software that would digitise Kenya's 2017 election. It wasn't the first time that Msando had appeared on television to talk about how he hoped technology that he had helped design and roll out would shape this pivotal vote. But it was an important appearance because he was forced to explain some major changes to the infrastructure, including what would happen after a court ruled that the National Tallying Centre was not allowed to alter electoral results.

Msando oozed confidence even though he had been less than two months on the job, replacing James Muhati, who had been suspended for failing to collaborate with the commission's audit department.[1] During the extended interview, Msando made easy reference to the laws and statutes that guided some of the changes that had been made to the KIEMS system. He joked with his colleagues on the panel and with the moderator. He fielded tough questions with the certainty of a man who knew what he was talking about.

According to his family and friends, he wasn't faking it. Msando was a conscientious and hardworking man who threw himself into the role with gusto. He frequently stayed late at the office – more so after his role was expanded. He was immensely proud of the system that they had built and was eager to see how it would be received by Kenyans. So even though the live, late night demonstration of how the KIEMS kit would work on election day would be aired at 10 p.m. he agreed.

Msando's family says that because it was a Friday, they didn't think much of his radio silence after the studio appearance. His brother Peter told a journalist they thought he was probably blowing off steam after another intense day of election preparation.[2] Texts were exchanged between Peter and Msando's wife speculating on his whereabouts but in the end they reassured each other that Msando would show up eventually.

On Saturday morning, 30 July, the official Twitter handle of the IEBC tweeted 'One of our ICT managers has gone missing. The Commission is working with Police and family to establish his whereabouts'.[3] Still Msando's family did not worry. Night clubs in Kenya frequently remain open until daybreak so that patrons don't have to drive home in the dark. Many have 'lodgings' attached to them – barebones rooms where a drunk patron can sleep off the alcohol and maybe even pay for sex. It is not unusual for a person who was at a club on Friday night not to show up until Saturday afternoon. Still, the IEBC tweet sent Kenya into a tailspin of speculation given that the election was just around the corner, even though Peter felt comforted by the fact that the police had responded so promptly to the family's concerns. He told himself the situation was under control.

At 1 a.m. on 31 July, Peter received a message on WhatsApp with a picture of his brother's car parked on the side of a highway that snaked away from the Central Business District. It wasn't a road that led to their home – it led in the opposite direction. Peter quickly forwarded the information to the Directorate of Criminal Investigations, Kenya's version of the FBI or Scotland Yard, which sent officers to the area to investigate further. The officers did in fact find that the car belonged to Msando but there was no sign of where he might be. The search continued – intensified even – and although his wife and brother grasped at the faintest hope that things would be different, Peter would later tell journalists that by this time he already knew what they would find.

The portly, bespectacled techie in charge of guiding Kenya through its first fully integrated digital election was dead.

The full impact of Chris Msando's murder was lost in the maelstrom of Kenya's chaotic 2017 election. A preliminary autopsy revealed that Msando had deep scratches in his hands and on his back consistent with torture, and that he had been strangled to death.[4] His body was found alongside that of a young woman, initially fuelling speculation of an extramarital affair that Msando's family denies. Wafula Chebukati, chair of the electoral commission, said categorically after helping identify the body 'there's no doubt that he was tortured and murdered'.

It is logical to infer that his death had something to do with the ICT infrastructure for the election. And while investigations into the killing may take years and never fully reveal the exact details, it does speak to the toxic environment in which the highly contested election happened. Msando was not a security expert. He was not a police officer or a soldier. He was a bureaucrat. And when bureaucrats start dying in the course of their work it's a sign that something is going terribly wrong.

And so many things did go terribly wrong with the digital infrastructure of Kenya's election. In fact the whole election was an unholy mess that threatened a repeat of the chaos of 2007. The 2017 election was supposed to finally represent the culmination of a slow process of digitalisation of Kenya's electoral system. This computerisation was a process that was more or less forced on the country as part of the political settlement to end the cycle of election violence that had plagued the country since 1992, culminating in the brutal aftermath of the 2007 election. It wasn't the same organic process that had led to the development of e-government systems, for example, but had its roots firmly in Kenya's history of violent elections, and represented a decade-long effort of trying to develop a better, less violent system for choosing political leaders.

The 1992 election violence was euphemistically labelled 'tribal clashes', as if it was a continuation of primordial tension between various ethnic groups. But, while the contours of the violence were indeed shaped by pre-existing cleavages, subsequent investigations revealed that the violence was orchestrated by politicians at the highest levels in order to destabilise specific regions and depress voter turnout in targeted regions in the build-up to the election.

By 1991, there was significant evidence that the one-party system would not survive given the large numbers of defections by key politicians in the Moi administration. Those loyal to the regime then changed tactics and began exploring various forms of intimidation to ensure that the ruling party won the election.[5] Klopp notes that one of Moi's staunchest supporters, the late Nicholas Biwott, gave a speech in 1991 in which he asserted that 'Kalenjins [his ethnic group] are not cowards'. He also gave an order to the crowd at the end of the speech that opposition politicians and politics were not allowed in the Rift Valley,[6] an order that would have some weight given his status as a community and national leader. This speech hinted at the desperation of the ruling party and its loyalists and the coming change in tactics.

Electoral violence in 1992 did overlap with and capitalised on many pre-existing tensions in the Rift Valley, including ethnic disputes over land and resettlement of communities viewed as outsiders. Ignoring the immediate trigger of Kenya's independence struggle, non-autochthonous groups were resettled in the most fertile regions of the country after independence as landed elites and colonial settler families kept hold of the land[7] that would have comprised their ancestral holdings. The land where they were resettled wasn't empty, and the subsequently displaced autochthonous groups were rarely adequately compensated. Many remained resentful, though pacified by an authoritarian state. The authoritarian state took advantage of these grievances to mobilise hostility against putative 'outsiders'.

Sources note that the people who carried out attacks in Rift Valley in 1992 appeared to be organised and coordinated to drive non-indigenous voters out of the area.[8] They were dressed alike and had similar weapons, unlike the ragtag groups that coordinated reprisal attacks. These attacks and reprisal attacks set off a nearly 12-month-long cycle of violence. By some estimates approximately 2,000 people died during this period, making these the deadliest elections in Kenyan history.[9]

In 1997 the pattern of pre-election violence continued in the same areas – Molo, Trans Nzoia and other cosmopolitan parts of the Rift Valley – but also expanded to include Nyanza and Coast provinces. In August, 104 people were killed in Likoni at the Coast in violence spread over several months.[10] The government portrayed it as armed violence but rights groups argued that it was a concerted effort to displace opposition voters so the president could acquire the required 25% of votes cast in Coast province and guarantee his victory.[11] Once again, because ethnicity correlates strongly with political affiliation in Kenya, armed groups targeted members of non-autochthonous groups as opposition voters and terrorised them for months, forcing them to leave the area. In December, just weeks before the election, 50 people were killed in Trans Mara district during an attack that locals said was triggered by local politicians whipping up supporters for political ends.[12]

While the 2002 election is broadly remembered as peaceful because it featured a change in government and violence on a much smaller scale, there were definitely incidents of intimidation. Amnesty International noted that opposition supporters attacked women who were attending a KANU rally in Nairobi, while the husband, daughter and five grandchildren of a KANU politician were burnt to death in their own home in Kiambu.[13] Still, on the whole, because the incumbent was no longer eligible to run and his chosen successor did not have the capacity for violence that he had created, the election ran fairly smoothly by Kenyan standards.

*

By the time there were negotiations on developing a new way of addressing political violence in 2007, Kenya had already been through three intense cycles of election violence. The standout vote in this period was not a general election but a vote on the new constitution in 2005 which was defeated by 58% of voters in a relatively peaceful if not fully transparent vote.[14] Even so, the referendum possibly triggered a series of events that culminated in the tensions of 2007. Political allegiances fractured as many who had campaigned for the referendum quit government to mount their presidential election campaigns and those that remained seemed rattled by the defeat.[15] The referendum campaign upped the ante on political rhetoric and organising.

Each wave of violence led to promises of decisive action that were never actioned. Commissions of Inquiry are a staple of political deflection in Kenya, giving the government the appearance of acting without actually doing anything. Many commission reports are never released to the public so the promise of a commission no longer inspires much confidence. In 1998 the Akiwumi Commission into Tribal Clashes was convened to address election violence in 1992 and 1997.[16] The explosive report identified many high-level individuals as part of the broader effort to destabilise various regions in the build-up to the two elections. Perhaps because of this the report was suppressed until the change of government in 2002, when it was made public by order of the high court.

These factors all fed into creating a greater sense of urgency regarding structural reform after the 2007 violence, which suggested that without drastic measures elections in Kenya were only going to become more violent. The principal political actors in that period signed a set of agreements known as the Kenyan National Dialogue and Reconciliation that involved many elements including the National Accord and Reconciliation Agreement, creating a power-sharing system between them.[17]

The process also mandated the establishment of various commissions to look into the causes of and suggest solutions to future electoral violence. Some of these were colloquially known as the Agenda 4 commissions because they were envisioned in the fourth Agenda item of the KNDR.[18] There were also commissions that focused on the specifics of the 2007/08 election. These included the Commission of Inquiry into the Post-Election Violence (CIPEV, or the Waki Commission) and the Independent Review Commission (IREC, or the Kriegler Commission, which focused solely on what went wrong with the electoral process).

The Kriegler Commission found that issues with the voting system were the immediate trigger for post-election violence in 2007.[19] It saw that at the heart of Kenya's broken electoral system was the lack of independence of the Electoral Commission. The commission argued that the existing system was not transparent and that results could not be verified. This triggered such uncertainty among politicians and voters that they were reluctant to accept electoral outcomes. The commission recommended amongst other things that Kenya should move to a digital electoral system – using computers for voter registration and identification, for vote tallying and transmission of results. They said that this would address the rampant rigging and alteration of results on their way to the national tallying centre that had indeed happened in every election, including in 2002, albeit on a less perceptible scale.[20]

The Kriegler Commission is also part of the reason why Kenya is one of the very few countries to have an electoral law embedded in its constitution. Fearing that like its predecessor, the Akiwumi Commission, the recommendations of the commission would be ignored or swept under the rug, much of the commission's report was translated into the constitution finally adopted by vote in 2010. Chapter 7, Section 81 of the constitution outlines exactly what an electoral system in Kenya is supposed to look like, including 'by secret ballot; free from violence, intimidation, improper influence or corruption; conducted by an independent body; transparent; and administered in an impartial, neutral, efficient and accountable manner'.[21] These details are all transliterations of the proposals contained in the Kriegler (and Waki) Commission.

The laws that flow from these constitutional chapters rely heavily on the commission's recommendations. For example, the 2011 amendment to the Kenya Elections Act required the IEBC to develop an integrated elections management system that allowed for computerised voter registration, identification and results transmission.[22] The law recognised that such an elaborate mechanism would require gradual implementation so it wasn't until 2017 that the KIEMS was supposed to be mandatory.

Yet the KIEMS in 2017 was anything but integrated. In 2016, the legislature passed a law that would permit the utilisation of a manual registration system alongside the KIEMS. This meant that even though the Electronic Voter Identity Devices (EVIDs) would be used for voter registration and identification at the polling centres, voters who were not in those registries could still be allowed to vote. The expectation was that these people would be few in number, so there was a requirement that the polling centre supervisor fill in a form for every vote that was cast in this way. Biometric Voter Registration was also an explicit recommendation of the commission and is envisioned as part of the IEBC's voter registration process but was not fully implemented in 2013 or 2017.[23]

Moreover on 6 August, just two days before the election, the IEBC issued a statement in which it announced that there would be adjustments to the RTS system: 11,155 polling centres, representing about one-third of the 40,883 centres in the country, would not be using electronic voter transmission.[24] The commission said that these locations did not have sufficient 3G coverage to allow for electronic transmission. Geographically, the stations were distributed across the country, with the highest concentration being in Kisii County. On social media, users rejected some of these assertions, arguing that they were in fact using 3G near the identified stations. Ultimately, the commission would disown the results portal that it used to keep the public informed about the election's progress, meaning that the entire RTS system failed in its core function of keeping people updated.

When you consider that the digitisation of Kenya's election was supposed to draw a line under the endless cycles of systematic abuse of the electoral system that ultimately fed into the 2007 violence, these and other failures become much more significant.

It's not just that elections in Kenya were manipulated. It was also that the manipulation was so insidious and pervasive that none of the major political actors trusted each other with anything. And trust is a key part of a functional democratic system. The actual voting process in Kenya is almost always peaceful, even under the highly contentious *mlolongo* (queueing) system. The challenge was maintaining peace before the election in the 1992, 1997 and 2013 elections, and in protecting the integrity of the tallying system in 2007 and 2017. So in many ways, these two elections bookend the decade because the same issues that caused uncertainty in 2007 recurred – how do we count votes in a way that stands up to both public scrutiny and the politicians?

The many checks and balances that are grafted onto Kenya's electoral system are designed to address these concerns. But the checks and balances mean nothing if the commission does not use them, and this can be particularly aggravating for voters considering they how much they cost. Even though in 2017 Kenya only had 19.2 million voters against the United States' 126 million or India's 214 million, Kenya's election was more expensive per capita, at $28, than those in both these countries. As outlined previously, both major political parties invested heavily in hiring IT experts and consultants. Contrast Kenya's multimillion-dollar fiasco with the Gambian election in 2016 in which the authoritarian ruler of 22 years standing, Yahya Jammeh, was voted out on a system that used marbles.[25]

Technology cannot purchase public trust – it has to be earned through a process of repeatedly conducting transparent and credible processes. The more Kenya tries to use technology to engender trust, the more expensive and opaque the electoral system becomes, and this complexity only engenders more anxiety as each level of operation comes under significant scrutiny from those with a vested interest in the process. Every five years, without fail, voters are expected to trust fully in a public institution that willingly forfeits its own credibility by announcing dramatic changes to procedures with only hours left before a crucial vote. The opposition feels helpless and panicked because it – generally rightly – suspects that the commission is working in tandem with the ruling party. And the ruling party papers over genuine concerns because the confusion ultimately works in its favour.

It's worth noting that the opposition made undercutting public trust in the IEBC's system a cornerstone of its campaign. Oftentimes, the IEBC offered ammunition. For example, the process through which the BVR and EVIDs kits were procured was not up to standard. By law, the IEBC is supposed to invite competitive bids for the procurement of such services. But according to local media reports, French company OT-Safran Morpho was awarded the contract after a single-sourced bid, meaning no other companies were allowed to tender.[26] Further investigation revealed that it was a multiyear contract that runs until 2020. The firm made a copy of the Kenya voter register as part of its work and retains it as their proprietary material.[27] The Kenyan auditor general also raised concerns about the financial details of the transactions when they were first entered into in 2013. Yet despite these questions and despite the fact that the kits repeatedly failed, OT-Safran Morpho retained the contract.

Sticking to the technological standards required by the law would have gone a long way towards making the 2017 election more credible than previous ones. Instead the IEBC chose to push on with the announcement on the 11th even though by this time it was clear that there were many operational and procedural issues with the vote.

*

On the morning of 9 August 2017, about 12 hours after the results started trickling in on the IEBC results transmission website, the leader of the largest opposition coalition Raila Odinga called a press conference to inform journalists that the public results portal on which interim results were being announced and on which media coverage was based had been hacked in order to underrepresent his share of the vote.[28] On Friday the 11th at 10:30 p.m., the chairman of the IEBC, Wafula Chebukati, declared the incumbent Uhuru Kenyatta the winner, triggering a flurry of protests in Nairobi and Kisumu.[29] In response to the protest, the police launched violent door-to-door raids and patrols that left 68 people dead.[30]

When Odinga announced that he was filing a petition challenging[31] the presidential results the expectation was that the court would go through the rigmarole of procedure but eventually dismiss the case for the sake of maintaining the political status quo. The petition set up one of the most intensely watched legal proceedings, in part because the technology for live broadcast was available but also because many viewers were hoping to hear more about Odinga's hacking claim. However, the hacking claim was never brought up in court. Instead, the trial focused on the many procedural failures that had made the entire process too unreliable to accept, and the discrepancies between the audited and the publicised results. Specifically, it hinged on the hybrid manual-electronic forms that had led to many forms of questionable origin and format being accepted as official documentation.

On 14 August, when the opposition filed its petition appealing the presidential election results at the Supreme Court, there was no reason to believe that the outcome of this petition would be any different from those filed in 1992 and 2013. In those cases, the leading opposition figure submitted to the court that there were far too many irregularities and illegalities conducted during the election for the result to stand. Even though there was in all three cases substantial evidence that these claims were grounded in law, the courts dismissed them. If there was a general thread uniting presidential election petitions in Kenya it would be that they conceded that there were in fact problems with the election but argued that they did not rise to the level required for the court to dismiss the results altogether.

By 14 August, all the major observation groups in the country had signed off on the election, calling it broadly free and fair. Former US Secretary of State John Kerry, who led the US-based Carter Center's observation mission, was adamant that the election was mostly above-board.[32] Kerry was operating from a context where the biggest fear was the recurrence of the 2007 violence – not unreasonable given most of the factors that triggered violence in 2007 were still in play. But it was a statement that misjudged the mood, the significance of the electronic processes that were built into the electoral system, and the influence that information circulating on social media would have. Especially when voters began contrasting photographs of their 34As – the constituency-level results forms certified by all party agents present – with what was being announced by the IEBC, the difference between what was published and what was shared triggered more incredulity around the results.

For most of the proceedings, which I watched closely, lawyers for the commission seemed to be confident in their case even though it appeared weak. They seemed to have come to court prepared to argue a case on hacking which the opposition did not make. For example, one lawyer for the IEBC admitted in open court that the results broadcast on the Results Transmission System was not actually transmitting election results. Seemingly taken aback by the claim, Chief Justice David Maraga made a rare intervention and pushed 'so if they weren't results what were they?' The lawyer had little more to offer than 'they were just statistics'. The lawyer and the commission gave little indication of where the statistics had come from and what they were supposed to represent, even though during the four-day period between the vote and the announcement of the results, those results were the only piece of information offered to the public.[33]

Still, it was more than a surprise when on 1 September, by a vote of four to two, the Supreme Court of Kenya agreed with the leader of the opposition and ruled that there were indeed too many irregularities and illegalities for the result to stand.[34] While legally it made sense to invalidate the presidential election result, it was still a great surprise when they actually did. This simply doesn't happen in Kenya where the judiciary regularly preserves the political status quo – a presumption grounded in 25 years of failed presidential election petitions, especially in 1992 and 1997 when the petitioner's case had arguably been stronger. The Supreme Court decision was ultimately guided by the protection that the constitution gave to the recommendations of the Kriegler Commission. The IEBC was being held to a higher standard than its predecessor institution because the laws that it was breaking were not just in violation of legislation passed by a partisan parliament but also protected in a constitution that had been approved by 68% of voters in a national plebiscite.

The Supreme Court decision triggered an unexpected period of political uncertainty. By law, the commission had 60 days from the day the decision was handed down to organise a fresh election. But 'fresh elections' in Kenya are governed by a complex network of the constitution, election law and regulations, as well as previous and current court decisions. Odinga was feeling emboldened. His NASA coalition made a list of what they called 'irreducible minimums' or conditions that would have to be met before he participated in the election.[35] Until that point, the letter of the law gave him reason to be cocky. Based on an obscure provision of the 2013 Supreme Court petition, at least on the surface of the law, his withdrawal meant that the commission was required to return to the nomination phase and start again.

However, some of his irreducible minimums were also arguably overreaching. For one thing, he wanted OT-Morpho Safran disqualified from providing election support during the election rerun. The firm was adamant that it had not been implicated in any wrongdoing during the election and that Odinga was making it a scapegoat for broader issues.[36] The company threatened a lawsuit in Kenya and in France for reputational harm. According to an internal audit of its systems, everything that it had control over worked perfectly. Regardless, 90 days required by the courts would have been far too short to source another supplier and get new systems in place.

With just a few days left to the election, Odinga announced that he was withdrawing from the race, which in theory should have led to the cancellation of the rerun.[37] In practice, it just fuelled more confusion. The detail in the 2013 decision he was relying on was in an advisory portion of the decision rather than the main decision itself, and it was never clarified whether it had the force of law. There was significant debate on this issue and some in the ruling coalition wanted President Kenyatta sworn in immediately.

The invalidation of the August vote meant that the election had not happened though, and another one was required by law. The day after Odinga withdrew from the race, a lower court added to the confusion by allowing one of the minor candidates back onto the poll[38] even though the 2013 decision had said candidates other than the nominal winner and their challenger were ineligible. This allowed the commission to evade the farce of Kenyatta running unopposed in a presidential election, but also led the commission to allow all other presidential candidates back onto the ballot. Moreover, the commission refused to recognise Odinga's withdrawal, arguing that he had not filed the proper paperwork. Odinga himself maintained that he would not file the paperwork even though he had in fact withdrawn.[39]

Two days before the 26 October vote, Odinga called for a boycott, urging a campaign of civil disobedience.[40] The news came in the shadow of the inability of the Supreme Court to hear a hastily filed petition from members of the public requesting that the 26 October vote be postponed. It was also overshadowed by the shooting of one of the guards providing the security detail for the deputy chief justice while she was in the car. For Odinga, calling for a boycott was a huge political gamble. His name was still on the ballot and he risked losing the election by a landslide thereby giving the ruling party more of a mandate than they could have claimed in August. It would have been an inauspicious way to close a nearly 40-year political career.

In the end, the 26 October election turned out to be a farce, even by Kenyan standards. With an official turnout of only 38%, more than half of the people who voted in August did not vote again in October.[41] Nearly a third of counties had a voter turnout of less than 15%. Moreover, the IEBC abandoned all pretext of using any of the electoral systems required by law. All votes were transmitted from the counties manually although the commission insisted this was merely a supplement to the electronic system.[42] The Electronic Voter Identification System was not used in a number of polling stations either.

The much-vaunted multimillion-dollar digital election was a massive flop.

Social media was a big part of this entire process. During the four-day wait for the results of the August election, individuals online began to notice irregularities with the data that was being represented on the RTS system. There were allegations that the president was maintaining a constant 11% lead against the leader of the opposition throughout the entire period, regardless of the size of constituencies or counties from which results were being announced. This is a statistical improbability. I myself tracked the number of rejected votes on the portal and was startled when they climbed to over 400,000 – nearly three times the number that was reported in 2013. Did Kenyans get dumber or did voting get harder in the five years between elections?

As a result of the recommendations of the Kriegler Commission, Kenyan electoral law requires each polling station to announce the result of an election before all agents of political parties present, have each of those agents sign the form and then post the form in a public place where any member of the public can see the result. Photographs of the form 34As posted at various polling stations circulated on social media, allegedly showing that the results being announced by the IEBC were incorrect. These rumours gained significant currency.

Moreover, after the result was announced at 9:30 p.m. there was an immediate flare-up of violence in parts of the country considered opposition strongholds. In my own neighbourhood sporadic gunshots in the nearby informal settlement began even before the ceremony at the national tallying centre began. Prior to the election, the police had identified a long list of opposition strongholds as 'hotspots' for electoral violence and sent many heavily armed riot police contingents to these neighbourhoods. On the day the result was announced the police responded to any form of protest in these neighbourhoods with disproportionate force.[43] Police officers allegedly fired rounds into people's homes and threw teargas while people were inside. In the end, the Kenyan National Commission on Human Rights (KNCHR) noted that over 37 people died as a direct result of these confrontations with the police.[44]

Kenya's traditional media initially refused to carry these reports even while victims of the violence circulated videos of police brutality on platforms like Facebook, Twitter and WhatsApp.[45] It fuelled a sense of ethnic profiling that would later take shape as the online movement #LuoLivesMatter. It was bad enough that the violence was happening, but the sense of a conspiracy of silence triggered accusations of genocide. The revelation that amongst the victims was a six-month-old baby who was clubbed to death by a police officer in her mother's arms, as well as a ten-year-old girl who was playing on her family's balcony triggered a shift in mood amongst the media establishment. By this time, the stories had gone viral on social media and only added to the sense that traditional media was increasingly censored and irrelevant.

The anger captured by #LuoLivesMatter raised the political temperature in the country considerably. On the eve of the Supreme

Court election announcement there was fear that not only would there be a large wave of protest but that there would also be a significant, violent backlash to it.[46] It seemed that the feared political violence would finally start.

The next day, however, the Supreme Court ruled that the presidential election result was invalid. Instead of protests in opposition strongholds, there was celebration. And on social media there was a renewed sense of importance and urgency around the potential organising that could be done. There may be many questions around the political expediency of the decision, but it undoubtedly doused the rising political temperature.

By the time the 26 October rerun rolled around, #KOTElection-Observer mission was ready, even if the IEBC was not. Form 34As were photographed, captured, disseminated and dissected online. The police were filmed and videos of brutality circulated at breakneck speed. Unlike in August, by October the IEBC did not have the benefit of the doubt and much of Kenya's social media community was primed for disbelief. The farcical election result only confirmed that they had been right to disbelieve.

At the time of writing, there was major discussion in North America about the ways in which social media sites like Facebook and Twitter had facilitated Russian interference in the 2016 US general election. There was panic among the US political class at the scale to which organisations and groups affiliated with the Russian government had purchased advertising that some argued had shifted preferences enough to alter the outcome of the election. Cambridge Analytica was on the chopping block, summoned by the UK Parliament to provide testimony regarding its interference in the Brexit vote that triggered the much-criticised process of Britain leaving the European Union.

The general counsels at Facebook, Twitter and Google – three of the largest tech companies in the world – had been summoned to Congress[47] to testify as to why their companies had failed to screen for and protect users from these groups. The conversation also included the impact of these bot farms on the Brexit vote in the UK.[48] Facebook especially, because its API provided CA with the infrastructure it needed for its data analytics operations, has been forced to give testimony before legislatures in the US, UK and Singapore,[49] and threatened with an investigation in the US[50] and the European Union.[51]

The broad argument that underpins these interventions is that we are all more polarised, stupid and less informed than we were before the internet became so closely connected to politics. Some articles argued that social media had allowed political opinions to harden so much that opinions and viewpoints that would previously have been unacceptable in public became normalised. Certainly, online radicalisation is a major contributing factor to the resurgence of right-wing extremism sweeping across the West, and the 2018 Cambridge Analytica investigation confirms that this radicalisation was propagated by a deliberate strategy of misinformation and manipulation.

What stands out in this conversation is that by and large communities outside the global north have been left out of it. Aside from a severe interrogation from the Singaporean parliament, these platforms are operating unchecked in the global south and in fact, as in the case of Ethiopia's authoritarian regime, collaborating with repressive regimes. The unspoken presumption is that the rest of the world will simply have to go along with whatever is decided in Washington DC or in Brussels, despite the fact that the impact of these platforms outside these countries is probably more severe. While regulators in Washington DC were worrying about Brexit or a Trump presidency, observers in Myanmar allege that Facebook was propagating a genocide.[52]

Digital technologies will continue to be an inevitable part of people's lives even if their shape and function will change as a result of the ongoing realisations and these efforts at reform and accountability matter a great deal. But the West is not the whole world, so the experiences of other parts of the world in relation to these developments must be part of designing better systems. As noted at the start of this book, the lesson from Kenya in 2017 is that social media especially is like salt: when mixed with water it is a fairly stable compound but when mixed with sulphuric acid the results can be explosive. Facebook, Twitter and Google represent the paradoxes of globalisation – rooted in countries with relatively strong legal systems but having significant impact on politics further away, where they are under less scrutiny and oversight. If they can cause this much disruption within a relatively strong legal context, how much more damage can they do further afield? More attention must be paid to how these systems are interacting with political cultures in other parts of the world.

In Kenya, technology was supposed to save an election but instead was used to compromise it. The lesson here is that technology cannot diminish political agency. People have to want things to change. The many failures of the system in Kenya were a function of people within the IEBC and within the political class wanting the system to fail; and so it did. Moreover, the choice of vendor and systems was not neutral – it reflected the interests of those who managed the systems.

Michel Foucault identifies the danger of ascribing neutrality to institutions that are not in fact neutral.[53] In this historical moment, the ideology of the dominant class is profit. OT-Safran Morpho's engagement with the Kenyan election was not out of benevolence, it was for profit. Cambridge Analytica didn't offer its services to the Jubilee party for free – the company made more money than any Kenyan vendor involved in the election at any level. The solution to constraints on democracy in the developing world therefore cannot be more technology, especially not technology for profit.

Following Kenya's 2017 experience, we are long overdue a conversation about morality, ethics and ideology in technology and new media. Should Facebook be held accountable if a political party creates hate speech and disseminates it on its platforms? Should a French company be able to purchase the private information of 19 million Kenyan citizens with limited civic oversight? Should a British or American data company be able to insert itself into a highly fraught political context halfway around the world? Should there be an obligation to prevent profit-making from elections? Until recently software developers have argued that their work in 'innovation' and 'disruption' could be profitable and still remain morally agnostic. To be sure, traditional media and other vendors have always made money from elections but not at the scale foreign companies made in Kenya in 2017. Moreover, when those profiting don't have a direct stake in the outcome of that politics – a form of digital colonialism that extracts profit but invests nothing in the country – the consequences can be dire. These are all questions triggered by the Kenyan experience that need to be part of the conversation as we decide what to do about new media in politics.

At the same time the conversation must be global. Sanya's feminist critique of technology insists that we 'move away from universalising representations of social change ... and [centre] localised agendas'.[54] With social media especially, these are US-listed companies and directly answerable to the US legislature and electorate, so understandably much of the focus has been on what is happening there. Of the three, only Google has a long-standing presence in Africa – Facebook opened its Johannesburg office in 2015[55] and Twitter runs its Africa operations from London. This perhaps explains why the Cambridge Analytica scandal prompted full-page apologies in newspapers in Europe and North America but not in Africa. What should the millions of people around the world who rely on these platforms and others to organise political protests, to challenge dominant political narratives or to simply find new ways of being and existing within their societies do? Where can they go and file their grievances? Who will speak up for them if the organisations don't even care enough to apologise for potential harms?

One powerful analytical tool in critical political theory is to shift the referent object of our analysis in order to see how the world looks when it is not built around the identities we consider to be 'natural' or 'given'. With social media, the implicit central object has always been the Western, white man. Until the panic around the Russian intervention, much of the disquiet around how women and people of colour were experiencing the spaces was roundly ignored. An investigation into the use of Russian bots revealed that many of the accounts that were linked to the broader conspiracy had been routinely harassing women of colour for years, but that the site had not responded to their concerns. #YourSlipIsShowing was crafted by black women to identify accounts that were posing as hostile black people in order to fuel racial discontent.[56] According to the report, the investigation into Russian interference revealed that many of these accounts were in fact part of a test of strategies to exacerbate racial tension in the US. If social networks had paid attention to these criticisms early enough, the broader catastrophe may have been avoided.

The same can be said for Cambridge Analytica's role in elections in Kenya, the UK and the US – what if we had been paying attention to what was happening in these elections beyond flattening tropes of ethnic politics? These technologies developed in the US are not developed with partly free countries such as Kenya in mind and there is still some surprise that people embrace them, so the technology intersects with politics in unpredictable ways. Certainly, Twitter did not set out to play a starring role in the Egyptian revolution, nor did Facebook have in its growth plan a desire to trigger conversations about class-consciousness in India. Both of these things happened because of human agency.

Today, we know that more social media doesn't automatically mean more democracy. But the evidence of youth organising in Chad, Togo, Uganda and other parts of the developing world in recent years confirms that these spaces are still tremendously important for dissenters in authoritarian spaces. And the case of Kenya shows how they are incubating a new political awareness and consciousness that is changing the country in dramatic ways. As governments in the West continue to deliberate over the future of these platforms, it is crucial for voices from around the world to be included, especially because, as the foregoing conversation on Kenya suggests, there is lots to be learnt from prior experiences here.

So is technology good or bad for politics? The truth, as always, is somewhere down the middle. In Kenya, as much as there are groups and parasites buying influence to create and sustain a misinformation ecosystem that undermines true political participation, there are groups like Maskani ya Taifa or Siasa Place that are using these spaces to inform the public and alter public consciousness. Both Maskani and Siasa Place connect their online work to offline organising, hosting public forums not just in Nairobi, where most of Kenya's social media users are based, but further afield in order to increase impact. They couldn't succeed if they only restricted their work to online organising. The impact of these platforms might not be immediately perceptible, especially in the face of the organised, systemic pushback highlighted here, but they will matter eventually. Depending on what people choose to do with it, technology has both undermined and enabled political progress in Kenya.

Consider the impact of digital spaces on one of the most important political identities in Kenya – ethnicity. Looking at how ethnicity collides with digital politics can be instructive for other parts of the world as identity re-emerges as a political instrument, taking on the characteristics of ethnic groups with a myth of common origin (hard work and determination), and a shared language on the ethos of accumulation. Kenya can teach the world a lot about ethnic politics. Ethnicity is the only political identity in Kenya that thrives in the ethereal, intangible plane of the deep state, where law is merely suggestion and institutions serve at the pleasure of unidentified patrons. It survives after all other political realities have been diluted or destroyed because it is a fiction that adapts to whatever reality it encounters. It is not tied to an immutable bio-logical characteristic like melanin or reproductive organs. A man can be asked to die for his ethnic group while a woman often loses hers as soon as she marries. It is literally an idea of where a person came from and where they can go to feel at 'home' that can provide reasons to fight one year and to form alliances five years later.

In itself, ethnicity is a morally neutral value – having an ethnic identity is not the issue. Issues arise when it becomes another basis for excluding people from power or access to resources. It is especially a problem when it is used to justify egregious violence against other groups. In his seminal work, *Orientalism*, Edward Said reminds us that the problem is not in realising that differences exist between groups but when these differences are essentialised and instrumentalised for political action.[57] When ethnic differences are used as a basis for hate speech, for example, they create space for systemic violence that is difficult to contain because they cannot easily be debated away.

It is this that makes ethnicity the most potent political identity in countries like Kenya precisely because it is so fluid. It is a useful tool for organising political communities and rationalising polit-ical behaviour without having to interrogate it. Yet this malleability also leaves people fighting shadows – imagined enemies that must be pre-emptively protected against. In this context, much of the discussion around Kenya's election violence has centred on ethnicity, and the idea of the ethnic group as the main spoiler to achieving 'real' democracy.

Can technology de-ethnicise a society, or at least defuse the political tension around it? That seemed to be the broad argument underpinning the Kriegler Commission's recommendations. The idea was that if the process of electioneering was professionalised and standardised then it would be easier for political opponents to accept results, making them less likely to instigate violence. A sterile bureaucracy would do more to contain ethnic conflict than one that was so easy to manipulate. This speaks to the broader belief in bureaucratisation and technology as simple ways of addressing broader social problems.

But as highlighted, technology can't fix problems online that people don't want to fix offline. Attempting to shift political accountability onto a digital system has created more problems in Kenya than it has fixed, burdening taxpayers with an expensive, dud system. The more complex the technology becomes, the more complex the efforts to circumvent it. It's also important to recall that ethnic identities are highly influenced by elections and other major political events – it's a mutually reinforcing cycle. This has to do with the nature of political contestation in the country. There's very rarely an appeal to national issues beyond cursory nods in party manifestos. So when the government threatens to punish people expressing offensive views online it simply drives the conversations back offline.

The good news from Kenya so far is that digital spaces can help considerably in overcoming the fluid yet toxic biases that ethnic identities sometimes engender. It's not that they flatten ethnic identities but that they give people the room to redefine the space their ethnicity occupies in their societies. They allow individuals to publicly surmount differences to create communities of collaboration around various issues which in turn undercuts the apparent immutability of these identities. Some of these have already been discussed – the women's rights movement, fundraising for various causes etc. Social networks are allowing people who want to operate outside the arbitrary lines that ethnicity draws in society to find each other and build new ways of belonging.

In countries where the physical public sphere is strongly controlled by the state, the digital public sphere takes on monumental importance, especially in coordinating public action. In Kenya, where the press is strongly controlled and influenced by the state, activists have used social media to mobilise for protest even when traditional media refused to cover stories. For example, the hashtag #StopExtrajudicialKillings was used to mobilise national protests in the first week of July 2016 against the kidnapping and murder of three individuals by state policemen.[58]

Such visible instances of inter-ethnic collaboration are critical to deconstructing and reconstructing ethnicity because they allow individuals to see that alternatives ways of organising public life are possible. Consider that much of the collaboration around online monitoring of the election in 2017 was spontaneous and happened across physical and ethnic divisions. This public performance of new ways of being also allows people to see that they have a significant amount of agency in deciding how they would like public life in their country to be organised. It allows the outliers to find each other and coalesce into a recognisable force. At the core of the tribe as a political entity is the question of trust: people assume that they are better off trusting people from the same ethnic background and are therefore more likely to share opportunities with them. In uncertain political or economic times, where the state offers no social safety nets, the tribe creates a basis for trust. Digital platforms allow people to experience trust across ethnic groups, reducing the need to collapse back into the ethnic group as the catch-all political safety net.

There are however limits to this, particularly with regard to hate speech. Many of the problems proliferating in online speech are created in another space – a failure in the education system, a dearth of inclusive physical public spaces, the slow death of the university as a space for genuine intellectual inquiry. Still, the internet does accelerate, amplify and even allow toxic ideas to coalesce with an imprimatur of authority. It allows people who hold offensive opinions to find each other in a manner that evades conventional scrutiny, which may give them the confidence to articulate these opinions publicly (hate speech) or even to act on them.

As such, social media in turn has paradoxically both reinforced and undermined ethnic identities in Kenya. Many people's ethnic biases have hardened, especially on the basis of microtargeted spin campaigns – the stratified form of advertising that firms like CA specialise in. Triggering ethnic hatred doesn't require evidence or proof or even a past record of performance. It simply requires repeating marginalisation tropes that sound true to people who have no alternative sources of information. It only requires subtle name-calling or finger-pointing. But many have also had their ethnic biases moderated through constant interaction with people from diverse backgrounds. Individuals routinely disprove claims that ethnic group X has either vastly profited from having one of their own in power and substantiate the denial with evidence in the form of video, articles or anecdotal evidence. Many go as far as directly confronting elected leaders – tagging them in posts that undercut their arguments – to show that blind allegiance to the ethnic group is not the blanket protection that political leaders promise. In Kenya this almost never happens offline.

Thus, Kenya is a reminder that action to regulate these spaces must be moderated by protecting the gains they create in diverse contexts. Unfortunately, the Kenyan legislature has taken the opposite approach, using real concerns over managing hate speech, for example, to create legislation designed to punish those who criticise the state. The Misuse of a Telecommunications Device Law was passed ostensibly to help manage harassment and threats online. In the end it was declared unconstitutional in 2016 because in its short life span it had been used primarily to punish people who dared criticise the government or its representatives. The Kenyan government's interests on social media are not in protecting individuals but in controlling dissent, and so far as this is their agenda, less regulation coupled with enhanced enforcement is actually better.

Although the regulatory agency National Cohesion and Integration Commission (NCIC) made social media the prime target of its regulation efforts around the 2017 election, in Kenya, given the relatively low numbers of people who use social media and their concentration in the capital, traditional media is more of a threat to social cohesion than social networking sites. This has been the case in the last two elections, where local language radio stations have been used to mobilise ethnic chauvinism and to incite violence against people seen to be 'outsiders' in certain areas. A 2017 report from the Election Observation Group Media Monitoring Project found that Kameme FM, a radio station owned by President Uhuru Kenyatta through his MediaMax company, had the highest rate of occurrence of hate speech in the lead-up to the 2017 election.[59] To date, there has been no punitive action against them.

When it comes to social media regulation, it's not tribalism online that scares the state but people organising across ethnic lines to complain about poor service delivery, state violence and exploitation. They are not interested in protecting women from online harassment; they do little to protect women from offline harassment and violence. If all that happened online in Kenya was complaining about other ethnic groups, there would be no impetus to control the space. The former is perfectly consistent with the status quo. The latter threatens to upend it, thereby taking out all who profit from it. It is the spread of legitimate criticism and evidence to back it up that has put the Kenyan government on a collision course with social media communities.

Which leaves the question – where will the sensible regulation come from? At the moment, it seems that Kenya will have to wait for regulation in the countries where these technologies are developed to rein in their excesses. At the time of publishing, for example, the General Data Protection Regulations (GDPR) implemented by the EU on 1 June 2018 have done more to protect the privacy of internet users in Kenya than any regulations issued by the Kenyan parliament.

Specifically with regard to social media, young activists in Kenya and beyond have embraced it as a space for political discourse, with mixed results. In more repressive states like Gabon, Cameroon, Ethiopia or Togo, social media has been revolutionary and states are running scared. Ethiopia, for example, switched off social media for almost two years to stop protesters from communicating with each other.[60] But most of these countries have small online communities, which makes such drastic measures more feasible. In South Africa, Nigeria and Kenya, there are so many social media users that an internet shutdown would not go unnoticed. At the same time, these countries have also embraced digitisation as an indication of modernity, and it would be self-defeating to destroy that image by embracing draconian shutdowns.

Kenya and other partially free societies cannot decide if they want digital democracy because they are struggling to control its analogue outcomes. The situation facing social media in Kenya is instructive. The PSCU headed by a former prominent blogger who himself was once deeply opposed to overregulation, has proposed legislation to govern what people can and cannot say on these platforms.[61] The proposal also includes the creation of a new authority – with a budget, a mandate and offices – to monitor what people post on social media. The Kenya Film Classification Board has also repeatedly attempted to curb what can and cannot be said on Twitter. On 18 March 2016 the KFCB declared on its official handle: 'Social media is a threat to national cohesion.'[62]

Is social media a threat to national cohesion in Kenya? It depends on how you define national cohesion and its role in fostering democracy. Much like Chase Bank, social media is only a threat to national cohesion if the foundations on which the country is built are weak, and digital organising in Kenya is constantly highlighting many of the state's weaknesses. If national cohesion is predicated on silencing, misinformation and misrepresentation then any platform that allows people to freely express themselves is a threat – whether it's a social network or a public meeting or a private meeting in a private members club.

Incidentally, the government of Kenya also has laws regulating public meetings precisely for this reason – silencing the aggregation of criticism. Public order ordinances are still used with alarming frequency to curtail online protest – requiring individuals to register protests with the police, pay deposits etc. These are physical efforts to censor the offline public sphere. So the state may have hoped that it could embrace a digital first strategy without replicating the offline protest dynamic. This has failed, leaving it lurching from one half-cooked legislative response to other real threats – like the proliferation of hate speech – to another.

As long as the government is desperate to maintain Kenya's reputation as a technological mecca, digital platforms will remain relatively open. As long the government wants to celebrate m-Pesa and Ushahidi as successes of Africa's silicon savannah, the state will need to maintain a healthy share of digital freedom. This gives activists and organisers in Kenya more latitude than their compatriots in many other developing countries. Political discourse happening in these spaces will continue to have significant impact on the country's politics.

But there are already questions of how sustainable these spaces will be in the long run. Social media companies are American companies answerable to the US government, meaning that if they upset the US government they could be summarily reformatted. And as long as they are beholden to profit motives, they will be vulnerable to capture by whatever entities have the deepest pockets or the greatest ability to impact 'growth'. Social networks are not public commons in the pure sense of the word. None of the social media platforms that have been created to date have survived indefinitely. The digital landscape around the world could look completely different in ten, or even five, years from now.

But the questions raised vis-à-vis citizen participation and democracy will linger. Technology will be an inevitable part of that future even if it is a case of three steps forward and two steps back. The only thing that is certain from the ten years between 2007 and 2017 is that Kenyans will continue to defend their agency over shaping that future.

Chapter 10

CONCLUSION

In March 2017, photographer turned activist Boniface Mwangi announced the launch of the Ukweli Party that would be the vehicle for his campaign for election as an MP in Nairobi's Starehe Constituency.[1] In his years as a photojournalist and activist, Mwangi had cultivated an audience of millions through his Facebook and Twitter presence, and hoped to translate that into votes even with a small, independent party. Mwangi also launched the first crowd-funded political campaign in Kenyan history, asking followers and friends who believed in his message to donate and help him take his fight for social justice to parliament.[2]

By the end of his campaign, Mwangi had raised 10 million shillings (approximately US$100,000) in a campaign that in many ways overturned Nairobi politics.[3] Mwangi's main challengers were a popular musician and a city millionaire who outspent him at every turn, particularly in offering bribes to voters. Other politicians copied his crowd-funding strategy, including former Prime Minister Raila in the build-up to the October rerun. At the end of the campaign, Mwangi spent days walking through the streets of Nairobi, scraping off his campaign posters from walls as a gesture to restore the city, a move that was quickly copied by other politicians.[4]

Boniface Mwangi did not win the Starehe election, and some analysts took it as a signal that work done on social media cannot stimulate change in Kenyan politics.[5] But this just hints at the narrow frame used to understand what politics is. Electoral politics is important but it is not the be all and end all of politics. Despite the loss, Mwangi's candidacy, with its embrace of clean politics and new media strategies, shifted political practice in Kenya.[6] The fact that other candidates were scrambling to copy his online and offline work signals that his presence was important. Losing in an election in Kenya may simply have been the outcome of introducing an idea ahead of its time.

Still, Mwangi's experience captures the state of the ongoing conversation on politics in the digital age replicated elsewhere as digital political cultures define themselves. After the fear of the 1990s and the blind optimism of the 2000s, there is a reset of public opinion on the normative dimensions of digital democracy. Kenya's first digital decade has been by turns heady and awe-inspiring, as shown by the successes of Ushahidi, m-Pesa and the new digital protest movements, but it has also been characterised by the frenetic convulsions of a schizophrenic state and the rise of new forms of exclusion. The spectacular failure of the 2007 election fuelled some of the most advanced electronic and political innovations in the world. Yet the fact so many of these failures were reproduced in 2017 suggests that Kenya's politics is determined to resist change.

Other movements on the continent have had similar experiences. The #ThisFlag movement in Zimbabwe may not have been directly responsible for the removal of Robert Mugabe after over 30 years in office, but it did galvanise public opinion and give focus to protests that were floundering after the official opposition joined the government. In Togo, #FaureMustGo protesters may not immediately have succeeded in their goal of removing long-serving President Fauré Gnassigbé from office, but they are drawing attention to the political plight of a small country that would otherwise have been ignored. In Ethiopia, social media galvanised anti-regime protests but also exposed activists to retribution through the information that the government accessed about them online. Outside the West, the terrain today is highly ambiguous.

In Kenya, digital platforms are spaces where the extent of people's agency and creativity is on full display beyond electoral politics – in their humour, melancholy, anger and confusion. They have allowed Kenyans to remind the world that there is life in Africa beyond elections, conflict and development. Elections may have catalysed Kenya's digital decade, but electoral politics is not the be all and end all of Kenya's online identity. Significantly, online spaces have amplified voices that would otherwise be unheard. In rural areas of Kenya, communities are participating in WhatsApp groups to set public agendas in their local communities.[7] Where traditional media remains obsessed with the woman as a mother or a mother in waiting, digital spaces are allowing women – young women especially – to define a broader existence. Kenya's radical feminists are organising to rewrite laws, to reclaim space and to occupy space. And when used with intention and the public interest at heart, as with the National Bureau of Statistics or the Open Government platform, the state has used digital technologies to enhance governance.

Yet digital spaces have also allowed the state to reach deeper into the private lives of citizens without necessarily raising the bar on state conduct towards its people. Kenya's surveillance state is one of the most elaborate in the developing world and this Panopticon is so far free of major legal constraint. The Cyber Crimes Act (2018) has focused on the threat of hacking or cyberterrorism, and the threat bloggers pose to politicians rather than the obligation to protect the privacy of Kenyans online.[8] These gaps attracted the worst of today's digital parasites. Companies that profit from selling political chaos are circling. Misogynists and ethnic chauvinists love the relative anonymity that social media gives them. The state, meanwhile, continues to oscillate between authoritarianism and ignorance.

The revelations about Cambridge Analytica's involvement in Kenya also underscore that digital colonialism is a real threat. Digital technologies have pulled developing countries with a sufficiently developed architecture into the heart of global politics. Today, we contend with a British firm experimenting with its political influence in the developing world seemingly unchecked because of the absence of a robust digital protection law in these countries. These are the absences de Sousa Santos warns about: 'the idea that time is linear and that at the cutting edge of time are to be found the core countries of the world system and, along with them, the dominant knowledges, institutions and forms of sociability'.[9] If the conversation on technology had included Kenya and other developing countries earlier, maybe things would have gone differently for everyone. Had there been a timely intervention to prevent foreign data companies from meddling in politics overseas, perhaps the normalisation of right-wing extremist politics or the march towards the unexpected Trump and Brexit victories would not have been consolidated. Maybe if more analysis had noticed earlier that digital technologies were weaving developing countries closer into global politics, 2017 would have been less of an *annus horribilis* all around.

Kenya's experience with digital democracy is a reminder of the importance of learning within political systems. The challenges posed by new media replicate those raised by local language radio during the 2007 election. Pretty soon, we will have to talk about WhatsApp and other Dark Social apps as more and more of the political organising and mobilisation highlighted here move to such platforms and away from public scrutiny. In Kenya, even political communities outside Nairobi are shifting major parts of their political work onto these platforms.[10] WhatsApp is already accused of taking the place of local language radio as the preferred site for the dissemination of hate speech.[11] What would enabling, effective, non-stifling regulation of that space look like?

Ultimately, democracy is about ideas. At the intersection of politics and technology is a simple question – what ideas does technology make possible? Which ideas does it constrain? Who has the power to share ideas and who doesn't? Whose ideas are given prominence and whose are shuttered? With increasing recognition that technology is not a morally neutral good we now have a better understanding that more technology is not inherently better for democracy. The shape and utilisation of technology reflects the moral values of those who develop and use it, and the foregoing discussion interrogates what ideas the current state of technology in politics in Kenya makes possible.

Kenya's first digital decade was bookended by two calamitous elections. When confronted by so much negative information on such an enormous scale, it is easy to believe that the story of Kenya's first digital decade is also a story of conflict and tension. But in between these extremes, significant innovation and creativity has been shown by citizens at all levels. Underneath all of this tension and upheaval is agency. Kenyans are taking on technology built for the West to tell their own story and chart their own political destiny for better or worse. Kenyan governments are choosing to embrace technology if only to sometimes discard it in response to analogue political pressure.

The only thing that is certain from 2007 to 2017 and everything in between is that Kenyans want agency over shaping that future, and will use whatever space they see in order to do that. Today that space is digital – in five or ten years it may be something else. This book captures the current state of play but the situation changes every day. In all this – in botched elections and animated online conversation, through the surveillance state and the explosion of mobile money – the underlying theme in the conversation is not conflict, it is agency.

NOTES

Preface

1   Touré (1959).
2   And there are some who argue that it doesn't exist. See Shivji (2017).
3   See e.g. Friederici, Ojanperä and Mark (2016).

Introduction

1   @MumbiKenya, 7:48 AM (US time), https://twitter.com/MumbiKenya/status/717302913568272385
2   Bloomberg (2017).
3   BBC (2017a).
4   Owaah (2016).
5   @chasebankKenya 10:10 a.m https://twitter.com/chasebankkenya/status/717338506687864832
6   Chase Bank (2016).
7   @jkemboe 7 April 2016, 6:24 AM, https://twitter.com/Jkemboe/status/718006549784952832
8   Central Bank of Kenya (2016).
9   Sambuli (2016).
10 Genga (2016).
11 Mwaniki (2016).
12 Karanja (2016).
13 Kazeem (2016).
14 Privacy International (2017a).
15 Devichand (2016).
16 DW.com (2016).
17 Brewster (2016).
18 See Ramanathan (2017).
19 Kuo (2017).
20 Alal and Matete (2017).
21 Said by Victor Nyamori, Advocate for the IEBC, during the Supreme Court proceedings on the Presidential Petition.
22 https://www.youtube.com/watch?v=VeJS5QrT2qg

23 See Muthuri (2017).
24 Mutai (2016).
25 Kenya National Commission on Human Rights (2017), p. 5.

Chapter 1

1   Matina Stevis @matinaStevis 17 October 2017 (accessed 11
    November 2017), available at https://twitter.com/MatinaStevis/
    status/920152509787893760
2   Dahir (2017).
3   Independent Election and Boundaries Commission (2017a; 2017b).
4   Ibid.
5   Nanjala Nyabola, @nanjala 1 '400454 Rejected Votes', 11 August 2017,
    available at https://twitter.com/Nanjala1/status/895898450486800386
6   Said by Victor Nyamori, Advocate for the IEBC, during the Supreme Court
    proceedings on the Presidential Petition.
7   Ngirachu (2017a).
8   Interview with Dr Roselyn Akombe, 18 November 2017.
9   Lang'at (2017).
10 Ngirachu (2017b).
11 Houreld and Miriri (2017).
12 BBC News (2017d).
13 Lang'at (2017).
14 Mbuthia (2017).
15 Magara (2009).
16 Perlez (1991).
17 Mutunga (2012).
18 See Adar and Munyae (2001).
19 Mutunga (2012).
20 Oluoch (2013a).
21 Press (1991).
22 See Adar and Munyae (2001).
23 Ibid.
24 Barkan (2004).
25 Murunga and Nasong'o (2006).
26 Bannon (2007).
27 Ibid.
28 Ibid., p. 1838.
29 Ibid., p. 1839.
30 Ibid., p. 1838.
31 BBC (2005).
32 Oluoch (2013b).
33 Mueller (2008).

34 International Parliamentary Union (2008).
35 Ibid.
36 Ibid.
37 Ibid.
38 See Kenya Elections Domestic Observation Forum (KEDOF) (2007);
    European Union Elections Observation Mission (EUEOM) (2008);
    Commonwealth Observer Group (2008).
39 See Ndungu (2008).
40 Human Rights Watch (2008), p. 22.
41 Ibid.
42 Author's recollection.
43 Human Rights House (2008).
44 Human Rights Watch (2008), p. 22.
45 Ibid., p. 24.
46 Ibid.
47 Author's recollection.
48 Nyassy (2013).
49 Ibid.
50 Ibid.
51 Cocks (2008).
52 Human Rights Watch (2008), p. 24.
53 Ibid., p. 27.
54 Nation Reporter (2011).
55 Human.Rights Watch (2008), p. 2.
56 See Reuters Staff (2008).
57 OECD (2012).
58 Ibid.
59 See Berkman Klein Internet Centre Blog (2008).
60 White African (2008).
61 Dialogue Africa Foundation (2009).
62 Kriegler Commission (2008), p. 35.

Chapter 2

1   See e.g. Sanya (2013).
2   See O'Neil (2016).
3   See Wallaroom Media (2017).
4   Wagner and Romm (2017).
5   See Eordorgh (2015).
6   See Bernstein (2017b).
7   See Internet World Stats (2018).
8   Stork, Calandro and Gillwald (2012), p. 6.
9   Communications Authority (2017a).
10 Communications Authority (2017b).

11 UNDP (2013), p. 10.
12 Stork et al. (2012), p. 6.
13 Bloggers Association of Kenya (2018), p. 4.
14 Banda, Fred Mudhai and Tettey (2009), p. 1.
15 See e.g. Spangler (2017).
16 Ya'u (2012), p. 374.
17 Habermas et al. (1974), p. 49.
18 Habermas (1992), p. 31.
19 Ibid., p. 42.
20 Roy (2004).
21 Mustapha (2012), p. 31.
22 Langman (2005), pp. 49–50.
23 Ya'u (2012), p. 87.
24 Ekeh (1975), p. 92.
25 Ibid., p. 96.
26 Benkler (2007).
27 Ibid., p. 212.
28 Ibid.
29 See de Sousa Santos (2012), p. 44.
30 Ibid., p. 58.
31 Schneider (1996), p. 375.
32 Langman (2005), p. 55.
33 Banda et al. (2009), p. 8.
34 See Mochama (2014).
35 See Wandia (2017).
36 See iHub Research (2014).
37 Merriam Webster: Press Release (2006).
38 See *The Guardian* (2018).
39 Sonnad (2017).
40 See e.g. Wakefield (2017).

Chapter 3

1   Some of the material in this chapter has been published as a research paper for the Electoral Institute for Sustainable Democracy in Africa (2018). It is republished with permission.
2   UNICEF Statistics (2013).
3   Mantzarlis (2017).
4   Wanzala (2017).
5   Elliot (2015).
6   Brand South Africa (2017).
7   Rusbriger (2017).
8   Ogola (2011), pp. 77–95.

9   Ibid., p. 81.
10   See Obiero Opondo (2014), pp. 27–35.
11   Ibid.
12   Ogola (2011), p. 81.
13   Ibid., p. 82.
14   Ibid.
15   Ibid.
16   Ibid., p. 85.
17   BBC Africa (2006).
18   Ibid.
19   One version of the coverage of the incident from Nation Television (NTV) is available on YouTube, https://www.youtube.com/watch?v=QrxpPHQ17SU. The state refused to prosecute the case against the first lady.
20   Chweya (2016)
21   See Trading Economics (2017).
22   Goldstein and Rotich (2008), p. 8.
23   Ibid., p. 4.
24   Mbugua (2013).
25   Committee to Protect Journalists (2016).
26   Allison (2016).
27   Galava (2016).
28   Allison (2016).
29   Committee to Protect Journalists (2017).
30   Africa Review (2017).
31   Sanya and Lutomia (2011), p. 70.
32   See Biersteker (2009).
33   See Stiglitz (1999).
34   See Naím (2000), pp. 86–103.
35   See Gertz (2009).
36   Upadaya and Johnson (2015).
37   See Buku and Meredith (2013).
38   Ibid., p. 390.
39   Ibid., p. 378.
40   Munda (2017).
41   See e.g. Cheutel (2016).
42   See Fildes and Aglionby (2017).
43   See Buku and Meredith (2013), p. 378.
44   Goldstein and Rotich (2008).
45   Ibid., p. 5.
46   See Ushahidi (2017a).
47   See Ushahidi (2017b).
48   Vota (2012).

49 See generally Mzalendo Website, info.mzalendo.com
50 Bright and Hruby (2015).
51 Ochieng' (2016a).
52 Ndemo (2015).
53 See Kenya Open Data Portal, http://www.opendata.go.ke/
54 See Ochieng' (2016b).
55 The Information Communications and Technology Practitioner's Bill (2016) http://kenyalaw.org/kl/fileadmin/pdfdownloads/bills/2016/Information CommunicationTechnologyPractitioners_Bill_2016.pdf
56 Nderitu (2016).
57 Omondi (2017).
58 Burke (2010).
59 Jubilee Manifesto (2012), p. 41.
60 USAID (2008).
61 *The Nation* (2013e).
62 Jubilee Manifesto (2012), p. 41.
63 Ngirachu (2016a).
64 Ibid.
65 Ngirachu (2016b).
66 See generally Salome (2015).
67 See e.g. Kisero (2015).
68 See Privacy International (2017b).
69 Otuki (2017).
70 Chimelu (2013).
71 See Privacy International (2017b).
72 A person suspecting that their spouse is cheating will send the minimum amount to the phone number of the suspect party. Once the money is received they will get a text message containing the full name, phone number and other details of the recipient. The person receiving the money cannot reject it. See Chimelu (2013).
73 See Kenyanito (2014).
74 See Benkler (2007).

Chapter 4

1   Some of the material in this chapter has been published as an article for the Electoral Institute for Sustainable Democracy in Africa (2018), published here with permission.
2   de Sousa Santos (2012), p. 52.
3   Merriam-Webster (2016).
4   United Nations (2011).
5   Stork et al. (2012).
6   Hatem Ali (2011).

7   Kenya Information and Communications Act, CAP411 A[Rev. 2009] Section 29: 'A person who by means of a licensed telecommunication system – (a) sends a message or other matter that is grossly offensive or of an indecent, obscene or menacing character; or (b) sends a message that he knows to be false for the purpose of causing annoyance, inconvenience or needless anxiety to another person commits an offence and shall be liable on conviction to a fine not exceeding fifty thousand shillings, or to imprisonment for a term not exceeding three months, or to both.'

8   See e.g. Nyamai (2016). Martha Wanjiru Miano was arrested by police attached to the Criminal Investigations Division for a series of Facebook posts in which she criticised Governor Nderitu Gachagua and his close relatives for duplicity in the disbursement of funds from the Constituency Development fund. See also Kiprono (2016).

9   Boyd and Ellison (2007), p. 211.

10 Ibid., p. 214.

11 Ibid., p. 215.

12 Ibid., p. 216.

13 Ibid., p. 217.

14 Ibid.

15 Ibid.

16 See Bloggers Association of Kenya (2018). See also Wyche et al. (2013), p. 1.

17 Wyche et al. (2013).

18 See e.g. Schroeder (2011).

19 United Nations (2011).

20 Privacy International (2017a).

21 Kroll (2018).

22 See Facebook (2014).

23 Ben-Ari (2009), p. 632.

24 Tufecki (2017).

25 Tsur and Rappoport (2012), p. 24.

26 Ibid., p. 25.

27 See Bloggers Association of Kenya (2018). See also *The Economist* (2014).

28 Ibid.

29 BBC News (2015a).

30 Tweet from @wacuka 28 February 2016 at 3:22 p.m., https://twitter.com/JustWacuka/status/704023890104811520

31 Tweet from the Wangari Maathai Foundation @WangariMaathai 5 March 2016 at 8:40 a.m., available at https://twitter.com/WangariMaathai/status/706096945593364480

32 Tweet by @erikooh, 28 February 2016 at 6:51 a.m., https://twitter.com/erikooh/status/703895256794845184

33 Kiberenge (2015).

34 Tweet by @InsecurityKE 28 November 2014 at 2:06 p.m., available at https://twitter.com/InsecurityKE/status/538393461771501568
35 See Portland Communications (2016).
36 Simon, et al. (2014).
37 See Nyabola (2016a).
38 Ecole Polytechnique Federale de Lausanne (2014).
39 Omanga (2015).
40 EPFL research, taken from *The Eeconomist* website.
41 Wainaina (2005).
42 See Madrigal (2012).
43 See Boyd (2017).
44 Madrigal (2012).
45 How et al. (2016).
46 Saner (2016).
47 Ibid.
48 Rawnsley, Woods and Treibert (2017).
49 See Muendo (2017).

Chapter 5

1   See generally BBC Africa (2016).
2   See Hatem Ali (2011).
3   BBC News (2017).
4   See Howden (2013).
5   See McConnell (2015).
6   Okwembah (2013).
7   Ombati and Obala (2013).
8   See McConnell (2015).
9   *Daily Nation* (2013d).
10 Barasa (2013).
11 *Daily Nation* (2013b).
12 *Daily Nation* (2013c).
13 *Daily Nation* (2013a).
14 Opiyo (2013).
15 Maina (2013).
16 Nation Correspondent (2014).
17 Munyori (2013).
18 Elbagir (2013).
19 @C_NyakundiH tweet at 8:22 a.m. 23 July 2015, available at https://twitter.com/C_NyaKundiH/status/624087221906329600
20 @durkchild tweet at 7:52 a.m. on 23 July 2015, available at https://twitter.com/durkchild/status/624079529720606720
21 @CKirubi tweet at 11:42 a.m. 23 July 2015, available at https://twitter.com/CKirubi/status/624137472822411264. For an excellent example

of using tweets alongside images, see Christian Dela (@xtiandela)
tweeting on the same issue here, available at https://twitter.com/xtiandela/
status/624163185709457408

22   See Beresford (2016).
23   See Karungu (2018).
24   Press Statement quoted in Mutiga (2015).
25   Tony Maddox quoted in Mutiga (2015).
26   Personal communications.
27   AJ+, 'Fake News and Election Fraud? Not in the US. This is Kenya', 10
      August 2017 (accessed 22 June 2018), available at https://twitter.com/ajplus/
      status/895831718493429760

Chapter 6

1   Bikozulu (2015).
2   Africa Cancer Foundation (2015).
3   Ibid.
4   Ibid.
5   Tweet by @kennytoonz (2015) 'This #Jadudi's thing is fast becoming a
     showbiz and celebrity moment for some people. Kenyans were touched, and
     contributed #JadudiReport' (accessed 16 March 2016), available at https://
     twitter.com/kennytoonz/status/641599724496285698
6   Biko (2015).
7   Zulu (2015).
8   Kimiyu (2015).
9   Pew Research Centre (2008).
10   See generally Bikozulu (2015).

Chapter 7

1   Some of the material in this chapter was published in an article by the author
     in *New African* magazine, November 2015, https://newafricanmagazine.com/
     news-analysis/politics/dress-choice/. Republished with permission.
2   Chege (2016).
3   Name changed to protect her privacy.
4   Specia (2014).
5   Maingi (2014).
6   See e.g. Milner Thornton (2012), pp. 45–47.
7   See generally Gikuyu Centre for Cultural Studies (2014).
8   See Anderson (2000).
9   Ekeh (1975), p. 93.
10   See Kepe and Hall (2018).
11   See Wipper (1975).

12 'The function, the very serious function of racism is distraction. It keeps you from doing your work. It keeps you explaining, over and over again, your reason for being. Somebody says you have no language and you spend twenty years proving that you do. Somebody says your head isn't shaped properly so you have scientists working on the fact that it is. Somebody says you have no art, so you dredge that up. Somebody says you have no kingdoms, so you dredge that up. None of this is necessary. There will always be one more thing.' Morisson (1975).

13 Tribbetts (1994), p. 32.

14 Constitution of Kenya (2010) Chapter 4: Bill of Rights.

15 Kenya National Bureau of Statistics (2018), p. 45.

16 Ligami (2017).

17 Sanya (2013).

18 Rugene (2013).

19 Maina (2013).

20 Kenya Today (2015).

21 See Makong (2018).

22 Kenya National Bureau of Statistics (2015).

23 Nyassy and Otieno (2016).

24 Chege (2016).

25 Wipper (1975).

26 Sami Omar @SamiaOBwana, available at https://twitter.com/SamiaOBwana/status/924864072570376192

27 Constitution of Kenya (2010) Article 81 (b).

28 See Sanya (2013).

29 See Tufecki (2016).

30 Bromwich, Victor and Isaac (2016).

31 Nyabola (2016b).

32 Munguti and Kakah (2016).

33 Wadell (2016).

34 Matfess (2017).

Chapter 8

1 Bernstein (2017a).

2 Ibid.

3 Mayer (2017).

4 Illing (2017).

5 Ibid.

6 Butcher (2017).

7 Mayer (2017).

8 Albright (2017).

9 Illing (2017).

10   de Sousa Santos (2012), p. 44.
11   Keter (2017).
12   Bright (2017).
13   Cambridge Analytica (2017).
14   Ibid.
15   Ibid.
16   Ibid.
17   Channel 4 (2018).
18   Bienkov (2018).
19   Channel 4 (2018).
20   See Ndlela (2015).
21   Channel 4 (2018).
22   BBC News (2013).
23   Warah (2013).
24   Ombara (2016).
25   See Hopkins (2013).
26   Jorgic (2013).
27   Ushahidi (2013), p. 23.
28   See generally, The Real Raila Facebook Page (accessed 4 November 2017).
29   Kelley (2017).
30   Aristotle Inc. (2017).
31   Houreld (2017).
32   Illing (2017).
33   See Lukes (2005).
34   Cilliza (2017).
35   Ndunde (2008).
36   Ibid.
37   Musila (2015), p. 115.
38   Ibid., p. 116.
39   Gathara (2017b).
40   *The East African* (2017).
41   Independent Elections and Boundaries Commission (2017c).
42   Odipo Dev (2017).
43   Wangari (2017).
44   Guy et al. (2010), p. 194.
45   Johannson-Stenman and Martinson (2005), p. 130.
46   See Broderick (2016).
47   Butcher (2017); O'Neil (2016).
48   Ibid.

Chapter 9

1   Ndonga (2017).

2   Griffin (2017).
3   @IEBCKenya on July 30 2017, https://twitter.com/IEBCKenya/status/ 891611472048115712
4   BBC News (2017b).
5   Klopp (2001), p. 486.
6   Ibid.
7   See Oyugi (1997).
8   Ibid.
9   See generally BBC News (1997). See also Press (1993).
10 Human Rights Watch (2002).
11 Maharaj (2002).
12 Canada: Immigration and Refugee Board of Canada (2001).
13 BBC News (2002).
14 See Andreassen and Tostensen (2006).
15 See BBC News (2005).
16 Kenya Judicial Commission Appointed to Inquire into Tribal Clashes in Kenya and Akiwumi (1999).
17 National Accord and Reconciliation Act No. 4 of 2008 (2008).
18 Kenya Law Reform Commission (2008).
19 Konrad Adenauer Foundation (2009).
20 Throup (2003).
21 Constitution of Kenya (2010) Chapter 7, Section 81 (e).
22 See Waweru (2017).
23 Mutahi (2016).
24 Mwangi (2017a).
25 See BBC Africa (2016).
26 Kamau (2017).
27 Private communications with a researcher investigating the firm.
28 de Freytas-tamura (2017).
29 Al Jazeera (2017a).
30 Ng'ethe (2017).
31 Al Jazeera (2017b).
32 van Heerden and Said-Morehouse (2017).
33 Olick and Kadida (2017).
34 Ombuor and Schemm (2017).
35 NASA Coalition (2017); NASA Coalition twitter account @CoalitionNASAKe
36 Nyambura-Mwaura (2017).
37 Burke (2017).
38 Mueni (2017).
39 Ondieki and Mutambo (2017).
40 Obulutsa and Houreld (2017).
41 Nation Newsplex (2017).

42 KTN News (2017).
43 See generally #StopMathareKillings and #StopKisumuKillings on Twitter.
44 Al Jazeera (2017c).
45 Gathara (2017a).
46 See Ochieng' (2017).
47 Illing (2017).
48 See Ball (2017).
49 See Government of Singapore (2018).
50 Scola (2018).
51 Cocco (2018).
52 See Hogan and Safi (2018).
53 Foucault (1980), p. 2.
54 Sanya (2013), p. 16.
55 BBC News (2015b).
56 Kendzior (2017).
57 Said (1979), p. 233.
58 See Kuo (2016); Shoo (2016).
59 Rajab (2017).
60 Phys.org (2017).
61 Wanyoro (2015).
62 Tweet from Kenya Film Classification Board.

Chapter 10

1   Mwangi (2017b).
2   Mwangi (2017c).
3   Mwangi (2017d).
4   Ngina (2017).
5   See Dahir (2017).
6   Agutu (2017).
7   See Omanga (forthcoming).
8   See Kenya Cyber Crimes Act (2018).
9   de Sousa Santos (2012), p. 52.
10 Omanga (forthcoming).
11 The Conversation (2017).

REFERENCES

Adar, Korwa A. and Munyae, Isaac M. (2001) 'Human Rights Abuse in Kenya under Daniel Arap Moi, 1978–2001', *African Studies Quarterly*, vol. 5, no. 1.

AFP (2016) 'Gambia Vote a Roll of the Marbles', *The Telegraph*, 29 November (accessed 4 November 2017), available at https://www.telegraph.co.uk/news/2016/11/29/gambia-vote-roll-marbles/

Africa Cancer Foundation (2015) The Jadudi Report (Nairobi: Africa Cancer Foundation), p. 4, available at https://thejadudireport.files.wordpress.com/2015/10/the-jadudi-report.pdf

African Media Development Initiative (AMDI) (2006) *African Media Development Initiative: Research Summary Report* (London: AMDI).

Africa Review (2017) 'Why NMG writer Walter Menya was Arrested', *East African Standard*, 18 June (accessed 13 November 2017), available at http://www.theeastafrican.co.ke/news/Why-NMG-writer-Walter-Menya-was-arrested/2558-3976408-r3f92h/index.html

Agutu, Nancy (2017) 'Boniface Mwangi Concedes After Jaguar Takes the Lead in Starehe', *The Star*, 9 August (accessed 28 March 2018), available at https://www.the-star.co.ke/news/2017/08/09/boniface-mwangi-concedes-after-jaguar-takes-lead-in-starehe_c1613123

Alal, Maurice and Matete, Faith (2017) 'Kenya Decides: Missing Names, KIEMS total failure in Kisumu', *The Star*, 8 August (accessed 25 October 2017), available at https://www.the-star.co.ke/news/2017/08/08/kenya-decides-missing-names-kiems-total-failure-in-parts-of-kisumu_c1612249

Albright, Jonathan (2017) 'Cambridge Analytica: The Geotargetting and Emotional Data Mining Scripts', *Medium*, 14 October (accessed 4 November 2017), available at https://medium.com/tow-center/cambridge-analytica-the-geotargeting-and-emotional-data-mining-scripts-bcc3c428d77f

Al Jazeera (2017a) 'Protests over Election Fraud Claim Turn Deadly in Kenya', Al Jazeera English, 10 August (accessed 9 November 2017), available at https://www.aljazeera.com/news/2017/08/kenya-police-protesters-clash-poll-fraud-claim-170809081850902.html

Al Jazeera (2017b) 'Kenya Opposition Files Challenge over Election Result', Al Jazeera English, 19 August (accessed 9 November 2017), available at http://www.aljazeera.com/news/2017/08/kenya-opposition-files-challenge-election-results-170819012525410.html

Al Jazeera (2017c) 'At Least 37 People were Killed in Election Violence' in Al Jazeera English, 9 October (accessed 7 November 2017), available at http://www.aljazeera.com/news/2017/10/37-people-killed-election-violence-171009081058361.html

Allison, Simon (2016) 'Blow to Kenya's Media after Editor Sacked for Criticising President', The Guardian Africa Network, 27 January (accessed 22 December 2016), available at https://www.theguardian.com/world/2016/jan/27/blow-to-kenyas-media-after-editor-sacked-for-criticising-president

Anderson, David M. (2000) 'Master and Servant in Colonial Kenya', Journal of African History, vol. 41, no. 3, pp. 459–485.

Andreassen, Bard Anders and Tostensen, Arne (2006) 'Of Oranges and Bananas: The 2005 Kenya Referendum on the Constitution', CMI Working Paper WP 2006:13 (accessed 14 November 2017), available at https://www.cmi.no/publications/2368-of-oranges-and-bananas

Aristotle Inc. (2017) 'About', Aristotle.inc (accessed 4 November 2017), available at http://aristotle.com/

Ball, James (2017) 'A Suspected Network of up to 13,000 Bots Pumped out Pro-Brexit Messages in the Run up to the EU Vote', Buzzed UK, 20 October (accessed 8 November 2017), available at https://www.buzzfeed.com/jamesball/a-suspected-network-of-13000-twitter-bots-pumped-out-pro?utm_term=.pue2WlJjm#.woz0bzvrG

Banda, Fackson, Mudhai, Okoth Fred and Tettey, Wisdom J. (2009) 'Introduction: New Media and Democracy in Africa – A Critical Interjection', African Media and the Digital Public Sphere, ed. Okoth Fred Mudhai, Wisdom Tetey and Fackson Banda (New York: Palgrave Macmillan).

Bannon, Alicia L. (2007) 'Designing a Constitutional Drafting Process: Lessons from Kenya', Yale Law Journal, vol. 116: 1824.

Barasa, Lucas (2013) '200 Kenyans Airlifted from Juba', Daily Nation, 30 December (accessed 14 November 2017), available at http://www.nation.co.ke/news/200-Kenyans-airlifted-from-Juba/1056-2129942-hea5en/index.html

Barkan, Joel D. (2004) 'Kenya after Moi', Foreign Affairs, vol. 83, no. 1, pp. 87–100.

BBC Africa (2006) 'Kenya Admits Raids on Paper', BBC Africa, 2 March (accessed 21 December 2016), available at http://news.bbc.co.uk/2/hi/4765250.stm

BBC Africa (2016) 'Uganda Election: Facebook and Whatsapp Blocked', 18 February (accessed 2 March 2016), available at http://www.bbc.com/news/world-africa-35601220

BBC News (1997) 'Kenya: A Political History', BBC News, 24 December (accessed 7 November 2017), available at http://news.bbc.co.uk/2/hi/special_report/for_christmas/_new_year/kenyan_elections/41737.stm

BBC News (2002) 'Kenya's Election Violence Condemned', BBC News, 23 December (accessed 7 November 2017), available at http://news.bbc.co.uk/2/hi/africa/2602819.stm

BBC News (2005) 'Kenyans Reject New Constitution', BBC World News, 22 November (accessed 31 October 2017), available at http://news.bbc.co.uk/2/hi/africa/4455538.stm

BBC News (2013) 'Did the ICC Help Kenyatta Win the Kenya Election', BBC News, 11 March (accessed 12 November 2017), available at http://www.bbc.com/news/world-africa-21739347

BBC News (2015a) 'Why #KOT is a Force for Change and Comedy', 23 July (accessed 2 March 2016), available at http://www.bbc.com/news/magazine-33629021

BBC News (2015b) 'Facebook Opens Its First Africa Office in Johannesburg', BBC News, 29 June (accessed 28 March 2018), available at http://www.bbc.com/news/world-africa-33310739

BBC News (2017a) 'Kenya's Chase Bank Placed Under Receivership by CBK', BBC Africa, 7 April (accessed 11 November 2017), available at http://www.bbc.com/news/world-africa-35989394

BBC News (2017b) 'Kenyan Election Official Chris Msando Tortured to Death', BBC News, 2 August (accessed 7 November 2017), available at http://www.bbc.com/news/world-africa-40807425

BBC News (2017c) 'After Trump: Big Data Firm Cambridge Analytica is Now Working in Kenya', BBC, 3 August 2017 (accused 3 November 2013), available at http://www.bbc.com/news/blogs-trending-40792078

BBC News (2017d) 'Rwanda Election: Paul Kagame Wins by Landslide', BBC News, 5 August (accessed 11 November 2017), available at http://www.bbc.com/news/world-africa-40822530

BBC Trust (2008) 'The Kenyan 2007 Elections and Their Aftermath: The Role of Media and Communication', The BBC Trust Policy Briefing No.1, April (accessed April 2011), available at http://downloads.bbc.co.uk/worldservice/trust/pdf/kenya_policy_briefing_08.pdf

Beers, David (2006) 'The Public Sphere and Online Independent Journalism', Canadian Journal of Education, vol. 29, no. 1, pp. 109–130.

Bell, Allan (1991) The Language of News Media (Oxford: Blackwell).

Ben-Ari, Elia (2009) 'Twitter: What's all the Chirping About?', BioScience, vol. 58, no. 7, p. 632.

Benkler, Yochai (2007) The Wealth of Networks: How Social Production Transforms Markets and Freedom (New Haven, CT: Yale University Press).

Beresford, Alexander (2016) 'Africa Rising?', Review of African Political Economy, vol. 43, no .147, pp. 1–7.

Berkman Klein Internet Centre Blog (2008) 'Blogs, SMS and the Kenyan Election', Internet and Democracy Blog at Harvard University, 3 January (accessed 13 November 2017), available at http://blogs.harvard.edu/idblog/2008/01/03/blogs-sms-and-the-kenyan-election/

Bernstein, Joseph (2017a) 'Hedge Fund Billionaire Robert Mercer Will Step Down from His Company Following Buzzfeed Expose', Buzzfeed News, 2 November (accessed 2 November 2017), available at https://www.buzzfeed.com/josephbernstein/hedge-fund-billionaire-robert-mercer-steps-down-from-his?utm_term=.odyAKDjR5#.gn3A3VKP8

Bernstein, Joseph (2017b) 'Alt-White: How the Breitbart Machine Laundered Racist Hate', Buzzfeed, 5 October (accessed 2 November 2017), available at https://www.buzzfeed.com/josephbernstein/heres-how-breitbart-and-milo-smuggled-white-nationalism?utm_term=.mlQZDGmab#.kxraAdJDB

Bhatia, Rahul (2016) 'The Inside Story of Facebook's Biggest Setback', The Guardian, 12 May (accessed 27 March 2018), available at https://www.theguardian.com/technology/2016/may/12/facebook-free-basics-india-zuckerberg

Bienkov, Adam (2018) 'Cambridge Analytica Whistleblower Says His Predecessor Was Allegedly Poisoned and the Police Bribed', Business Insider, 27 March (accessed 28 March 2018), available at http://uk.businessinsider.com/cambridge-analytica-whistleblower-christopher-wylie-illegal-trump-brexit-2018-3?IR=T

Biersteker, Ann (2009) 'Horn of Africa and Kenya Diaspora Websites as Alternative Media Sources', Media and Identity in Africa, ed. Kimani Njogu and John Middleton (Bloomington, IN: Indiana University Press and International African Institute).

Biko, Jackson (2015) 'Helping Jadudi Raise Sh. 6.4 Million in Less Than Two Days Made Me Feel Divine', Daily Nation, 13 August (accessed 16 March 2016), available at http://www.nation.co.ke/lifestyle/family/Helping-Jadudi-made-me-feel-proud-and-purposeful-/-/1954198/2831366/-/11vedjgz/-/index.html

Biko Zulu (2015) 'To Be Clear', Bikozulu.co.ke, 22 October (accessed 16 March 2016), available at http://www.bikozulu.co.ke/to-be-clear/

Bikozulu (2015) 'That Thing In Jadudi's Head', Bikozulu.co.ke, 2 August (accessed 15 March 2016), available at http://www.bikozulu.co.ke/that-thing-in-jadudis-head/

Bloggers Association of Kenya (2018) State of the Internet in Kenya: 2017 (Nairobi, Kenya: BAKE).

Bloomberg (2017) 'Company Overview Chase Bank (Kenya) Limited', Bloomberg.com, 11 November (accessed 11 November 2017), available at https://www.bloomberg.com/research/stocks/private/snapshot.asp?privcapId=100705830

Bowles, Nellie (2017) 'How Doxxing Became a Mainstream Tool in the Culture Wars', New York Times, 30 August (accessed 14 November 2017), available at https://www.nytimes.com/2017/08/30/technology/doxxing-protests.html

Boyd, Danah M. and Ellison, Nicole (2007) 'Social Network Sites: Definition, History and Scholarship', Journal of Computer-Mediated Communication, vol. 13, no. 1, pp. 210–230.

Boyd, Joshua (2017) 'What is Dark Social and How Can you Track it?', Brandwatch. com, 8 September (accessed 14 November 2017), available at https://www. brandwatch.com/blog/dark-social-definition-traffic-track/

Brand South Africa (2017) 'A Guide to South African Newspapers', Brand South Africa website (accessed 13 October 2017), available at https://www. brandsouthafrica.com/south-africa-fast-facts/media-facts/a-guide-to-south-african-newspapers

Brewster, Kelly (2016) 'Ethiopian Government Accused of Arresting Family of Melbourne Protesters', ABC Australia news, 2 December (accessed 19 December 2016), available at http://www.abc.net.au/news/2016-12-02/ethiopia-accused-of-arresting-family-of-melbourne-protesters/8075236

Bright, Jake and Hruby, Aubrey (2015) 'The Rise of Silicon Savannah and Africa's Tech Movement', TechHub, 23 July (accessed 3 November 2017), available at https://techcrunch.com/2015/07/23/the-rise-of-silicon-savannah-and-africas-tech-movement/

Bright, Sam (2017) 'After Trump "Big Data" Firm Cambridge Analytica is Now Working in Kenya', BBC Trending, 3 August (accessed 4 November 2017), available at http://www.bbc.com/news/blogs-trending-40792078

Broderick, Ryan (2016) 'This is How Facebook is Radicalising You', Buzzfeed News, 16 November (accessed 6 November 2017), available at https://www.buzzfeed.com/ryanhatesthis/the-far-right-is-a-meme?utm_term=.paNparNlw#.gwG52B1yv

Bromwich, Jonah Engel, Victor, Daniel and Isaac, Mike (2016) 'Police Use Surveillance Tool to Scan Social Media, ACLU Says', New York Times, 11 October (accessed 7 November 2017), available at https://www.nytimes.com/2016/10/12/technology/aclu-facebook-twitter-instagram-geofeedia.html

Buku, Mercy W. and Meredith, Michael W. (2013) 'Safaricom and M-Pesa in Kenya: Financial Inclusion and Financial Integrity', Washington Journal of Law, Technology and Arts, vol. 8, no. 3, pp. 375–400.

Burke, Benjamin (2010) 'Beyond the Online Transaction: Enhancement of Citizen Participation via the Web in Ontario Provincial Government', Handbook of Research on Overcoming Digital Divides: Constructing an Equitable and Competitive Information Society (IGI Global), pp. 500–514.

Burke, Jason (2017) 'Kenya: Odinga Withdraws from Election Rerun', The Guardian, 10 October (accessed 9 November 2017), available at https://www.theguardian.com/world/2017/oct/10/kenya-raila-odinga-withdraws-election

Butcher, Mike (2017) 'Cambridge Analytica CEO Talks to TechCrunch about Trump, Hillary and the Future', TechCrunch.com, 6 November (accessed 6 November 2017), available at https://techcrunch.com/2017/11/06/cambridge-analytica-ceo-talks-to-techcrunch-about-trump-hilary-and-the-future/amp/

Cambridge Analytica (2017) 'Case Studies: Kenya', CA-Political.com, (accessed 4 November 2017), available at https://ca-political.com/casestudies/case studykenya2013

Campbell, Vincent, Gibson, Rachel, Gunter, Barrue and Touri, Maria (2010) 'News Blogs, Mainstream News and News Agencies', *Web Journalism: A New Form Of Citizenship?*, ed. Sean Tunney and Garret Monaghan (Eastbourne: Sussex Academic Press).

Canada: Immigration and Refugee Board of Canada (2001) 'Kenya: Reports of Tribal Clashes in Trans Mara in 1997 and 1999; Which Tribes were Involved; Reasons for the Clashes; Response of the Government', 16 July, KEN37431.E (accessed 7 November 2017), available at http://www.refworld.org/docid/3df4be5219.html

Carter, Cynthia and Steiner, Linda (2004) 'Introduction', in *Critical Readings: Media and Gender*, ed. Cynthia Carter and Linda Steiner (Maidenhead: Open University Press).

Central Bank of Kenya (2016) Press Release: Chase Bank Limited, 7 April (accessed 10 April 2016), available at https://www.centralbank.go.ke/images/docs/MPC%20Press%20Releases/Press_Release_Chase_Bank_Limited_April_7_2016.pdf

Channel 4 (2018) 'Cambridge Analytica Uncovered: Secret Filming Reveals Election Tricks', YouTube.Com, 19 March (accessed 20 March 2018), available at https://www.youtube.com/watch?v=mpbeOCKZFfQ

Chase Bank (2016) Press Statement, 6 April (accessed 4 May 2016), available at https://twitter.com/chasebankkenya/status/717656479445172226

Chege, Njoki (2016) 'City Girl: How to Be a Twitter Feminist in Kenya', *Daily Nation*, 8 January (accessed 16 March 2016), available at http://nairobinews.nation.co.ke/news/city-girl-how-to-be-a-twitter-feminist-in-kenya/

Cheutel, Lynsey (2016) 'Vodacom has Given Up on Revolutionary Service Mobile Money m-Pesa in South Africa', Qz.com, 2 May (accessed 7 November 2017), available at https://qz.com/679059/vodacom-has-given-up-on-revolutionary-mobile-money-service-m-pesa-in-south-africa/

Chimelu, Chiponda (2013) 'Privacy Concerns in Kenya as Users Turn to m-Pesa to Catch Cheating Partners', *Deutsche Welle*, 12 July (accessed 14 November 2017), available at http://www.dw.com/en/privacy-concerns-in-kenya-as-users-turn-to-m-pesa-to-catch-cheating-partners/a-16947446

Chweya, Edward (2016) 'Gitobu Imanyara Recalls Lucy Kibaki's Slap: Mourns her Death', Tuko.co.ke, July (accessed 21 December 2016), available at https://www.tuko.co.ke/122930-former-mp-slapped-lucy-kibaki-say-death.html

Cilliza, Chris (2017) 'Donald Trump Just Claimed He Invented "Fake News"', CNN International, 26 October (accessed 6 November 2017), available at http://www.cnn.com/2017/10/08/politics/trump-huckabee-fake/index.html

Cocco, Frederica (2018) 'EU to Investigate Facebook and Cambridge Analytica Data Usage', *Financial Times*, 19 March (accessed 27 March 2018), available at https://www.ft.com/content/7ded83bc-2b67-11e8-9b4b-bc4b9f08f381

Cocks, Tim (2008) 'Mutilated Bodies Found after Kenya Massacre', Reuters.com, 8 January (accessed 13 November 2017), available at https://www.reuters.com/article/us-kenya-violence-church/mutilated-bodies-found-a-week-after-kenya-massacre-idUSL0847034820080108

Committee to Protect Journalists (2016) 'Gado Blames Government Pressure as Cartoonists Contract at the Nation Ends', CPJ.org, 17 March (accessed 22 December 2016) available at https://cpj.org/blog/2016/03/gado-blames-government-pressure-as-cartoonists-con.php

Committee to Protect Journalists (2017) 'Kenyan Journalist Murdered by Unknown Assailants in Eldoret Town', cpj.org, 1 May (accessed 13 November 2017), available at https://cpj.org/2015/05/kenyan-editor-murdered-by-unknown-assailants-in-el.php

Commonwealth Observer Group (2008) 'Kenya General Election 27 December 2007: The Report of the Commonwealth Observer Group', 7 January.

Communications Authority (2017a) 'First Quarter Statistics Report for the Financial Year 2017/2018', Communications Authority, January 2018 (accessed June 2018), available at http://www.ca.go.ke/images/downloads/STATISTICS/Sector%20Statistics%20Report%20Q1%20%202017-18.pdf

Communications Authority (2017b) 'Kenya's Mobile Penetration Reaches 88%', First Quarter Sector Statistics Report for the Financial Year 2015/2016, Communications Authority, December 2016 (accessed 2 November 2017), available at http://www.ca.go.ke/images/downloads/STATISTICS/Sector%20%20Statistics%20Report%20Q1%202015-16.pdf

Constitution of Kenya (2010) Chapter 7, Section 81 (e).

The Conversation (2017) 'Kenya Targets WhatsApp Admins in its Fight Against Hate Speech', *The Star*, 1 September (accessed 24 June 2018), available at https://www.the-star.co.ke/news/2017/09/01/kenya-targets-whatsapp-admins-in-its-fight-against-hate-speech_c1627669

Cornwall, Andrea (2005) 'Introduction', in *Readings in Gender in Africa*, ed. Andrea Cornwall (Bloomington, IN: Indiana University Press).

Curran, James (2002) 'Newspapers: The Sociology of the Press', in *The Media: An Introduction*, ed. Adam Briggs and Paul Cobley (Harlow: Pearson Education).

Dahir, Abdi Latif (2017) 'Kenya is Set to Hold One of the Most Expensive Elections in Africa', *Quartz Africa*, 18 July (accessed 12 November 2017), available at https://qz.com/1030958/kenyas-elections-will-cost-1-billion-in-government-and-campaign-spend/

Daily Nation (2013a) 'Pain, Desperation at Kenyatta and Mbagathi Hospitals as Doctors Down Their Tools', Daily Nation.com, 10 December (accessed

22 December 2016), available at http://www.nation.co.ke/news/Kenyatta-Mbagathi-Hospitals-Doctors-Strike/1056-2106882-26dxefz/index.html

Daily Nation (2013b) 'Gunmen Kill 8 Kenyans Near Somali Border', Daily Nation, 13 December (accessed 22 December 2016), available at http://www.nation.co.ke/news/africa/Gunmen-kill-eight-Kenyans-near-Somali-border/1066-2106890-rvbnqu/index.html

Daily Nation (2013c) 'Media Owners to Fight New Law Gagging Reporters', Daily Nation, 17 December (accessed 22 December 2016), available at http://www.nation.co.ke/news/politics/Media-owners-to-fight-the-new-law--gagging-reporters/1064-2116536-q2kohm/index.html

Daily Nation (2013d) 'Kenyans Unite in Marking 50 Years of Independence', Daily Nation, 12 December (accessed 22 December 2016) available at http://www.nation.co.ke/news/Kenyans-unite-in-marking-50-years-of-independence/1056-2109544-70ami/index.html

Daily Nation (2013e) Profile: Anne Waiguru, 25 December (accessed 10 January 2017), available at http://www.nation.co.ke/news/politics/Profile-Anne-Waiguru/1064-1757980-tr5xc4z/index.html

de Freytas-tamura, Kimiko (2017) 'Kenya Election Returns Were Hacked', New York Times, 9 August (accessed 7 November 2017), available at https://www.nytimes.com/2017/08/09/world/africa/kenya-election-results-raila-odinga.html

De Smedt, Johan (2009) 'No Raila! No Peace! Big Man Politics and Election Violence at the Kibera Grassroots', African Affairs, vol. 108, no., pp. 581–598.

de Sousa Santos, Boaventura (2012) 'Public Sphere and Epistemologies of the South', Africa Development, vol. 37, no. 1, pp. 43–67.

Devichand, Mukul (2016) 'Did Aylan Kurdi's Death Change Anything?', BBC Trending, 2 September (accessed 11 November 2017), available at http://www.bbc.com/news/blogs-trending-37257869

Dialogue Africa Foundation (2009) 'Kreisler and Waki Reports: Summarised Version', Dialogue Africa Foundation (Nairobi: Konrad Adenauer Foundation).

DW.com (2016) 'Internet Shutdowns: An Explainer', DW.com, 12 December (accessed 23 December 2016), available at http://www.dw.com/en/internet-shutdowns-an-explainer/a-36731481

The East African (2017) 'Kenya's Campaign Now in Doubt as Poll Costs Shoot to $500 Million', East African, 16 July (accessed 14 November 2017), available at http://www.theeastafrican.co.ke/news/Kenya-most-expensive-elections-in-the-world-/2558-4016484-5dw5jhz/index.html

Ecole Polytechnique Federale de Lausanne (2014) 'Surveying African Cities Using Twitter', 30 April (accessed 27 February 2016), available at http://actu.epfl.ch/news/surveying-african-cities-using-twitter/

The Economist (2014) 'Baobab: A Million Conversations Now', 7 May (accessed 27 February 2015), available at http://www.economist.com/blogs/baobab/2014/05/twitter-kenya

Ekeh, Peter (1975) 'Colonialism and the Two Publics in Africa: A Theoretical Statement', *Comparative Studies in History and Society*, vol. 17, no. 1, pp. 91–112.

Elbagir, Nima (2013) 'Armed and Ready to Vote', CNN International website, 28 February (accessed 9 March 2016), available at http://edition.cnn.com/videos/international/2013/02/28/elbagir-kenya-armed.cnn

Elliot, Roxana (2015) 'Data on Newspaper, Magazine Readership in Kenya', GeoPOll Surveys, 13 February (accessed 31 October 2017), available at http://blog.geopoll.com/data-on-newspaper-magazine-readership-in-kenya

Eordorgh, Fruszina (2015) 'Inside an Instagram Bot Farm', Motherboard, 10 August (accessed 13 November 2017), available at https://motherboard.vice.com/en_us/article/4x3zy9/inside-an-instagram-bot-farm

European Union Elections Observation Mission (EUEOM) (2008) 'Preliminary Statement: Doubts about the Credibility of the Presidential Results Hamper Kenya's Democratic Progress', 1 January.

Facebook (2014) 'The New Facebook Login and Graph API 2.0', Facebook.com, 30 April (accessed 27 March 2018), available at https://developers.facebook.com/blog/post/2014/04/30/the-new-facebook-login

Fairclough, Norman (2001) *Language and Power* (Harlow: Pearson Education).

Fildes, Nic and Aglionby, John (2017) 'Vodafone Transfers Stake in Kenya Operator Safaricom to Vodacom', *Financial Times*, 15 May (accessed 7 November 2017), available at https://www.ft.com/content/bbbb386e-3956-11e7-ac89-b01cc67cfeec

Filipovic, Jill (2007) 'Blogging White Female: How Internet Misogyny Parallels Real-World Harasment', *Yale Journal of Law and Feminism*, vol. 19, pp. 295–304.

Foucault, Michel (1980) *Power/Knowledge: Selected Interviews and Other Writings 1972–1977* (New York: Vintage).

Friederici, Nicolas, Ojanperä, Sanna and Graham, Mark (2016) 'The Impact of Connectivity in Africa: Grand Visions and the Mirage of Inclusive Digital Development', *Electronic Journal of Information Systems in Developing Countries*, available at https://papers.ssrn.com/sol3/papers.cfm?abstract_id=2855398

Galava, Dennis (2016) 'Mr. President Get Your Act Together This Year', *Saturday Nation*, 1 January (accessed 22 December 2016), available at http://www.nation.co.ke/oped/Editorial/Mr-President-get-your-act-together-this-year/-/440804/3018414/-/pwgeuq/-/index.html

Gathara, Patrick (2017a) 'Broken News: Kenyan Media's Election Coverage Betrayed Kenya', *The Elephant*, 14 September (accessed 7 November 2017), available at https://www.theelephant.info/media-analysis/2017/09/14/broken-news-kenyan-medias-election-coverage-betrayed-kenyans/

Gathara, Patrick (2017b) 'Betrayal in the Kenyan Media', *Gathara's World*, 20 August (accessed 4 November 2017), available at http://gathara.blogspot.co.ke/2017/08/betrayal-in-kenyan-media.html

Genga, Bella (2016) 'Chase Bank Executives Resign After Earnings Restated', *Bloomberg Africa*, 6 April (accessed 11 April 2016), available at http://www.bloomberg.com/news/articles/2016-04-06/chase-bank-kenya-says-operations-are-sound-as-results-restated?cmpid=twtr1

Gertz, Geoffrey (2009) 'Kenya's Trade Liberalisation of the 1980s and 1990s: Policies, Impacts and Limitations', Background Paper to the Impact of the Doha Round on Kenya, available at https://carnegieendowment.org/files/kenya_background.pdf

Gikuyu Centre for Cultural Studies (2014) 'Gikuyu Sexual Training for Youth – Ngwiko', Gikuyu Centre for Cultural Studies blog, 4 July (accessed 14 November 2017), available at https://mukuyu.wordpress.com/tag/kikuyu-sexual-practices/

Goldstein, Joshua and Rotich, Juliana (2008) 'Digitally Networked Technology in Kenya's 2007 – 2008 Post-Election Crisis', Internet and Democracy Series for the Berkman-Klein Centre for Internet and Society at Harvard University, September (accessed 11 March 2016), available at https://cyber.harvard.edu/publications/2008/Digitally_Networked_Technology_Kenyas_Post-Election_Crisis

Government of Singapore (2018) 'Facebook's Statement and Conduct on the Cambridge Analytica Data Breaches', YouTube.com, 22 March (accessed 27 March 2018), available at https://www.youtube.com/watch?v=A7gJPjLt4Dw

Griffin, Tamerra (2017) 'Who Killed Chris Msando', Buzzed News, 5 October (accessed 7 November 2017), available at https://www.buzzfeed.com/tamerragriffin/kenya-chris-msando-murder?utm_term=.tbeXxB7Ew#.krl3QRVel

The Guardian (2018) 'The Cambridge Analytica Files: A Year Long Investigation into Facebook, Data, and Influencing Elections in the Digital Age', *The Guardian*, March (accessed 27 March 2018), available at https://www.theguardian.com/news/series/cambridge-analytica-files

Guy, Ido, Zwerdling, Naama, Ronen, Inbal, Carmel, David and Uziel, Erel (2010) 'Social Media Recommendation Based on People or Tags', in SIGIR'10, 19–23 July 2010, Geneva, Switzerland, pp. 194–201.

Habermas, Jürgen, et al. (1974) 'The Public Sphere: An Encyclopedia Article (1964)', *New German Critique*, no. 3, pp. 49–55.

Habermas, Jürgen (1992) *The Structural Transformation of the Public Sphere* (London: Polity).

Hargittai, Eszter, Gallo, Jason and Kane, Matthew (2008) 'Cross-Ideological Discussions among Conservative and Liberal Bloggers', *Public Choice*, vol. 134, pp. 67–86.

Hatem Ali, A. H. (2011) 'The Power of Social Media in Developing Nations: New Tools for Closing the Global Digital Divide and Beyond', *Harvard Human Rights Journal*, vol. 24.

Haugerud, Angelique (1993) *The Culture of Politics in Modern Kenya* (Cambridge: Cambridge University Press).

Hogan, Libby and Safi, Michael (2018) 'Revealed: Facebook Hate Speech Exploded in Myanmar during Rohignya Crisis', *The Guardian*, 3 April (accessed 22 June 2018), available at https://www.theguardian.com/world/2018/apr/03/revealed-facebook-hate-speech-exploded-in-myanmar-during-rohingya-crisis

Holland, Patricia (2004) 'The Politics of the Smile', *Critical Readings: Media and Gender*, ed. Cynthia Carter and Linda Steiner (Maidenhead: Open University Press).

Hopkins, Curt (2013) 'How Technology is Shaping Kenya's Decisive Elections', *Daily Dot*, 13 February (accessed 4 November 2017), available at https://www.dailydot.com/layer8/kenyan-election-2013-technology-umati/

Houreld, Katherine (2017) 'Foreigners Working with Kenyan Opposition Manhandled by the Police before being Deported', Reuters.com, 6 August (accessed 4 November 2017), available at https://www.usnews.com/news/world/articles/2017-08-06/foreigners-working-with-kenyan-opposition-manhandled-by-police-before-being-deported

Houreld, Katherine and Miriri, Duncan (2017) 'Kenyan President Kenyatta Wins 98% of Vote in Repeat Election', Reuters, 30 October (accessed 11 November 2017), available at http://www.reuters.com/article/us-kenya-election-kenyatta/kenyan-president-kenyatta-wins-98-percent-of-vote-in-repeat-election-idUSKBN1CZ1SE

How, Tan Tarn, Hui, Ting Ying and Yeo, Andrew (2016) 'Slow Beginnings: WhatsApp as a Political Communication Tool', IPSCommons, 2 April (accessed 14 November 2017), available at https://www.ipscommons.sg/will-whatsapp-swing-bukit-batok/

Howden, Daniel (2013) 'Terror in Nairobi: The Full Story behind Al Shabaab's Mall Attack', *The Guardian*, 4 October (accessed 14 November 2017), available at https://www.theguardian.com/world/2013/oct/04/westgate-mall-attacks-kenya

Human Rights House (2008) 'I acted under pressure – says Electoral Commission Chairman, Kivuitu,' Nairobi, 2 January, also available at https://humanrightshouse.org/articles/i-acted-under-pressure-says-electoral-commission-chairman-kivuitu/ (accessed, February 24, 2008).

Human Rights Watch (2002) 'Case Study: Armed Political Violence at the Coast', in *Playing with Fire: Weapons Proliferation, Political Violence and Human Rights in Kenya* (New York: HRW), available at https://www.hrw.org/reports/2002/kenya/Kenya0502-06.htm

Human Rights Watch (2008) *Ballots to Bullets: Organised Political Violence and Kenya's Crisis of Governance* (New York: HRW).

iHub Research (2014) *Umati: Monitoring Dangerous Online Speech: October 2012 to January 2013* (Nairobi: iHub), available at https://files.ihub.co.ke/ihubresearch/uploads/2013/february/1361013008_819_929.pdf

Illing, Sean (2017) 'Cambridge Analytica: The Shady Data Firm that Might be a Key Trump-Russia Link, Explained', Vox.Com, 22 October (accessed 4 November 2017), available at https://www.vox.com/policy-and-politics/2017/10/16/15657512/cambridge-analytica-trump-kushner-flynn-russia

Independent Election and Boundaries Commission (2017a) 'Electronic Voter Identification System (EVID)', (accessed 7 November 2017), available at https://www.iebc.or.ke/election/technology/?Electronic_Voter_Identification_System_(EVID)

Independent Election and Boundaries Commission (2017b) 'Electronic Voter Identification System (EVID)', (accessed 7 November 2017), available at https://www.iebc.or.ke/election/technology/?Results_Transmission_And_Presentation_(RTS)

Independent Elections and Boundaries Commission (2017c) 'Nominated Candidates for the August 8 2017 General Election', *The Kenya Gazette*, no. 6253, 27 June 2017.

The Information Communications and Technology Practitioner's Bill (2016) http://kenyalaw.org/kl/fileadmin/pdfdownloads/bills/2016/Information CommunicationTechnologyPractitioners_Bill_2016.pdf

International Parliamentary Union (2008) 'Kenya: National Assembly', IPU website, (accessed 13 November 2017), available at http://archive.ipu.org/parline-e/reports/arc/2167_07.htm

Internet World Stats (2018) Kenya: Internet World Stats and Market Reports, 20 November 2017 (accessed 21 June 2018), available at https://www.internetworldstats.com/af/ke.htm

Johannson-Stenman, Olaf and Martinson, Peter (2005) 'Honestly, Why Do You Drive a BMW?', *Journal of Economic Behaviour and Organisation*, vol. 60, pp. 129–146.

Jorgic, Drazen (2013) 'Kenya Tracks Facebook, Twitter for Hate Speech', Reuters, 3 February (accessed July 2018), available at https://www.reuters.com/article/net-us-kenya-elections-socialmedia/kenya-tracks-facebook-twitter-for-election-hate-speech-idUSBRE9140IS20130205?feedType=RSS&feedName e=internetNews

Jubilee Manifesto (2012) 'Information and Communication Technology (ICT): Digital Takeoff', The Harmonised Jubilee Coalition Manifesto by H.E. President Uhuru Kenyatta.

Kamau, John (2017) 'Puzzle of French Hand in Electoral Body's Deals', *Daily Nation*, 1 April (accessed 7 November 2017), available at http://www.nation.co.ke/news/puzzle-of-french-hand-in-iebc-deals/1056-3873860-h82288z/index.html

Karanja, Michael (2016) 'Chase Bank Placed under Receivership: Branches and ATMs Closed', *Citizen Digital*, 7 April (accessed 11 April 2016), available at http://citizentv.co.ke/news/chase-bank-placed-under-receivership-branches-and-atms-closed-121656/

Karungu, Francis (2018) 'Runaway Corruption in Kenya is a Project of Political Leadership', *The Star*, 31 May (accessed 22 June 2018), available at https://www.standardmedia.co.ke/article/2001282408/runaway-corruption-in-kenya-is-a-project-of-political-leadership

Katz, James E. and Lai, Chih-Hui (2009) 'News Blogging in Cross-Cultural Contexts: A Report on the Struggle for Voice', *Knowledge Technology and Politics*, vol. 22, pp. 95–107.

Kazeem, Yomi (2016) 'Politics and Activism are Driving Africa's Twitter Conversations to New Highs', *Quartz Africa*, 6 April (accessed 22 December 2016), available at http://qz.com/654958/politics-and-activism-are-driving-africas-twitter-conversations-to-new-highs/

Kelley, Kevin J. (2017) 'Deported US Data Boss Phillips Tells of Painful Experience', *Daily Nation*, 7 August (accessed 28 March 2018), available at https://www.nation.co.ke/news/Deported-US-data-firm-boss-Phillips-tells-of-painful-experience/1056-4049056-kde90tz/index.html

Kendzior, Sarah (2017) 'Russia's Social Media Propaganda Was Hiding in Plain Sight', NBC News.com, 2 November (accessed 8 November 2017), available at https://www.nbcnews.com/think/amp/ncna816886

Kenya Judicial Commission Appointed to Inquire into Tribal Clashes in Kenya, and Akiwumi, A. M. (1999) *Report of the Judicial Commission Appointed to Inquire into Tribal Clashes in Kenya* (Nairobi, The Commission).

Kenya Cyber Crimes Bill (2016) (Proposed).

Kenya Elections Domestic Observation Forum (KEDOF) (2007) 'Preliminary Press Statement and Verdict of the 2007 Kenya General Election', 31 December.

Kenya Information and Communications Act, CAP411 A[Rev. 2009] Section 29.

Kenya Law Reform Commission (2008) 'Our Work', KLRC.com, 2017 (accessed 7 November 2017), available at http://www.klrc.go.ke/index.php/our-work/national-accord-and-agenda-four-commissions

Kenya National Bureau of Statistics (2015) K*enya Demographic and Health Survey: Domestic Violence* (Nairobi: KNBS).

Kenya National Bureau of Statistics (2018) *Women and Men in Kenya: Facts and Figures 2017* (Nairobi: KNBS).

Kenya National Commission on Human Rights (2017) *Mirage at Dusk: A Human Rights Account of the Kenyan 2017 Election* (Nairobi, Kenya: KNCHR).

Kenya Today (2015) '#JusticeForKhadija: IG Boinett Promises Justice for Mandera Girl Burnt by Her Husband', *Kenya Today*, 3 May (accessed 30 March 2016), available at https://www.kenya-today.com/news/justiceforkhadija-ig-joseph-boinnet-promises-justice-for-mandera-girl-burnt-by-husband

Kenyanito, Ephraim (2014) 'Surveillance in a Legal Vacuum: Kenya Considers Massive New Spying System', AccessNow.org, 13 June (accessed 14 November 2017), available at https://www.accessnow.org/surveillance-in-a-legal-vacuum-kenya-considers-massive-new-spying-system/

Kepe, Thembele and Hall, Ruth (2018) 'Land Distribution in South Africa: Towards Decolonisation or Recolonisation', *Politikon: South African Journal of Political Studies*, vol. 45, no. 1, pp. 128–137.

Keter, Gideon (2017) 'Uhuru hires data firm behind Trump, Brexit Victories', *The Star*, 10 May (accessed 3 November 2017), available at https://www.the-star.co.ke/news/2017/05/10/uhuru-hires-data-firm-behind-trump-brexit-victories_c1557720

Kiberenge, Kenfrey (2015) 'How Jubilee Lost the Social Media Plot', *Nairobi News*, 8 December (accessed 9 March 2016), available at http://nairobinews.nation.co.ke/news/digital-vs-analogue-the-sad-tale-of-uhurutos-presidency/

Kimiyu, Hillary (2015) 'Scandal: The Sh 7 Million Rip-Off that was the Jadudi Campaign', *Nairobi News*, 21 October (accessed 16 March 2016), available at http://nairobinews.nation.co.ke/news/what-kenyans-werent-told-about-the-scandalous-jadudi-campaign/

Kiprono, Dennis (2016) '"Misuse of a Telecoms Device" Abuses the Constitution', 1 February (accessed 2 March 2016), available at http://www.the-star.co.ke/news/2016/02/01/misuse-of-licensed-telecoms-device-abuses-the-constitution_c1285726

Kisero, Jaindi (2015) 'How Managing Finances Separates Performers from Banana Republics', *Daily Nation*, 28 July (accessed 10 January 2017), available at http://www.nation.co.ke/oped/Opinion/How-managing-finances-separates-performers-from-banana-republics/440808-2812398-d5mra8z/index.html

Klopp, Jacqueline M. (2001) '"Ethnic Clashes" and Winning Elections: The Case of Kenya's Electoral Despotism', *Canadian Journal of African Studies*, vol. 35, no. 3, pp. 473–517.

Konrad Adenauer Foundation (2009) The Kriegler and Waki Commission Reports: Summarised Version (Berlin, Germany), available at http://www.kas.de/kenia/en/publications/16094/v

Kriegler Commission (2008) Summary and Recommendations.

Krippendorf, Klaus (2004) *Content Analysis: An Introduction to its Methodology* (London: Sage).

Kroll, Andy (2018) 'Cloak and Data: The Real Story behind Cambridge Analytica's Rise and Fall', *Mother Jones*, May/June (accessed 27 March 2018), available at https://www.motherjones.com/politics/2018/03/cloak-and-data-cambridge-analytica-robert-mercer/

KTN News (2017) 'Commission Reverts to Manual Transmission of Results', KTN News, 15 October (accessed 9 November 2017), available at https://www.youtube.com/watch?v=DPAyiiM9Zo0

Kuo, Lily (2016) 'Kenya Police are Routinely Killing Citizens and The Public is Finally Saying Stop', *QZ*, 4 July (accessed 14 November 2017), available at https://qz.com/723039/kenyan-police-are-routinely-executing-citizens-and-the-public-is-finally-saying-stop/

Kuo, Lily (2017) 'A Quarter of Kenya's Electronic Voting Stations Won't Have Network Coverage to Send the Results', *QZ Africa*, 7 August (accessed 25 October 2017), available at https://qz.com/1047519/a-quarter-of-kenyas-electronic-voting-stations-wont-have-network-coverage-to-send-the-results/

Kweyu, Dorothy (2008) 'Let's Not Forget About Justice in Our Quest for Peace', *Daily Nation*, 8 January.

Lang'at, Patrick (2017) 'Wafula Chebukati: I Can't Guarantee Credible Election on October 26', *Daily Nation*, 18 October (accessed 7 November 2017), available at http://www.nation.co.ke/news/Wafula-Chebukati-on-repeat-presidential-election/1056-4145232-oyj67sz/index.html

Lang'at, Patrick (2017) 'IEBC: Here's Our Proof of 7.6 m Turnout in Kenya's Repeat Poll', *Daily Nation*, 1 November (accessed 11 November 2017), available at http://www.nation.co.ke/news/IEBC-Kenya-repeat-election-turnout-/1056-4164536-adhopgz/index.html

Langman, Lauren (2005) 'From Virtual Public Spheres to Global Justice: A Critical Theory of Internetworked Social Movements', *Sociological Theory*, vol. 23, no. 1, pp. 42–74.

Li, Xigen (2006) 'News of Priority Issues in Print versus Internet Newspapers', in *Internet Newspapers*, ed. Xigen Li (New Jersey: Lawrence Erlbaum Associates).

Ligami, Christine (2017) 'Kenya Lifts Ban on Sending Domestic Workers Overseas', *NewsDeeply*, 13 December (accessed 28 March 2018), available at https://www.newsdeeply.com/womensadvancement/articles/2017/12/13/kenya-lifts-ban-on-sending-domestic-workers-to-the-middle-east

Lukes, Steven (2005) *Power: A Radical View* (Basingstoke: Macmillan).

Madrigal, Alexis C. (2012) 'Dark Social: We have the Whole History of the Internet Wrong', *The Atlantic*, 12 October (accessed 14 November 2017), available at https://www.theatlantic.com/technology/archive/2012/10/dark-social-we-have-the-whole-history-of-the-web-wrong/263523/

Magara, Emeka-Makaya (2009) 'The Incident that Transformed Kenya into a De Facto One Party State', *Daily Nation*, 23 October (accessed 13 November 2017), available at http://www.nation.co.ke/news/politics/1064-676220-76oxayz/index.html

Maharaj, Davan (2002) 'Rights Group Blames Ruling Party for 1997 Kenyan Violence', *LA Times*, 1 June (accessed 7 November 2017), available at http://articles.latimes.com/2002/jun/01/world/fg-kenya1

Maina, Samwel Born (2013) 'Jubilee on the Spot Over the Unfulfilled Promises', *Daily Nation*, 30 December (accessed 22 December 2016), available at http://www.nation.co.ke/news/Jubilee-on-the-spot-over-the-unfulfilled-promises/1056-2129946-159v3liz/index.html

Maina, Simon (2013) 'Women Demand Justice for Liz', *Daily Nation*, 31 October, (accessed 30 March 2016), available at http://www.nation.co.ke/photo/-/1951220/2056168/-/aw2lc8/-/index.html

Maingi, Muthoni (2014) 'Letter from Nairobi: Mother's Mobilise for Women's Rights Using Social Media', BDLive, 18 November (accessed 23 March 2016), available at http://www.bdlive.co.za/opinion/columnists/2014/11/18/letter-from-nairobi-mothers-mobilise-for-womens-rights-using-social-media

Makinen, Maarit and Kuira, Mary Wangu (2008) 'Social Media and Postelection Crisis in Kenya', International Journal of Press/Politics, vol. 13, pp. 328–355.

Makong, Bruhan (2018) 'Wajir Leaders Condemn the Use of Maslaha to Resolve Rape Cases', Daily Nation, 26 February (accessed 28 March 2018), available at https://www.nation.co.ke/counties/wajir/Use-of-maslaha-to-resolve-rape-cases/3444790-4320604-dt3yxp/index.html

Mantzarlis, Alexios (2017) 'Most Kenyans Have Seen Fake News', Poynter.org, 20 July (accessed 13 November 2017), available at https://www.poynter.org/news/most-kenyans-have-seen-fake-news-according-new-report

Matfess, Hilary (2017) 'Three Years Later, A Look at the #BringBackOurGirls Catch-22', The Daily Beast, 14 April (accessed 9 November 2017), available at https://www.thedailybeast.com/three-years-later-a-look-at-the-bringbackourgirls-catch-22

Mayer, Jane (2017) 'The Reclusive Hedge Fund Behind Trump's Presidency', The New Yorker, 27 March (accessed 4 November 2017), available at https://www.newyorker.com/magazine/2017/03/27/the-reclusive-hedge-fund-tycoon-behind-the-trump-presidency

Mbugua, Ng'ang'a (2013) 'Uhuru and Ruto's State House Show', Daily Nation, 23 April (accessed 22 December 2016), available at http://www.nation.co.ke/news/politics/Uhuru-and-Rutos-State-House-show/1064-1756672-7gy0fe/index.html

Mbuthia, Wambui (2017) 'Statement by IEBC over KIEMS Kit Triggered an Uproar from Kenyans on Social Media', The Standard U Report, 30 October (accessed 12 November 2017), available at https://www.standardmedia.co.ke/ureport/article/2001258820/statement-by-iebc-over-kiems-kits-triggered-an-uproar-from-kenyans-on-social-media

McConnell, Tristan (2015) 'Close Your Eyes and Pretend To be Dead: What Really Happened Two Years Ago in the Bloody Attack in Nairobi's Westgate Mall', Foreign Policy, 20 September (accessed 14 November 2017), available at http://foreignpolicy.com/2015/09/20/nairobi-kenya-westgate-mall-attack-al-shabab/

Merriam Webster: Press Release (2006) '2006 Word of The Year', Merriam-Webster.com, December (accessed 22 December 2016), available at https://www.merriam-webster.com/press-release/2006-word-of-the-year

Mikell, Gwendolyn (1997) 'Introduction', in African Feminism: The Politics of Survival in Sub-Saharan Africa, ed. Gwendolyn Mikell (Philadelphia, PA: University of Pennsylvania Press).

Milner Thornton, Juliette Bridgette (2012) *The Long Shadow of the British Empire: The Ongoing Legacies of Race and Class in Africa* (Basingstoke: Palgrave Macmillan).

Mochama, Tony (2014) 'Why I Stopped Being a "Concerned Kenyan Writer"', *The Standard*, 27 December (accessed 27 March 2017), available at https://www.standardmedia.co.ke/lifestyle/article/2000145978/no-longer-at-ease-why-i-stopped-being-a-concerned-kenyan

Morisson, Toni (1975) 'A Humanist View', 30 May, part of the Black Studies Centre for Dialogue (lecture) (accessed 14 November 2017), available at https://soundcloud.com/portland-state-library/portland-state-black-studies-1

Mudhai, Okoth Fred; Tettey Wisdom and Banda, Fackson (eds) (2009) *African Media and the Digital Public Sphere* (New York: Palgrave Macmillan).

Mueller, Susanne D. (2008) 'The Political Economy of Kenya's Crisis', *Journal of Eastern African Studies*, vol. 2, no. 2, pp. 185–210.

Muendo, Mercy (2017) 'Kenya Targets WhatsApp Admins in Its Fight Against Hate Speech', *The Star*, 1 September (accessed 19 June 2018), available at https://www.the-star.co.ke/news/2017/09/01/kenya-targets-whatsapp-admins-in-its-fight-against-hate-speech_c1627669

Mueni, Jemimah (2017) 'Fresh Twirl as Court Orders IEBC to Include Aukot in October 26 Poll', Capital FM, 11 October (accessed 9 November 2017), available at https://www.capitalfm.co.ke/news/2017/10/fresh-twirl-court-orders-iebc-include-aukot-oct-26-poll/

Munda, Constant (2017) 'Transactions through Mobile Money Platforms Close to Half of GDP', *Business Daily*, 2 August (accessed 14 November 2017), available at http://www.businessdailyafrica.com/news/Yearly-mobile-money-deals-close-GDP/539546-4041614-f1vjudz/index.html

Munguti, Richard and Kakah, Maureen (2016) 'Deputy President William Ruto Sues Activist Boniface Mwangi for Defamation', *Daily Nation*, 7 October (accessed 23 December 2016), available at http://www.nation.co.ke/news/Ruto-sues-activist-Boniface-Mwangi-for-defamation/1056-3408304-ujh256/

Munyori, Wagema (2013) 'Golden Jubilee Fete sets Twitter Abuzz', *Daily Nation*, 12 December (accessed 22 December 2016), available at http://www.nation.co.ke/news/Golden-jubilee-fete-sets-Twitter-abuzz--/1056-2109996-uy23caz/index.html

Murunga, Godwin R. and Nasong'o, Shadrack W. (2006) 'Bent on Self-Destruction: The Kibaki Regime in Kenya', *Journal of Contemporary African Studies*, vol. 24, no. 1, pp. 1–28.

Musila, Grace (2015) *A Death Retold in Truth and Rumour: Kenya, Britain and the Julie Ward Murder* (London: James Currey).

Mustapha, Abdul Raufu (2012) 'The Public Sphere in 21st Century Africa: Broadening the Horizons of Democratisation', *African Development*, vol. 37, no. 1, pp. 27–41.

Mutai, Edwin (2016) 'Internet, Phones Blocked as House Debates Election Laws', 20 December (accessed 21 December 2016), available at http://www.businessdailyafrica.com/Internet--phones-blocked-as-House-debates-election-laws/539546-3493404-ucr0v7z/

Mutahi, Patrick (2016) 'Eight Years Later, Little Has Been Learnt from the Kriegler Commission', *Daily Nation*, 16 May 2016 (accessed 7 November 2017), available at http://www.nation.co.ke/oped/opinion/-little-has-been-learnt-from-the-Kriegler-Commission/440808-3204984-6rgechz/index.html

Muthuri, Robert (2017) 'Internet Speed Throttling Surrounding Repeat Election', Strathmore University Centre for Intellectual Property and Information Technology Law (CIPIT) blog, 29 October (accessed 7 November 2017), available at http://blog.cipit.org/2017/10/29/internet-speed-throttling-surrounding-repeat-election/

Mutiga, Murithi (2015) 'CNN Executive Flies to Kenya to Apologise over "Hotbed of Terror" Claim', *The Guardian*, 14 August (accessed 9 March 2016), available at http://www.theguardian.com/world/2015/aug/14/cnn-kenya-apologise-obama

Mutunga, Kamau (2012) 'Moment of Bravado that Changed Kenya', *Daily Nation*, 31 July (accessed 13 November 2017), available at http://www.nation.co.ke/lifestyle/dn2/How-1982-coup-changed-Kenya/957860-1467488-13vl42az/index.html

Mwangi, William (2017a) 'Over 11,000 Polling Stations Lack Network Coverage, Returning Officers to "Move" to Relay Results', *The Star*, 6 August (accessed 7 November 2017), available at https://www.the-star.co.ke/news/2017/08/06/over-11000-polling-stations-lack-network-coverage-returning-officers_c1611185

Mwangi, William (2017b) 'Boniface Mwangi Launches Ukweli Party, Promises to Take Street Fights to Parliament', *The Star*, 20 March (accessed 28 March 2018), available at https://www.the-star.co.ke/news/2017/03/20/boniface-mwangi-launches-ukweli-party-promises-to-take-street-fights_c1528032

Mwangi, William (2017c) 'Supporters Raise Sh. 160,000 for Boniface Mwangi Starehe MP Campaign', *The Star*, 24 March (accessed 28 March 2018), available at https://www.the-star.co.ke/news/2017/03/24/supporters-raise-sh160000-for-boniface-mwangi-starehe-mp-campaign_c1531083

Mwangi, William (2017d) 'I'll Account for the 10 Million Raised for my Starehe MP Campaign – Boniface Mwangi', *The Star*, 20 August (accessed 28 March 2018), available at https://www.the-star.co.ke/news/2017/08/20/ill-account-for-the-sh10-million-raised-for-my-starehe-mp-campaign_c1619742

Mwaniki, Charles (2016) 'Chase Bank Shocks Market with 8 Billion Secret Insider Loans', *Business Daily*, 7 April (accessed 11 November 2017), available at http://www.businessdailyafrica.com/corporate/Chase-Bank-shocks-market-with-Sh8bn-secret-insider-loans/539550-3149358-2txgo3z/index.html

Naím, Mosés (2000) 'Washington Consensus or Washington Confusion?', *Foreign Policy*, no. 118, pp. 86–103.

Nakashima, Ellen (2007) 'Sexual Threats Stifle Some Female Bloggers', *The Washington Post*, 30 April (accessed 10 January 2010), available at http://www.washingtonpost.com/wp-dyn/content/article/2007/04/29/AR2007042901555.html

NASA Coalition (2017) 'NASA Position Paper on Irreducible Minimums Before The Fresh Elections are Held', NASA Coalition website, October (accessed 9 November 2017), available at https://twitter.com/coalitionnasake/status/907619216416788480?lang=en and https://twitter.com/coalition nasake/status/907619664922103808?lang=en

Nation Newsplex (2017) 'Rift Valley Voters Drop by a Quarter, October Poll Data Shows', *Daily Nation*, 30 October (accessed 9 November 2017), http://www.nation.co.ke/newsplex/repeat-election-Kenya-voter-turnout/2718262-4162738-ldtvr7/index.html

Nation Reporter (2011) 'Key Events in Kenya since the Signing of the National Accords', *Daily Nation*, 27 February (accessed 13 November 2017), available at http://www.nation.co.ke/news/politics/Key-events-in-Kenya-since-signing-of-National-Accord-/1064-1115972-i6ml4dz/index.html

National Accord and Reconciliation Act No 4 of 2008 (2008).

Ndemo, E.B. (2015) 'Political Entrepreneurialism: Reflections of a Civil Servant on the Role of Political Institutions in Technology Innovation and Diffusion in Kenya', *Stability: International Journal of Security and Development*, vol. 4, no. 1, p. Art. 15

Nderitu, Charles (2016) 'Press Release: Government Rejects ICT Practitioner's Bill', All Africa.com, 30 August (accessed 3 November 2017), available at http://allafrica.com/stories/201608310260.html

Ndlela, Martin Nkosi (2015) 'Social Media and Elections in Kenya', in *The Routledge Companion to Social Media and Politics*, ed. Alex Bruns, Gunn Enli, Eli Skogerbo, Anders Olog Larsson and Christian Christensen (Abingdon: Routledge), pp. 460–469.

Ndonga, Simon (2017) 'IEBC Appoints Acting ICT Director after Sending Muhati on Compulsory Leave', Capital FM.com, 27 May (accessed 7 November 2017), available at https://www.capitalfm.co.ke/news/2017/05/iebc-appoints-acting-ict-director-sending-muhati-compulsory-leave/

Ndunde, Hezron (2008) 'From Cyberspace to Public: Rumor, Gossip, Hearsay and the Paradoxes of the 2007 Election in Kenya', 12th Annual CODESRIA General Assembly.

Ndungu, Njoki (2008) 'Kenya: The December 2008 Election Crisis', *Mediterranean Quarterly*, vol. 19, no. 4, pp. 111–121.

Ng'ethe, Vincent (2017) 'Police Killed over 214 People as of October', Nation Newsplex, 4 November (accessed 4 November 2017), available at http://www.

nation.co.ke/newsplex/Kenya-police-shooting/2718262-4173542-o46a6f/index.html

Ngina, Fay (2017) 'Boniface Mwangi Embarks on Removing His Posters – A Sign of Moving On', *Standard U Report*, 12 August (accessed 28 March 2018), available at https://www.standardmedia.co.ke/ureport/story/2001251075/boniface-mwangi-embarks-on-removing-his-own-posters-a-sign-of-moving-on

Ngirachu, John (2016a) 'MPs, Auditor General Declare Online Procurement System Ineffective', *Daily Nation*, 3 March (accessed 10 January 2017), available at http://www.nation.co.ke/news/MPs-Auditor-General-say-ifmis-ineffective/1056-3101988-do8rvyz/index.html

Ngirachu, John (2016b) 'Audit Reveals how Brazen Forgery bled Sh1.8 billion from NYS Coffers', *Daily Nation*, 9 June (accessed 10 January 2017), available at http://www.nation.co.ke/news/-how-brazen-forgery-bled-Sh1-8bn-from-NYS-coffers/1056-3240626-1d1i69/index.html

Ngirachu, John (2017a) 'Roselyn Akombe Resigns from Poll Agency', *Daily Nation*, 18 October (accessed 11 November 2017), available at http://www.nation.co.ke/news/IEBC-commissioner-Roselyn-Akombe-resigns/1056-4144480-7lyoqhz/index.html

Ngirachu, John (2017b) 'Ezra Chiloba Takes a Break as Poll Chiefs Explain Bias Claims', *Daily Nation*, 20 October (accessed 11 November 2017), available at http://www.nation.co.ke/news/Chiloba-takes-three-week-break-ahead-of-poll/1056-4147754-iwo67f/index.html

Ngirachu, John and Okoth, Edwin (2017) 'Kenya Electoral Agency Calms Fears over Network Coverage Before Polls', *Africa Review*, 7 August (accessed 11 November 2017), available at http://www.africareview.com/news/Polls-agency-moves-to-calm-fears-over-network-coverage/979180-4048190-nnkx6i/index.html

NTV (2017) 'Government Reiterates There are No Plans to Shut Down the Internet Come August 8', NTV News, 23 July (accessed 9 November 2017), available at https://www.youtube.com/watch?v=VeJS5QrT2qg

Nyabola, Nanjala (2016a) 'Je Ne Suis Pas Garissa', *Foreign Policy*, 2 April (accessed 13 November 2017), available at http://foreignpolicy.com/2016/04/07/je-ne-suis-pas-garissa-kenya-al-shabab/

Nyabola, Nanjala (2016b) 'Free Basics is an African Dictator's Dream', *Foreign Policy*, 16 October (accessed 10 November 2017), available at http://foreignpolicy.com/2016/10/27/facebooks-plan-to-wire-africa-is-a-dictators-dream-come-true-free-basics-internet/

Nyamai, Faith (2016) 'Blogger Arrested for Insulting Nyeri Governor's Relatives', *Daily Nation*, 2 March (accessed 2 March 2016), available at http://mobile.nation.co.ke/counties/-/1950480/3098394/-/format/xhtml/item/0/-/5t29qyz/-/index.html

Nyambura-Mwaura, Helen (2017) 'French Supplier of Kenya Vote System Says Being Scapegoated', Bloomberg, 15 September (accessed 7 November 2017), available at https://www.bloomberg.com/news/articles/2017-09-15/french-supplier-of-kenya-vote-system-says-it-s-being-scapegoated

Nyassy, Daniel Tsuma (2013) 'Truck Mechanic Tells of how Kiambaa Church was Set Ablaze', Daily Nation, 18 September (accessed 31 October 2017), available at http://www.nation.co.ke/news/politics/How-Kiambaa-church-was-set-ablaze-/1064-1998426-1hveoxz/index.html

Nyassy, Daniel Tsuma and Otieno, Winnie (2016) 'Jubilee Supporters in Mombasa Demand Apology from Millie Adhiambo over Uhuru Remarks', Daily Nation, 21 December (accessed 23 December 2016), available at http://www.nation.co.ke/counties/mombasa/apology-demand-Millie-Odhiambo/1954178-3493862-r6rwvoz/

Nzomo, Maria (1997) 'Kenyan Women in Politics and Public Decision Making', in African Feminism: The Politics of Survival in Sub-Saharan Africa, ed. Gwendolyn Mikell (Philadelphia, PA: University of Pennsylvania).

Obiero Opondo, Paul (2014) 'Kenyatta and Odinga: The Harbingers of Ethnic Nationalism in Kenya', Global Journal for History, Archaeology and Anthropology, vol. 14, no. 3, pp. 27–35.

Obulutsa, George and Houreld, Katherine (2017) 'Kenya Opposition Leader Urges Vote Boycott, Civil Disobedience', Reuters.Com, 25 October (accessed 9 November 2017), available at https://www.reuters.com/article/us-kenya-election/kenya-opposition-leader-urges-vote-boycott-civil-disobedience-idUSKBN1CU0KR

Ochieng', Justus (2017) 'Wyong'o Cautions Police Ahead of Supreme Court Ruling', Daily Nation, 1 September (accessed 8 November 2017), available at http://www.nation.co.ke/counties/kisumu/Nyongo-Luo-lives-matter/1954182-4078950-k63lk7/index.html

Ochieng', Lilian (2016a) 'Safaricom to Manage Kenya Power's Fiberoptic Network', Daily Nation, 5 April (accessed 3 November 2017), available at http://www.nation.co.ke/business/corporates/Safaricom-to-manage-Kenya-Power-fibre-optic-/1954162-3147204-lufqi2z/index.html

Ochieng', Lillian (2016b) 'Investors Raise Concern over Multi-Billion Konza City Plan', Daily Nation, 26 January (accessed 3 November 2017), available at http://www.nation.co.ke/lifestyle/smartcompany/Investors-raise-concerns-over-multi-billion-Konza-City-plan/1226-3049122-dibjgez/index.html

Odipo Dev (2017) '3 Things We Discovered from 3 Months of Investigating Fake News in Kenya', Medium, 12 July (accessed 6 November 2017), available at https://medium.com/@OdipoDev/3-things-we-discovered-from-3-months-of-investigating-fake-news-in-kenya-dfaa6f4e1857

OECD (2012) 'Kenya: Emigrant Population, Person's Born in Kenya Living Abroad', Keepek.com, 26 July (accessed 13 November 2017), available at http://www.keepeek.com/Digital-Asset-Management/oecd/social-issues-migration-health/connecting-with-emigrants/key-statistics-on-diaspora-from-kenya_9789264177949-graph161-en#.Wgjl4bCZ3LY

Ogola, George (2011) 'The Political Economy of the Media in Kenya: From Kenyatta's Nation-Building Press to Kibaki's Local-Language FM Radio', *Africa Today*, vol. 57, no. 3, pp. 77–95.

Okolloh, Ory (2009) '"Ushahidi", or "Testimony": Web 2.0 Tools for Crowdsourcing Crisis information', in *Change at Hand: Web 2.0 for Development*, ed. Holly Ashley et al. (Nottingham: IIED).

Okwembah, David (2013) '#WeAreOne: How Westgate United Kenyans', BBC Africa.com, 27 September (accessed 22 December 2016), available at http://www.bbc.com/news/world-africa-24305277

Olick, Felix and Kadida, Jillo (2017) 'IEBC says Portal for President is only Statistics', *The Star*, 26 August (accessed 7 November 2017), available at https://www.the-star.co.ke/news/2017/08/26/iebc-says-portal-for-president-is-only-statistics_c1623729

Oluoch, Fred (2013a) 'Agitation that Shaped Today's Politics', *Daily Nation*, 7 October (accessed 31 October 2017), available at http://www.nation.co.ke/lifestyle/dn2/Kenya-Multiparty-politics/957860-2020838-14ea6gp/index.html

Oluoch, Fred (2013b) 'Attack on Standard Group Shakes Media', *Daily Nation*, 24 November (accessed 31 October 2017), available at http://mobile.nation.co.ke/lifestyle/Attack-on-Standard-Group-shakes-media/1950774-2086370-format-xhtml-x8vvr1/index.html

Omanga, Duncan (2015) '"Chieftaincy" in the Social Media Space: Community Policing in a Twitter Convened Baraza', *Stability: International Journal of Security & Development*, vol. 4, no. 1, pp. 1–16.

Omanga, Duncan (forthcoming) 'Whatsapp, Tweet-ups and Digital Publics: The "Nakuru Analysts" and the Evolution of Public Participation in County Governance'.

Ombara, Omwa (2016) 'Kenyans Try the International Criminal Court on Social Media', The Hague Trials Kenya, 20 January (accessed 14 November 2017), available at http://allafrica.com/stories/201601210702.html

Ombati, Cyrus and Obala, Roselyne (2013) 'Police Want Journalists John-Allan Namu and Mohammed Ali over Westgate Story', *The Standard*, 23 October (accessed 20 July 2018), available at https://www.standardmedia.co.ke/article/2000096092/police-want-journalists-john-allan-namu-and-mohammed-ali-over-westgate-story

Ombuor, Raell and Schemm, Paul (2017) 'Kenya's Supreme Court Annuls Vote for Irregularities, Orders New Vote', *The Washington Post*, 1 September (accessed 9 November 2017), available at https://www.washingtonpost.com/world/kenya-supreme-court-cancels-presidential-election-result-for-irregularities-orders-new-election/2017/09/01/ceee81d6-8ef4-11e7-84c0-02cc069f2c37_story.html?utm_term=.255497497aaa

Omondi, Dominic (2017) 'A Glimpse into Kenya's Billion Shillings Wee Hour Business Oiling the Economy', *The Standard*, 21 March (accessed 3 November 2017), available at https://www.standardmedia.co.ke/business/article/2001233461/a-glimpse-into-kenya-s-wee-hour-business-oiling-the-economy

Ondieki, Elvis and Mutambo, Aggrey (2017) 'Raila Hits out at Poll Observers during London Speech', *Daily Nation*, 13 October (accessed 7 November 2017), available at http://www.nation.co.ke/news/Raila-says-he-will-not-sign-Form-24A/1056-4138774-14ia985/index.html

O'Neil, Cathy (2016) *Weapons of Math Destruction: How Big Data Increases Inequality and Threatens Democracy* (New York: Crown).

Opiyo, Dave (2013) 'Kenya "Moving in the Wrong Direction" Survey Finds', *Daily Nation*, 24 December (accessed 22 December 2016), available at http://www.nation.co.ke/news/Cost-of-living--insecurity-top-challenges-for-Kenyans/1056-2124352-te9sp8/index.html

Osborn, Michelle (2008) 'Fuelling the Flames: Rumour and Politics in Kibera', *Journal of Eastern African Studies*, vol. 2, no. 2, pp. 315–327.

Otuki, Neville (2017) 'Safaricom gets 7.5 Billion Payout for Security Network Job', *Business Daily*, 3 January (accessed 14 November 2017), available at http://www.businessdailyafrica.com/Corporate-News/Safaricom-paid-Sh7-5-billion-for-security-network-contract/539550-3505148-15li5rm/

Owaah (2016) 'The Sack of Imperial Bank', Owaahh.com, 16 February (accessed 30 April 2016), available at http://owaahh.com/the-sack-of-imperial-bank/

Oyugi, Walter O. (1997) 'Ethnicity in the Electoral Process', *Africa Journal of Political Science*, vol. 2, no. 1, pp. 41–69.

Perlez, Jane (1991) 'Defying Kenya's One Party State, Dissident Plans Opposition Group', *New York Times*, 14 February (accessed 13 November 2017), available at http://www.nytimes.com/1991/02/14/world/defying-kenya-s-one-party-state-dissident-plans-opposition-group.html

Pew Research Centre (2008) 'Where Trust is High, Crime and Corruption are Low', Pew Research Centre, 15 April (accessed 22 June 2018), available at http://www.pewglobal.org/2008/04/15/where-trust-is-high-crime-and-corruption-are-low/

Phillips, Anne (1991) *Engendering Democracy* (Cambridge, UK: Polity).

Phys.org (2017) 'Internet, Social Media back in Ethiopia after Block', Phys.Org, 8 June (accessed 9 November 2017), available at https://phys.org/news/2017-06-internet-social-media-ethiopia-block.html

Pole, Antoinnete (2009) *Blogging the Political: Politics and Participation in a Networked Society* (London: Routledge).

Portland Communications (2016) 'Press Release: Africa Outstrips US and UK in Using Twitter for Political Conversations', Portland Communications, 6 April (accessed 27 February 2016), available at http://www.howafricatweets.com/Press-Release/International-Press-Release.pdf

Press, Robert M. (1991) 'Kenya's Moi Bows to Calls for Multiparty Elections', *Christian Science Monitor*, 4 December (accessed 31 October 2017), available at https://www.csmonitor.com/1991/1204/04041.html

Press, Robert M. (1993) 'Tribal Clashes in Kenya Continue', *Christian Science Monitor*, 27 September (accessed 7 November 2017), available at https://www.csmonitor.com/1993/0927/27091.html

Privacy International (2017a) 'Track, Capture, Kill: Inside Communications Surveillance and Counterterrorism in Kenya', March (accessed 27 March 2018), available at https://privacyinternational.org/sites/default/files/ 2017-10/track_capture_final.pdf

Privacy International (2017b) 'State of Privacy in Kenya', Privacy International, 12 July (accessed 14 November 2017), available at https://www.privacy international.org/state-privacy/1005/state-privacy-kenya

Rajab, Ramadhan (2017) 'Kameme FM Leads in Hate Speech, Media Survey Shows', *The Star*, 7 July (accessed 27 March 2018), available at https://www.the-star.co.ke/news/2017/07/07/kameme-fm-leads-in-hate-speech-media-survey-shows_c1591993

Ramanathan, Usha (2017) 'Who is Opposing the Aadhar Project?', *The Wire*, 6 June (accessed 7 November 2017), available at https://thewire.in/144204/aadhaar-uid-opposition-criticism/

Rawnsley, Adam, Woods, Eric and Treibert, Christiaan (2017) 'The Messaging App Fuelling Syria's Insurgency', *Foreign Policy*, 6 November (accessed 7 November 2017), available at http://foreignpolicy.com/2017/11/06/the-messaging-app-fueling-syrias-insurgency-telegram-arms-weapons/?utm_content=buffer79913&utm_medium=social&utm_source=twitter.com&utm_campaign=buffer

The Real Raila Facebook Page (accessed 4 November 2017), available at https://www.facebook.com/pg/TheRealRaila/about/?ref=page_internal

Reuters Staff (2008) 'Kenya Lifts Ban on Live Broadcasts: Government Spokesman', Reuters, 4 February (accessed 13 November 2017), available at http://www.reuters.com/article/us-kenya-crisis-media/kenya-lifts-ban-on-live-broadcasts-govt-spokesman-idUSL0413662520080204

Rheault, Magali and Tortora, Bob (2011) 'African's Speak on the Meaning of Being Well Governed', *Harvard International Review*, 6 March (accessed 2 June 2011), available at http://hir.harvard.edu/india-in-transition/confidence-in-institutions

Roy, Arundhati (2004) 'The 2004 Sydney Peace Prize Lecture' for the Sydney

Peace Prize, 4 November (accessed 3 November 2017), available at http://sydney.edu.au/news/84.html?newsstoryid=279

Rugene, Njeri (2013) 'Brave Busia Girl Battles as Her Rapists Go Scott Free', *Daily Nation*, 7 October (accessed 30 March 2016), available at http://www.nation.co.ke/lifestyle/DN2/When-rapists-go-scot-free/-/957860/2022572/-/skd9s8z/-/index.html

Rusbriger, Alan (2017) 'Fiscal Blackmail', Committee to Protect Journalists, 25 April (accessed 31 October 2017), available at https://cpj.org/2017/04/fiscal-blackmail.php

Said, Edward (1979) *Orientalism* (London: Vintage Anchor).

Salome, Nyambura (2015) 'e-Government Platforms in Kenya – Evidence of Change or "Politics for Show"', Making All Voices Count.org, 23 September (accessed 13 November 2017), available at http://www.makingallvoicescount.org/blog/e-government-platforms-in-kenya-evidence-of-change-or-politics-for-show/

Sambuli, Nanjira (2016) 'Chase Bank Is in Receivership Because of Chase Bank, not Because of Social Media', *Daily Nation*, 8 April (accessed 11 April 2016), available at http://www.nation.co.ke/oped/blogs/chase-bank-receivership-social-media/-/620/3151826/-/1gy0shz/-/index.html?utm_content=buffer6f21a&utm_medium=social&utm_source=twitter.com&utm_campaign=buffer

Saner, Emine (2016) 'From Political Coups to Family Feuds: How WhatsApp became our Favourite Way to Chat', *The Guardian*, 3 July (accessed 14 November 2017), https://www.theguardian.com/technology/2016/jul/03/from-political-coups-to-family-feuds-how-whatsapp-became-our-favourite-way-to-chat

Sanya, Brenda Nyandiko (2013) 'Disrupting Patriarchy: An Examination of the role of e-Technologies in Rural Kenya', *Feminist Africa*, vol. 18, pp. 12–24.

Sanya, Brenda Nyandiko and Lutomia, Anne Namatsi (2011) 'Archives and Collective Memories: Searching for African Women in the Pan-African Imaginary', *Feminist Africa*, vol. 20, pp. 69–75.

Schneider, Steven M. (1996) 'Creating a Democratic Public Sphere through Political Discussion: A Case Study of Abortion Conversation on the Internet', *Social Science Computer Review*, vol. 14, pp. 373–393.

Schroeder, Stan (2011) 'Facebook Privacy: 10 Settings Every User Should Know', Mashable.com, 7 February (accessed 22 December 2016), available at http://mashable.com/2011/02/07/facebook-privacy-guide/#uGUAoWmfakqA

Scola, Nancy (2018) 'US Regulator Confirms Investigation of Facebook', Politico.com, 26 March (accessed 27 March 2018), available at https://www.politico.eu/article/us-regulator-confirms-investigation-of-facebook-cambridge-analytica-data/

Shivji, Issa (2017) 'The Metamorphosis of the Revolutionary Intellectual', IssaBinMariam.com, available at https://apnews.com/6d16a08f5b1d4587b0df 886b122eb52c

Shoo, Elizabeth (2016) 'Follow the Hashtag #StopExtrajudicialKillings', Deutsche Welle, 5 July (accessed 14 November 2017), available at http://www.dw.com/ en/dwnews-kenyans-protest-to-stopextrajudicialkillings/av-19377983

Simon, T., Goldberg, A., Aharonson-Daniel, L., Leykin, D. and Adini, B. (2014) 'Twitter in the Cross Fire – The Use of Social Media in the Westgate Mall Terror Attack in Kenya', PLoS ONE, vol. 9, no. 8, pp. e104136. doi:10.1371/ journal.pone.0104136

Somolu, Oreoluwa (2007) '"Telling Our Own Stories": African Women Blogging for Social Change', Gender and Development, vol. 15, no. 3, pp. 477–489.

Sonnad, Nikhil (2017) 'This is now What Happens When You Try to Post Fake News on Facebook', QZ.com, 19 March (accessed 2 November 2017), available at https://qz.com/936503/facebooks-new-method-of-fighting-fake-news-is-making-it-hard-for-people-to-post-a-false-story-about-irish-slaves/

Spangler, Todd (2017) 'Buzzed News Twitter Live Daily Morning Show to Debut in September', Variety.com, 10 August (accessed 13 November 2017), available at http://variety.com/2017/digital/news/buzzfeed-news-twitter-live-daily-morning-show-launch-date-1202522459/

Specia, Megan (2014) 'Brutal Mob Assault in Kenya Triggers #MyDressMyChoice', Mashable, 14 November (accessed 16 March 2016), available at http:// mashable.com/2014/11/14/kenya-mydressmychoice/#Kk2dE0JriGqy

Stiglitz, Joseph (1999) 'More Instruments and Broader Goals: Moving Towards the Post-Washington Consensus', Villa Borsig Workshop Series 1998 (German Foundation for International Development), available at https://pdfs. semanticscholar.org/657d/d9ec1d1631b3d46e19e6657bad7a8de5de4f.pdf

Stork, Christoph, Calandro, Enrico and Gillwald, Alison (2012) Internet Going Mobile: Internet Access and Usage in Eleven African Countries, Proceedings of the 19th ITS Biennial Conference 2012, Bangkok, Thailand.

Sustein, Cass R. (2008) 'Neither Hayek nor Habermas', Public Choice, vol. 134, pp. 87–95.

Throup, David (2003) 'The Kenya General Election: 2002', Centre for Strategic and International Studies Briefing, 14 January (accessed 7 November 2017), available at https://csis-prod.s3.amazonaws.com/s3fs-public/legacy_files/files/ media/csis/pubs/anotes_0301b.pdf

Touré, Sékou (1959) 'The Political Leader as the Representative of a Culture', speech, Rome, Italy.

Trading Economics (2017) 'Kenya Inflation Rate: 2005–2017', Trading Economics.com, (accessed 13 November 2017), available at https://tradingeconomics.com/ kenya/inflation-cpi

Tribbetts, Alexandra (1994) 'Mamas Fighting for Freedom in Kenya', *Africa Today*, vol. 41, no. 4, Kenyan Politics, What Role for Civil Society?, pp. 27–48.

Tsur, Oren and Rappoport, Ari (2012) 'What's in a Hashtag? Content Based Prediction of the Spread of Ideas in Microblogging Communities', WSDM'12, 8–12 February, Seattle, Washington, USA.

Tufecki, Zeynep (2017) *Twitter and Teargas: The Power and Fragility of Networked Protest* (New Haven, CT: Yale).

UN Broadband Commission (2010) 'About', UN Broadband Commission website (accessed 22 December 2016), available at http://www.broadbandcommission.org/about/Pages/default.aspx

UNDP (2013) *Kenya's Youth Employment Challenge* (Kenya: UNDP).

UNICEF Statistics (2013) 27 December (accessed 13 November 2017), available at https://www.unicef.org/infobycountry/kenya_statistics.html

United Nations (2011) Report of the Special Rapporteur on the Promotion and Protection of the Right to Freedom of Opinion and Expression, Frank La Rue*, A/HRC/17/27, available at http://www2.ohchr.org/english/bodies/hrcouncil/docs/17session/A.HRC.17.27_en.pdf

Upadaya, Radha and Johnson, Susan (2015) 'Transformation of Kenya's Banking Sector, 2000 to 2012', in *Kenya's Financial Transformation in the 21st Century*, ed. Amrik Heyer and Michael King (Nairobi: FSD Kenya), available at http://opus.bath.ac.uk/48797/1/Upadhyaya_and_Johnson_Kenya_s_fin_transformation_2015_Ebook_Chapter_1.pdf

USAID (2008) 'Integrated Financial Management and Information Systems: A Practical Guide, Edwin Rodin-Brown', available at http://pdf.usaid.gov/pdf_docs/PNADK595.pdf

Ushahidi (2013a) Umati: Monitoring Online Dangerous Speech: October 2012 – January 2013 (Nairobi, Kenya).

Ushahidi (2017b) 'About Ushahidi', Ushahidi.com, 2008–2017 (accessed 13 November 2017), available at https://www.ushahidi.com/about

Ushahidi (2017) 'Brck', back.com (accessed 13 November 2017), available at https://www.brck.com/

Vail, Leroy (1989) 'Introduction: Ethnicity in Southern African History', *Creation of Tribalism in Southern Africa*, ed. Leroy Vail (London: James Currey).

van Heerden, Dominique and Said-Morehouse, Lauren (2017) 'Kerry: Every Kenyan's Vote is Protected', CNN International, 11 August (accessed 9 November 2017), available at http://www.cnn.com/2017/08/10/africa/kenya-elections/index.html

Vavrus, Mary Douglas (2002) *Postfeminist News: Political Women in Media Culture* (New York: State University of New York).

Vota, Wayan (2012) 'Dead Ushahidi: A Stark Reminder for Sustainability Planning in ICT4D', ICT Works, 9 July (accessed 3 November 2017), available a https://

www.ictworks.org/dead-ushahidi-stark-reminder-sustainability-planning-ict4d/#.WrvEp5NubLY

Wadell, Kaveh (2016) 'Why Google Quit China – and Why It May Go Back', *The Atlantic*, 19 January (accessed 7 November 2017), available at https://www.theatlantic.com/technology/archive/2016/01/why-google-quit-china-and-why-its-heading-back/424482/

Wa Githinji, Mwangi and Holmquist, Frank (2008) 'Kenya's Hopes and Impediments: The Anatomy of a Crisis of Exclusion', *Journal of Eastern African Studies*, vol. 2, no. 2, pp. 344–358.

Wagner, Kurt and Romm, Tony (2017) 'Live Updates: Facebook, Google and Twitter Testified before Congress Again', Recode.net, 1 November (accessed 2 November 2017), available at https://www.recode.net/2017/11/1/16588374/live-updates-facebook-google-twitter-testify-senate-congress-russia-president-election

Wainaina, Binyavanga (2005) 'Inventing a City: Nairobi', *National Geographic* (September) accessed 28 February 2016, available at http://ngm.nationalgeographic.com/ngm/0509/feature2/

Wakefield, Jane (2017) 'Facebook's Fake News Experiment Backfires', BBC News, 7 November (accessed 13 November 2017), available at http://www.bbc.com/news/technology-41900877

Wallaroom Media (2017) 'Facebook Newsfeed Algorithm History', last updated 12 October (accessed 13 November 2017), https://wallaroomedia.com/facebook-newsfeed-algorithm-change-history/#nine

Wandia, Tess (2017) 'Enhancing Internet Freedom in Kenya for Women', iHub Research, 18 June (accessed 27 March 2018), available at https://ihub.co.ke/blogs/30328/enhancing-internet-freedom-in-kenya-for-women

Wang, Selina (2017) 'Twitter Sidestepped Russian Account Warnings, Former Worker Says', Bloomberg.com, 3 November (accessed 8 November 2017), available at https://www.bloomberg.com/news/articles/2017-11-03/former-twitter-employee-says-fake-russian-accounts-were-not-taken-seriously

Wangari, Njeri (2017) 'GeoPoll and Portland Launch a Survey Report on Fake News in Kenya', GeoPoll.com, 19 July (accessed 6 November 2017), available at http://blog.geopoll.com/geopoll-and-portland-launch-a-survey-report-on-fake-news-in-kenya

Wanyoro, Charles (2015) 'Government to Prepare Law on How Kenyans Use Facebook, Twitter – Itumbi', *Nairobi Now*, 6 June (accessed 6 June 2016), available at http://nairobinews.nation.co.ke/news/govt-prepare-law-kenyans-use-facebook-twitter-itumbi/

Wanzala, James (2017) 'Kenya Now Has 39.4 Million Internet Users', *The Standard*, 20 April (accessed 13 November 2013), available at https://www.standardmedia.co.ke/business/article/2001236985/kenya-now-has-39-4-million-internet-users

Warah, Rasna (2013) 'Did the Kenya Media do Justice to the 2013 Election?', *Sahan Journal*, 26 August (accessed 14 November 2017), available at http://sahanjournal.com/kenyan-media-election-coverage/#.WgtYU7CZ3LY

Waweru, Nduta (2017) 'How Technology is Changing Elections in Kenya', *Daily Vox*, 2 August (accessed 7 November 2017), available at https://www.thedailyvox.co.za/how-technology-is-changing-elections-in-kenya-nduta-waweru/

Weintraub, Jeff (2005) 'The Theory and Politics of the Private/Public Distinction', in *Private and Public in Thought and Practice: Perspectives on a Grand Dichotomy*, ed. Jeff Weintraub, and Krishan Kumar (Chicago, IL: University of Chicago Press).

White African (2008) 'Mashada Forums: Kenya's First Digital Casualty', whiteafrican.com, 29 January (accessed 13 November 2017), available at http://whiteafrican.com/2008/01/29/mashada-forums-kenyas-first-digital-casualty/

Willis, Justin (2008) 'What has He Got up His Sleeve? Advertising the Kenyan Presidential Candidates in 2007', *Journal of Eastern African Studies*, vol. 2, no. 2, pp. 264–271.

Wipper, Audrey (1975) 'The Maendeleo Ya Wanawake Organization: The Co-Optation of Leadership', *African Studies Review*, vol. 18, no. 3, pp. 99–120.

Woodruff, Betsy and Ackerman, Spencer (2017) 'Russian Probe now Investigating Cambridge Analytica, Trump's "Psycographic Gurus"', *The Daily Beast*, 11 October (accessed 6 November 2017), available at https://www.thedailybeast.com/russia-probe-now-investigating-cambridge-analytica-trumps-psychographic-data-gurus?via=twitter_page

Wyche, Susan P., Forte, Andrea and Schoenboek, Sarita Yardi (2013) 'Hustling Online: Understanding Consolidated Facebook Use in an Informal Settlement in Nairobi', CHI 2013, 27 April–2 May, Paris.

Ya'u, Yunusa Z. (2012) 'Ambivalence and Activism: Netizens, Social Transformation and African Virtual Publics', *African Development*, vol. 37, no. 1, pp. 85–102.

Zuckerman, Ethan (2008) 'Meet the Bridgebloggers', *Public Choice*, vol. 134, pp. 47–65.

INDEX

regarding, 171; shut down of, 11 (in Ethiopia, 208; in Uganda, 101); space for challenging narratives, 60; threatening to governments, 145; thrives in Kenya, 153; use of algorithms, 172–3; used to disseminate hate speech, 163; viewed as threat to national cohesion, 208

sociology of absence, 79, 160

Somali people, 140

Somalia, xix

#SomeoneTellCNN, 106, 111, 113

South Africa, 50; Cambridge Analytica operations in, 160; social media in, 208

South Asian community in Kenya, 104

South Sudan, violence in, 105

Speakers' Corner, 40

speaking to power, xiv

Standard, 50, 53, 54

Standard Media Group, 46; offices raided, 22, 55

state, retreat of, 63

state capture, 53

#StopExtrajudicialKillings, 205

Stork, Christoph, 80

Strategic Communications Laboratories, 158

stripping attacks, 128–9, 131, 136, 137

superusers on Twitter, 91, 111, 120, 121, 153

Supreme Court, ruling on 2017 election, 193, 197

surveillance, 153, 213; by governments, 7, 70; installation of cameras, 74

Swahili language, 42, 128; used in tweets, 89

tea, invitations to State House, 57–8

Team banana, 22

Team orange, 22

technology, 209; critique of, 202; intersection with politics, xiv; not agnostic, 166; portrayed as neutral, 31; role of, 214–15

telecommunications, liberalisation of, 36

Telecoms Kenya, 64, 68

Telegram, usage of, in Syria, 96–7

#Telema, 153

television, 42, 49, 53; as state monopoly, 52

terrorism, 129

texting and SMS, 67

Thiong'o, Ngugi wa, 20

#ThirdwayKE, 89

#ThisFlag, 212

thought leader status, on Twitter, 111

Togo, 201, 212; social media in, 207

Touré, Sékou, xvii

traditional media, 38, 41, 46–7, 49, 50, 61, 62, 75, 144, 147, 154, 200; diminishing of women, 138; fixation on women, 213; irrelevance of, 196; loss of credibility of, 28, 169; manipulation of, 167; popular distrust of, 60; threat to social cohesion, 206–7

transparency, 71, 104

trending, 97, 130, 154; measurement of, 88–9

trends are not movements, 155

tribalism, 175–7, 184; difficult to diagnose, 176; fears of, 172

tribe, 137, 174; as basis of trust, 205; definition of, 125; use of term, 115

Tribe.com, 84

#TribelessYouthKE, 177

Trump, Donald, election of, 158–9, 161, 170, 214; uses term 'fake news', 167 *see also* elections, in USA

Women and the War on Boko Haram: Wives, Weapons, Witnesses
BY HILARY MATFESS

'An original, innovative, and much-needed addition to the growing literatures on both women and conflict in Africa and the Boko Haram insurgency.'

Brandon Kendhammer, Ohio University

'The author's intensive fieldwork reveals previously unseen layers of complexity. Matfess is right to conclude the fate of Nigeria is tied to the fate of its women, and her book is an important contribution to that discussion.'

Valerie Hudson, Texas A&M University

Congo's Violent Peace: Conflict and Struggle Since the Great African War
BY KRIS BERWOUTS

'Essential reading for all those who want to understand the current situation. *Congo's Violent Peace* has all the makings of a classic.'

Séverine Autesserre, author of *The Trouble with the Congo and Peaceland*

'Few people have a better grasp of the key players than Kris Berwouts. From diplomat parties to refugee camps, from warlords to the presidential entourage, this book is essential reading for anyone truly interested in the DRC.'

David Van Reybrouck, author of *Congo: The Epic History of a People*

Africa: Why Economists Get It Wrong
BY MORTEN JERVEN

'A highly readable and absolutely devastating critique of an increasingly extensive and influential body of work by economists seeking to explain "what's wrong with Africa".'

James Ferguson, Stanford University

'Morten Jerven provides a valuable reminder of the need not just to cite statistics but to question them.'

Financial Times